NEW Brewing Lager Beer

Other technical books by Brewers Publications include:

Principles of Brewing Science
By George Fix

Dictionary of Beer and Brewing
Compiled by Carl Forget

Evaluating Beer
Compiled by Brewers Publications

Victory Beer Recipes
America's Best Homebrew

North American Brewers Resource Directory
Compiled annually by the Institute for Brewing Studies

Brewery Planner
A Guide to Opening Your Own Small Brewery

For a complete list of titles, please refer to page 365, or contact Bre
Publications at (303) 546-6514, orders@aob.org or FAX (303) 447-2825.

NEW Brewing Lager Beer

*The Most Comprehensive Book
for Home- and Microbrewers*

Completely Revised and Expanded

GREGORY J. NOONAN

New Brewing Lager Beer
Copyright 1986, 1996 by Gregory J. Noonan

Copy Editor: Merilee Eggleston
Technical Editor: Darryl Richman
Book Project Editor: Theresa Duggan

The illustration "Hardness of Ground Waters" on pages 38 and 39 is
from *Water Atlas of the United States,* by James J. Geraghty, and was
used with permission of the publisher.

Printed in the United States of America
10 9 8 7 6 5 4 3 2 1

Published by Brewers Publications, a division of the Association of
Brewers: PO Box 1679, Boulder, Colorado 80306-1679; (303) 447-
0816; and FAX (303) 447-2825.

Direct all inquiries/orders to the above address.

Cover design by Marylin Cohen and Stephanie Johnson
Cover illustration by Molly Gough
Interior design by PS Studios
All illustrations by Gregory J. Noonan unless otherwise noted.

Library of Congress Cataloging-in-Publication Data

Noonan, Gregory J.
    New brewing lager beer / Gregory Noonan : foreword by
Charlie Papazian.
      p.   cm.
    Includes bibliographical references (p.   -) and index.
    ISBN 0-937381-46-2
    1. Brewing—Amateurs' manuals. 2. Beer. I. Title.
TP570.N583 1996   95-25594
541.8'73—dc20   CIP

DEDICATION

To the brewing of better beer, and to those who brew it.

TABLE OF CONTENTS

PART 1: BREWING CONSTITUENTS

Tables

FOREWORD

It is difficult to improve a classic. Yet as all master brewers know, the process of learning about beer and brewing is never-ending. Ten years ago, Greg Noonan captured the essence of fine brewing and presented his knowledge of and appreciation for brewing great beers in his original *Brewing Lager Beer* (Brewers Publications, 1986). Now Greg brings us all up to date with the best cutting-edge brewing information and techniques in this new and expanded revision, *New Brewing Lager Beer*.

I had the great privilege of being the technical editor for the first edition of *Brewing Lager Beer*. After initially reviewing the original manuscript, I was awed and spellbound. It was during those moments that I really began to appreciate how much I didn't know about brewing's finer points. Indeed, what I was reading was about to help improve the quality of homebrewed beer as no other advanced book on applied brewing had.

With its release in 1986, *Brewing Lager Beer* became Brewers Publications' cornerstone and the standard by which the Association of Brewers and all of its other divisions have measured their work. Greg's original book was a first of its kind, and the research and experience that went into it has benefited brewers around the globe.

American homebrewers were the first to embrace Greg's practical and applied approach to brewing lager beers. Then as the homebrewing hobby gained the respect it still enjoys today, professionals came to cite this classic work as a reference, one that is still unequaled.

In fact, *Brewing Lager Beer* has become a standard for aspiring and veteran small brewers everywhere. Greg's devotees sometimes refer to themselves as "Noonanites." I have encountered their enthusiasm, appreciation, and most excellent beers during my travels through South America, Asia, Africa, Australia, and Europe. Just as I know when I've tasted a great beer, I know that when I encounter a Noonanite, I have come upon the "best of the best" among homebrewers — someone who has been infected with Greg's contagious enthusiasm and respect for the art of brewing.

As Greg states in his introduction to this new edition, ten additional years of brewing experience is an invaluable resource that can't be bought. His success in the microbrewing industry and his gracious efforts to share his increased knowledge provide us all with continued inspiration and even better beers.

New Brewing Lager Beer is the new touchstone for those of us who choose to advance our knowledge of beer and brewing. Like me, you probably thought it couldn't get any better. Thanks, Greg, for showing us otherwise.

Charlie Papazian, Founding President
Association of Brewers
and author of *The New Complete Joy of Home Brewing*
and *The Home Brewer's Companion*
January 3, 1996

PREFACE

A lot has changed in the world of craft brewing in ten years, and the updating of *Brewing Lager Beer* is long overdue. It is surprising to me that the book has endured, and that so may brewers still refer to their dog-eared copies.

Brewing Lager Beer never really was just about lager brewing. The lager tradition is really the culmination of the brewing theories of all the other European brewing traditions. By examining lager techniques and technology, any student of brewing is being exposed to brewing dissected to its vital principles. Before 1985, Dave Line's still-classic *Big Book of Brewing* (Amateur Winemaker Publications, 1985) was the only readily available reference for homebrewers and the pioneers of microbrewing; in deference to him, I chose the title so as not to compete with his groundbreaking work.

This edition retains the title, but broadens its scope to include more of the spectrum of craft-brewing techniques and more information specific to ale brewing. Besides updating the work and including more useful information for serious brewers, a lot of factual and editing errors that appeared in the original have been corrected.

The trickle of knowledge available to craft and homebrewers when this book was first published has become a flood; I am proud to have *Brewing Lager Beer* continue to be part of most serious brewers' libraries.

Greg Noonan
Burlington, Vermont
July 1, 1995

ACKNOWLEDGMENTS

Thanks to my wife, Nancy, Martha and John Murtaugh, Darryl Richman, George Fix, Charlie Papazian, Charles Kochenour, and everyone else who contributed to the publication of this book.

INTRODUCTION

Outline of Brewing

Brewing begins with malted barley, which is the sprouted, then dried and/or roasted, barley seed. The malt is coarsely crushed and mixed with hot water to form a mash. During the mash, compositional changes occur, brought about by enzymes in the malt. The hot aqueous solution leaches the contents out of the crushed malt kernels and gelatinizes the starch; the enzymes reduce them to soluble fractions. This extract is rinsed from the insoluble malt particles during sparging. The sweet solution is called wort.

The wort is boiled with the flowerlike cone of the hop vine for bitterness and flavor, and to clarify the wort. The wort is cooled, and active brewers' yeast is added to ferment it. The yeast forms carbon dioxide and alcohol from the sugars extracted from the malt; carbon dioxide carbonates the beer. This fermentation may be carried out in several stages, and the beer moved from one vessel to another to separate it from flavor-impairing sedimented yeast, malt, and hop residues.

The beer is bottled, kegged, or casked so that it may be served carbonated.

Reference Units

The volume, temperature, and density (weight) of a solution all have various terms by which they may be expressed. Throughout this book, U.S. gallons, degrees Fahrenheit, and density as degrees Plato have been given, with liters, degrees centigrade, and specific gravity parenthetically appended. The term original gravity (OG) refers to the density of the boiled wort (original extract, OE), and final gravity (FG) to the density of the fermented beer (apparent extract, AE). Specific gravity (sp gr) refers to the usual metric system (sp gr 1.046), gravity (SG) to a simpler form of expression preferred by brewers (1046), and excess gravity (G) to an abbreviated form (46) commonly used in equations.

Other abbreviations used in this book include:

ASBC American Society of Brewing Chemists
EBC European Brewing Convention
IOB Institute of Brewing (British)
°F Temperature, degrees Fahrenheit
°C Temperature, degrees Centigrade
°Plato Density, degrees Plato
°SRM Wort color, standard reference method
°L Malt color, degrees Lovibond (often used interchangeably with SRM)
°HCU Homebrew color units (sum of °L of goods)
°EBC Color, degrees EBC
°IOB Color, degrees IOB
DBFG Laboratory extract potential, dry basis fine grind
DBCG Brewhouse extract potential, dry basis coarse grind
FG-CG Malt modification, fine grind minus coarse grind
HWE Hot water extract, extract potential, IOB method
CWE Cold water extract, modification, IOB method
TN Total nitrogen
% P Percent protein (TN/6.25)

TSN Total soluble nitrogen
SNR Soluble nitrogen ratio (TSN/TN)
DP Diastatic power
IBU International bittering units, iso-alpha acid in solution
BU Bittering unit (IBU x 1.125)
HBU Homebrew bitterness units, identical to AAU (alpha acid units, ounces of hops x % alpha acid)
DU Dextrinizing units
MC Moisture Content
ppm Parts per million
mg/L Milligrams per liter

For those more familiar with standards other than those used herein, tables are provided in appendix D for conversion of U.S. standards to metric and British units. Other useful tables of measure and conversion formulas for brewing are also found in the appendixes.

Classic Lager Types

The range of lager beers is represented by seven recognized types, which are identified by the brewing centers where they evolved. They are:

Pilsener (Pilsner, Pils), Bohemia, Czech Republic. 11 to 14 °Plato (OG 1044 to 1057). Golden color, distinctive hop palate, medium body, well carbonated, dry. 4 to 5.2 percent alcohol by volume (3.2 to 4.1 w/w). After the style set by the classic Pilsner Urquell (Plzensky Prazdroj). Served at 48 to 50 degrees F (9 to 10 degrees C).

Dortmunder (Dort, Export), Westfalen, Germany. 12 to 14 °Plato (OG 1049 to 1057). Light, golden-blond color, moderate hop palate, medium body; rich, mellow, and yet sharp. 5 to 5.7 percent alcohol by volume (3.9 to 4.5 w/w). Served at 48 to 50 degrees F (9 to 10 degrees C).

Vienna (Wiener/Spezial, Märzenbier/Oktoberfest),

Lower Austria and Bavaria. 12.5 to 15 °Plato (OG 1050 to
1061). Reddish-amber or copper color, moderately hopped,
medium body; malt to toasted-malt flavor. Viennas tend to
be somewhat drier and more bitter than Oktoberfests. 4.9
to 5.7 percent alcohol by volume (3.8 to 4.5 w/w). Served
at 50 to 55 degrees F (10 to 13 degrees C).

Dark Munich (Münchener dunkel), Bavaria,
Germany. 12 to 14 °Plato (OG 1048 to 1057). Dark-brown
color, lightly hopped, medium to full body; slightly sweet,
malty flavor. 4.5 to 5.5 percent alcohol by volume (3.5 to
4.3 w/w). Served at 35 to 45 degrees F (2 to 7 degrees C).

Light Munich (Münchener helles), Bavaria,
Germany. 11 to 12 °Plato (OG 1044 to 1049). Amber color,
lightly hopped, medium bodied; slightly sweet, malty character. 4 to 5 percent alcohol by volume (3.2 to 3.9 w/w).
Served at 45 to 50 degrees F (7 to 10 degrees C).

Bock, Bavaria, Germany. 16 to 18 °Plato (OG 1065
to 1074). Light- to dark-brown color, rich and malty flavor,
medium to full body. Darker bocks usually have a roasted-
malt and hop flavor. 6 to 7.5 percent alcohol by volume
(4.7 to 5.9 w/w). Served at 50 to 65 degrees F (10 to 18
degrees C).

Dopplebock, Bavaria, Germany. Most often the brand
name ends in the suffix -ator. 18 to 28 °Plato (OG 1074 to
1112). Light- to dark-brown color, often having a roasted-
malt flavor. Medium to very full bodied. 7.5 to 13 percent
alcohol by volume (5.9 to 10.2 w/w). Served at 50 to 65
degrees F (10 to 18 degrees C).

Myriad variations of the classic lager types exist: eisbocks that are partially frozen to increase the concentration
of alcohol; schwarzpils and dark Pilseners, some with and
some without roast-malt character; smoked lagers; spiced
lagers; and American Pilseners, the much-maligned fizz-water
that many Americans still think is the only kind of beer.

Lagers are defined by the process used to brew them. They are essentially distinguished from ales, the other beer family, by relatively slower fermentation at cool (40 to 55 degrees F [4 to 13 degrees C]) temperatures, followed by a relatively longer period of cold conditioning. By definition, lagers have low levels of esters and vicinal diketones; devoid of significant "yeast character," they rely solely upon the interplay of the malt, hops, and water for their aromas and flavors.

BREWING CONSTITUENTS PART ONE

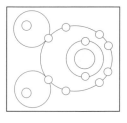

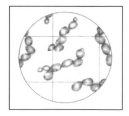

CHAPTER 1

Barley

Barley has been the brewer's preferred source of fermentable extract since prehistory. The barley kernel is readily malted, contains adequate enzymes to convert its starch to sugars, and upon mashing, yields a very complete, highly soluble extract that is relatively free of unwieldy constituents. Barley gives beer its characteristic sweet-to-malty taste, as well as its body, head, and color. Other grains such as wheat, oats, and rye do not lend themselves so readily to brewing.

The barley kernel is the seed of a plant of the grass family (Gramineae). It is one of the hardiest of all the cereal grains and is able to grow under widely varying conditions from Alaska to the equator; it grows best, however, in cool, dry climates.

The seeds grow in two, four, or six rows, called *heads*, along a central stem. The number of seed rows is determined by the number of fertile flowers; in two-row types only two of the six flower clusters are fertile, whereas all the flowers of six-row barley are fertile. Long,

Barley

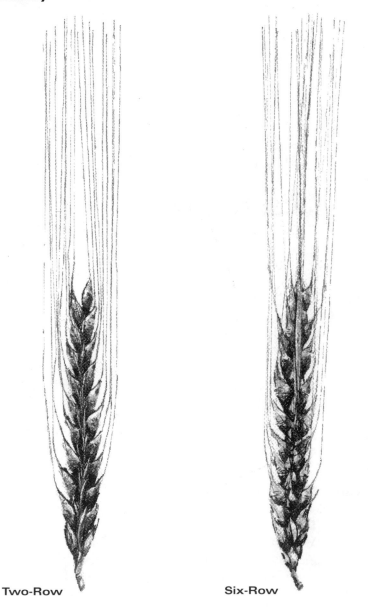

Two-Row   Six-Row

thin bristles protrude from each seed, producing a "bearded" grain that closely resembles wheat.

Harvested when fully ripe, malting barley is dried from a moisture content of 15 to 25 percent down to below 14 percent and is binned for six to eight weeks before being malted. It is then graded; only the largest (greater than three-thirty-seconds of an inch in width) of the four standard grades is considered suitable for malting.

One bushel of brewing-grade barley weighs forty-eight pounds, and it should be at least 95 percent germinant. The kernels should be of uniform size, glossy, uniformly straw colored (light to dark yellow), plump, and have a clean grain aroma. There should be no rancid, moldy, or musty smell, nor any slender, immature grains with greenish-white husks. The husks should be thin, finely wrinkled, and tightly jacket the kernels. The endosperm (starch) must be opaque, white, and mealy, not translucent, grayish, steely, or glassy. Steely grains are excessively high in nitrogen, contain a greater percentage of poorly soluble protein, and do not take up moisture as readily. Consequently, nitrogen content should not exceed 1.6 percent where the barley will not be well modified or where the malt will be infusion mashed. Except where the wort will contain a high percentage of adjuncts, the nitrogen content should never exceed 2 percent. The protein-to-carbohydrate ratio should suit the type of beer being brewed and the processes used to brew it.

European brewers prefer superior two-row, thin-husked, large-berried barley varieties, which give the best brew-house yield, clarity, and flavor. These have a more favorable starch-to-protein/husk ratio than other barleys and yield a mellow flavor and good clarity.

Six-row barley is the most economical to grow because the greater number of rows per head increases the per-acre yield. It is a warm-climate barley and is the type

Dehusked Barley Kernel

Lateral

Dorsal

Ventral

Barley Corn

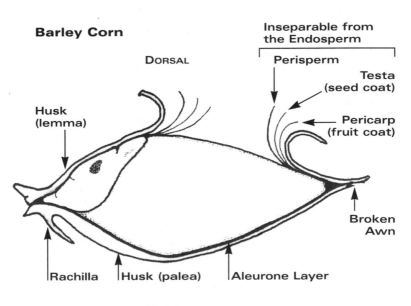

DORSAL

Inseparable from
the Endosperm

Perisperm

Testa
(seed coat)

Husk
(lemma)

Pericarp
(fruit coat)

Broken
Awn

Rachilla   Husk (palea)   Aleurone Layer

VENTRAL

Barley Head, top view

Two-Row

Four-Row

Six-Row

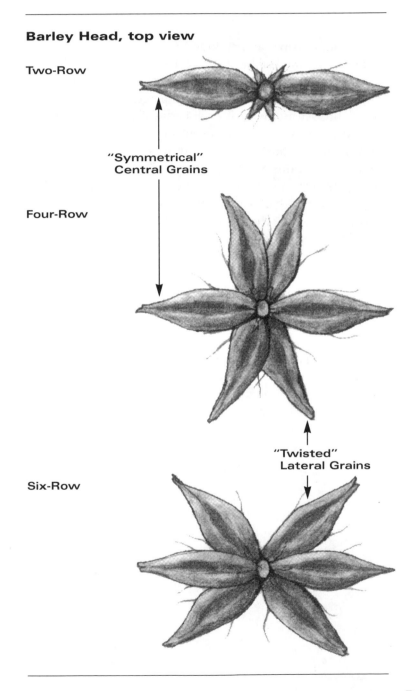

"Symmetrical"
Central Grains

"Twisted"
Lateral Grains

most widely grown in the United States. It is favored by domestic commercial breweries because it is rich in the enzymes needed to convert the adjuncts they employ (adjuncts may account for up to 60 percent of the extract in U.S. brews). Because six-row barley is high in protein, in all-malt brews it presents problems with clarity and stability. Its higher husk content improves mash filterability but can contribute harsh flavors, especially when brewhouse practices cause hot-side aeration.

Four-row barley is still grown and malted in Northern Europe, where it has long been prized for its hardiness in the cold climate. It is not widely used elsewhere, however, because of its steeliness and low yield. It is actually a six-row barley that appears to form four rows, rather than six, because of its thin, elongated head.

Modern barley varieties have been selected for improved field and maltings yields. Improved varieties have replaced older cultivars several times during the past twenty years, and will continue to do so. Thus far, the only appreciable improvement in brewing quality that has been realized is the lower nitrogen of six-row varieties, and in many cases "improved" varieties have been rejected by brewers.

CHAPTER

Malted Barley

Because malt is organic, and subject to the meteorological and soil conditions under which the barley type is grown, malts of the same type can vary substantially in appearance and composition, depending on the season and where and how they are grown. For instance, moist, cool seasons produce more starch and less protein and fat, whereas nitrogen-based fertilizers applied too heavily or too late in the season increase the protein content. A lack of nutrients and minerals will also affect growth and composition. Malt quality depends as well on the circumstances of its malting and subsequent handling. Furthermore, the different barley types are each composed of several varieties.

For these reasons, it is advisable to ask for a lot analysis of any malt to guide adjustments in the mash program so that a wort consistent with previous brews can be made. Commercial breweries evaluate malt at the time of purchase. Craft brewers and homebrewers should too, using the lot analysis provided by the maltster. At the minimum, the lot analysis should give information about the moisture content, color, dry basis fine grind extract, fine-coarse difference, diastatic power, total nitrogen (protein), soluble nitrogen ratio, mealiness, and size distribution of the particular batch of malt.

The lot analysis is generally given on a "dry basis"; that is, the parameters given in the analysis are adjusted to give values as if the malt were oven-dried to 0 percent moisture content. This makes comparisons between lots of malt easier, because no adjustments need to be made for varying percentages of moisture in the malt.

Maltsters generally publish "typical" analyses so that brewers can evaluate their products before purchase. A typical analysis should not be accepted as a substitute for a lot analysis; unless the brewer knows the laboratory parameters of the malt actually on hand, adjustments to brewing procedures cannot be made, and brew-to-brew consistency is not possible. Lot analyses that vary considerably from the parameters stated in the typical analysis are reason to find a new source of malt.

Typical and lot analyses provide the brewer with essential data regarding the general quality of a malt and the barley it is made from, and the suitability of a particular malt for a given mashing method. Without referring to a lot analysis, the brewer cannot know whether a given malt is suitable for infusion mashing or if it requires a protein rest, and if it does, what the duration of the rest should be. Lot-to-lot adjustments to the brew house program usually need to be made in response to changes in the parameters of the malt on hand.

"Base" malts are those malts that form the basis of the brew, usually making up 60 to 100 percent of the grain bill. They usually provide the bulk of the extract and the enzymes to produce it. Lager, Pilsen, Brewers', Pale,

Vienna, light Munich, and British mild ale malts are base malts. The last three resemble British pale malt, except that their colors are higher, and during malting, Vienna and Munich malts are converted somewhat less (fine grind–coarse grind difference 1.5 to 2.0 percent, lower soluble nitrogen ratio) than the British ale malts. Vienna malts have a diastatic power similar to European lager malts, while the range of diastatic power of Munich malts is similar to British malt. Consequently, Munich malt presents the potential for conversion problems if it is at all undermodified by the maltster, and cannot be used as a base malt in high-adjunct mashes.

Pilsen and lager malts originating in Britain and America usually resemble the brewers' malts of those countries in everything but color; they need to be handled in the brew house accordingly. Generally, malts purchased from the country of origin of the beer style give better results than those originating elsewhere.

Any analysis is only of use to brewers if they understand the significance and acceptable ranges of the quoted values. For lot analyses, the common parameters are:

Moisture content, percent: The upper limit for acceptable moisture content in any malt is 6 percent. The closer a malt is to 1.5 percent moisture content, the less risk of mold growth and the less flavor and aroma loss there will be in storage. For the last two reasons especially, colored malts should never be higher in moisture content than 4 percent. Of the base malts, British ale malts have the lowest moisture content.

The moisture content reflects upon the quality of the malting; high moisture-content malts are very often lacking in other areas as well. Furthermore, each 1 percent increase in the moisture content adds 1 percent to the real cost of the malt.

Table 1

Malt Analysis, Dry Basis, Comparative Analysis of Acceptable Ranges					
Malt Analysis Dry Basis Acceptable Ranges	Traditional 2-Row Lager	European 2-Row Lager	American 2-Row Brewers	American 6-Row Lager	British 2-Row Best Pale
Moisture content, %	3.5–4.5	3.5–4.5	3.5–4.5	3.5–4.5	1.5–3.5
Color, SRM (°L, ASBC)	1.2–1.6	1.4–1.8	1.4–2.0	1.4–2.0	2.0–2.7
Color, °EBC	2.0–3.0	2.5–3.5	2.5–4.0	2.5–4.0	4.0–6.0
Extract, DBFG	80.0–82.0	80.0–82.0	79.0–81.5	78.0–79.5	80.5–82.5
Extract, DBCG	78.0–80.5	78.0–80.5	77.0–80.5	76.0–78.1	79.0–81.5
FG-CG, difference	1.5–2.2	1.5–2.0	1.0–2.0	1.4–2.0	1.0–1.5
HWE (L°/kg at 20°C), .2M	309–316	309–316	305–315	301–307	311–318
CWE	16–18	18–20	18–21	18–21	18–22
Hartong 45°, %	30–34	32–38	36–42	38–42	36–42
Alpha-amylase, DU	44–48	40–48	40–45	35–45	25–35
DP, °Lintner	70–100	75–110	100–150	125–160	50–70
DP, °WK	200–325	220–350	375–450	400–500	150–220
Conversion, min	10–15	10–15	5–10	5–10	10
Protein, %	9.0–11.0	9.0–11.0	11.5–12.5	12.0–13.5	9.0–10.0
Soluble protein, %	3.0–4.2	3.5–4.6	4.2–5.3	4.8–5.8	3.5–3.8
TN, %	1.4–1.75	1.4–1.75	1.8–2.0	1.9–2.2	1.4–1.55
TSN, %	.48–.67	.50–.75	.65–.85	.7–.93	.5–.6
SNR, % (S/T, SN/TN, %)	33–38	36–42	36–42	40–45	38–42
Mealy, %	92–97	95–97	95–97	92–97	97–99
Half-glassy, %	2–8	2–4	2–4	2–8	1–3
Glassy, %	0–1	0–1	0–1	0–1	0
Friability, %	80–85	80–90	80–90	75–85	85–95
On 7/64" scrn.-plump %	75–85	75–85	60–70	45–55	80–85
On 6/64" screen %	10–20	10–20	20–30	35–45	10–20
On 5/64" scrn. %<2.2 mm	0–3	0–3	7–13	10–20	0–2
Thru 5/64" scrn.-thin %	0–2	0–2	0–2	0–2.5	0
Wort pH	5.8–5.9	5.7–5.9	5.7–5.9	5.7–5.9	5.5–5.8
Viscosity, cP	165–1.75	1.55–1.65	1.52–1.62	1.60–1.70	1.45–1.55
Odor of mash	Aromatic	Aromatic	Aromatic	Aromatic	Aromatic
Speed of filtration	Norm.–Slow	Norm.–Rapid	Normal	Norm.–Slow	Norm.–Rapid
Degree of clarity	Clr.–Sl. hazy	Clear	Clear	Sl. Hazy	Clear

The brewer always needs to take into account the moisture content of each lot of malt to calculate its real extract potential. Given two malts with 81 percent DBFG extract (see below), malt at 6 percent moisture content will give only 76.1 percent potential extract as-is, while a malt at 3 percent moisture content will give 78.6 percent.

Color, SRM (°Lovibond, ASBC color): The color given for the lot of malt being evaluated should be within, or close to, the color parameters given in tables 1 and 16. Moreover, for batch-to-batch beer consistency, the grain bill needs to be adjusted to reflect malt color change, especially regarding highly colored malts.

Color may not be stated as SRM/ASBC/°L units. Where EBC units are given, the formula ASBC = (°EBC + 1.2)/2.65 gives reasonable but not entirely accurate transposition. The color for English malts is often given as Color IOB, EBC method. IOB color is only approximately 80 percent of EBC color. Where IOB units are given, the formula ASBC = [(IOB/.80) + 1.2]/2.65 can be used.

HCU color units are a summary measurement of wort color that is equal to the sum of the SRM/°Lovibond of all the malts used to make a wort. HCU units and SRM wort color are comparable up to about 10 °SRM; after that, corrections must be made. See the conversion chart in table 15 to convert from HCU color to approximate °SRM.

The color ranges for most malt types vary widely, depending on the country of origin and the maltster. From the maltster's point of view, it is of some advantage to have a "unique" color range, since it requires any brewer using the malt to make serious adjustments in the brew house program in order to switch suppliers. To some extent, this diversity also benefits brewers, but on the whole, color variation in the same nominal malt types is a problem for the brewer seeking predictable results.

Extract, DBFG: Extract yield, dry basis (0 percent moisture content) fine grind, from an ASBC laboratory mash. The "fine grind" is standardized as being crushed on a Buhler-Miag disc mill at a .2 millimeter setting (often given as 2 Miag), giving 10 percent (±1 percent) of the yield held on a .0232-inch screen, or 40 percent flour. The fine-grind extract gives the maximum potential yield of any malt. It indicates the quality of the barley and the proficiency of its malting. The higher the DBFG extract, the better the malt. Any base malt that does not give at least 78 percent DBFG extract is substandard.

Extract, DBCG: Extract yield, dry basis coarse grind, from an ASBC standard laboratory mash, to 113 degrees F (45 degrees C), malt ground at .7 millimeters on a Buhler-Miag disc mill (7 Miag), giving 75 percent (±1 percent) of the yield as grits held on a .0232-inch screen, or 20 percent flour. Again, extract is given on the dry basis of the malt, for ease of comparison. DBCG indicates the yield that the malt is capable of giving, because it approximates the crush experienced in the brew house. Brew house yield, however, is always lower than the coarse-grind figure predicts, because the value is given on a dry basis (see above), and because the laboratory crush and mash are always more efficient than that actually experienced in the brewery.

In reality, brew-house efficiency is only 85 to 95 percent of what coarse grind predicts. The brew-house yield can be calculated from the dry basis coarse grind by adjusting it to account for the moisture content given in the lot analysis (as-is coarse grind), then factoring in the anticipated brew-house efficiency:

DBCG/(1 + moisture content) - .002 = AICG (as-is coarse grind)

For example, where DBCG is 80 percent and moisture content is 5 percent, the result would be

$$(.80/1.05)-.002 = .7599$$

Seventy-six percent is the yield a brewer could expect from the malt if mashing and lautering were 100 percent efficient. For a brew house averaging 92 percent efficiency, anticipated brew-house yield would be

$$[(.80/1.05)-.002].92 = .699, \text{ or } 70\% \text{ brew-house yield}$$

The adjusted brew-house extract yield can be used to predict the degrees Plato or specific gravity that each pound of malt will give in a gallon of wort by the formulas

Adjusted yield x 11.486 = °Plato of 1 lb. of malt in 1 gal. of wort
Adjusted yield x 46.214 = excess gravity, 1 lb. in 1 gal. of wort
.699 x 11.486 = 8.02 °Plato
.699 x 46.214 = G 32.3, or SG 1032.3

Conversely, the actual density of the wort yielded can be used to calculate the brew-house efficiency:

Brew-house efficiency = [(°Plato x gal. of wort)/11.486]/[DBCG/(1 + moisture content) - .002)] x lb. of malt

FG-CG, difference: The fine grind–coarse grind difference indicates the modification of the malt. When a "steely" (vitreous) malt is crushed at 7 Miag, the large grits are not as accessible to diastatic enzymes as grits from a mealy malt. The difference between the extract yield of the

fine-grind and coarse-grind mashes will be greater with a
steely malt. An FG-CG difference of up to 2.2 percent is
acceptable if a decoction or step mash is being employed,
but brewers are well advised to purchase malts with a difference less than 2.0 percent, and below 1.8 percent when
infusion mashing.

HWE (hot-water extract, liter degrees/kilogram at
68 degrees F [20 degrees C], dry basis): The IOB method of
measuring the dissolved extract from malt. A loose laboratory EBC Congress mash is made from fine-ground malt.
L°/kg expresses the excess gravity of one liter of wort that
a kilogram of the given malt could produce. The HWE can
be compared to ASBC DBFG by dividing it by the factor
3.86 (300/3.86 = 77.7 percent). A reasonably good malt
gives at least 300 L°/kg, dry basis, and a good malt 305 to
315 L°/kg.

An IOB lot analysis may give the HWE at 7 Miag,
which is equivalent to the DBCG rather than the DBFG;
the yield from such a lot will be correspondingly lower. It
can be compared to the DBCG by dividing it by 3.86.

HWE (pounds per quarter): Expressing the hot water
extract in pounds per quarter, or pounds per barrel, is an
outmoded British means of measuring extract potential. It
was based on dividing the weight of a barrel of extract
derived from a quarter of malt (336 pounds) by the weight
of one UK barrel of plain water (360 pounds). The weight of
the wort in excess of the weight of the water gives the
pounds of extract per barrel:

Brewer's pounds per barrel = weight of wort - 360,
or G (excess gravity) x .36

Brew-house extract was expressed as pounds per
quarter of malt:

Pounds per quarter = [(G - 360) x barrels of wort)/(pounds of malt/336)]

Specific gravity was obtained by the formula

sg gr = weight of 1 UK barrel of the wort/360

CWE (cold-water extract): The amount of soluble material that is present in any malt before mashing, obtained from a three-hour stirred mash of coarse-ground malt at 68 degrees F (20 degrees C), containing ammonia to inhibit enzyme activity. It is an indicator of malt modification; the higher the CWE value, the more complete the beta-glucanase dissolution of endosperm cell walls has been, and the more soluble starch and protein the malt contains. A CWE of 18 percent indicates well-modified malt, and higher than 20 percent "forced" or overmodified malt. The range of 18 to 22 percent is acceptable for infusion mashing, and 15 to 18 percent for decoction and step mashing; for Vienna and Munich malts, 17 to 20 percent is more usual. The CWE as an indicator of modification should be judged in relationship to the soluble nitrogen ratio (see below) for a more complete picture of the malt character.

Hartong 45 degrees: An expression of malt modification, based upon mashing a lot sample by the Congress mash method and at 113 degrees F (45 degrees C). The yield obtained from the 45-degree mash as a percentage of the yield obtained from the Congress mash is given as the Hartong 45-degree percentage, or VZ45 value. Like CWE and SNR, it is an indicator of malt modification.

Another value, known as the Hartong extract, compiled from mashes at four different temperatures, was used to indicate malt quality, with well-modified malt giving a value greater than 5. The Hartong extract is no longer commonly used.

Alpha-amylase, DU: ASBC measurement of dextrinizing units/100 grams, dry weight. Each unit represents the quantity of alpha-amylase that dextrinizes one gram of soluble starch in one hour at 68 degrees F (20 degrees C). One hundred grams of six-row malt should give thirty-five to forty-five units, and American two-row malts forty to fifty. Pilsener malts, because they are kilned at lower temperatures, should range between forty-four and forty-eight, and higher-kilned lager and Vienna malts in the range of forty to forty-five. Munich and ale malts give the least alpha-amylase, because extensive conversion and higher kilning temperatures have caused greater enzyme depletion.

Overly modified malts generally have low DU values. On the other hand, the less well modified a malt is, the greater the DU value needs to be for it to be infusion mashed. When a lot analysis gives an alpha-amylase value below the quoted ranges and modification indicators are relatively usual, the mash may need to be thicker and longer for it to yield the usual brew-house efficiency.

DP, °Lintner (diastatic power ASBC, .25 maltose equivalent): Diastatic power expresses the combined alpha- and beta-amylase strength of the malt. DP measures digestion of a standard starch solution by titration with ferricyanide. Diastatic power is compared to dextrinizing units as a measure of beta-amylase strength, and considered together with mealiness/vitreosity as a measure of how well a malt will respond to mashing. The DP may be as low as 35 to 40 for a well-converted, low-protein ale malt, 100 for a lager malt, 125 for an American high-protein two-row lager malt, and as high as 160 for six-row brewers' malt. Diastatic power decreases as malt color increases.

IOB DP units give values similar to °Lintner.

DP, °WK (diastatic power, degrees Windisch-Kolbach, WK units): The EBC unit of measurement for diastatic strength. °WK may be as low as 100 for ale malts or as high as 600 for green malt. The °WK value can be converted to degrees Lintner by the formula °Lin = (°WK + 16)/3.5. The reciprocal equation is °WK = (°Lin x 3.5) - 16.

Conversion time, min: Indicates modification and diastatic power under real, albeit ideal, mash conditions, by the time it takes a laboratory mash to reach iodine end point. "Base" malts such as pale and Pilsener should convert within fifteen minutes, British ale malts within ten, and better converted, high-enzyme base malts, such as brewer's two- and six-row, in less than ten minutes.

Protein, percent: Equal to the total nitrogen times a factor of 6.25. For all-malt beers, protein should not exceed 12 percent; 9 to 10 percent is usual for European lager and British ale malts.

Soluble protein, percent: See TSN, percent, below.

TN, percent: Expresses the total nitrogen as a percentage of the weight of the malt. Since 30 to 40 percent of malt nitrogenous matter ends up as "permanently soluble nitrogen" and composes 5 to 6 percent of the dissolved solids in the boiled wort, the nitrogen content of any malt is of concern to the brewer. Total nitrogen includes poorly soluble proteins and polypeptides, and affects extract yield, clarity, head formation, and fermentation. There needs to be enough nitrogen, but not too much; malt of 2 percent or more nitrogen creates the risk of haze problems in an all-malt beer.

TSN, percent (total soluble nitrogen, percent of total nitrogen by weight): The percentage of nitrogen in solution in a wort. Generally, about half the soluble nitrogen in wort is formed by proteolysis during mashing; the other half exists in the malt. TSN is used in the soluble nitrogen ratio, below.

SNR (Kolbach Index, S/T, SN/TN, soluble nitrogen/total nitrogen ratio): The soluble nitrogen (or protein) figure, divided by the percent total nitrogen (or protein) is another indicator of malt modification. The higher the percentage, the more highly modified the malt sample is. For traditional lager malts, 30 to 33 percent indicates undermodification, and 37 to 40 percent over-modification. Malts to be infusion mashed should have an SNR of 38 to 42 percent. Malt is seldom rejected on the basis of the SNR unless it approaches 50 percent for infusion mashing, and 40 percent for decoction mashing. At 50 percent SNR, the beer brewed will inevitably lack body. Generally, when the percentage given exceeds that recommended for the type of malt, the brewer increases the temperature or shortens the duration of protein and saccharification rests; when it is lower, the saccarifica-tion rest is lengthened or the temperature is lowered, or a protein rest is added or extended.

Mealy, percent: By convention, malt is classi-fied as being mealy, half-glassy/glassy-ends, and glassy (steely or vitreous). Mealy kernels are those in which the endosperm is not more than 25 percent glassy. Half-glassy endosperm is 25 to 75 percent glassy, and the endosperm of glassy kernels is more than 75 percent vitreous. The better and more extensive the malting, the higher the percentage of mealy kernels. Glassy malt does not crush well and is not readily hydrolyzed because it contains a higher percentage of beta-glucans and complexed protein, so it gives less extract than mealy malt. If a malt is to be infusion-mashed, it must be at least 95 percent mealy, and for any mash program should be at least 90 percent mealy. Where mealiness is expressed as mealy/half-glassy/glassy, for base malts the ratio should be 92/7/1 percent or better for decoction and step mashing, and 95/4/1 percent or better for infusion mashing.

Friability, percent (vitreosity): Another method of analyzing malt conversion. The ASBC/EBC method measures the percentage friable and the percentage unmodified by standardized crushing, sieving, and weighing. Any malt should be at least 80 percent friable, and for infusion mashing 85 percent friable.

By another method sometimes used, a sample of thirty or so kernels are split lengthwise in a farinator box, then examined and classified. The factor 1 expresses vitreous, glassy endosperm, .5 is half-glassy, .25 indicates glassy ends, and 0 is the value given to completely modified (mealy) kernels. The average result is given. The range is 0 to 1.0, with a vitreosity of 0 to .25 preferred. By itself, the vitreosity value is of questionable use, since it doesn't clearly pinpoint either the exact problem or the extent to which it occurs. Moreover, it is very subjective.

Size (plump/thin, screen separation less than 2.2 millimeters): Size is most clearly expressed as screen separations, but is just as commonly given as plump/thin. European malts often list only the percentage that can be sieved through 2.2-millimeter openings (thins, 5/64 inch diameter and smaller). Generally, the plumper the kernels, the better the yield; however, the uniformity of malt size is just as important. Because of this, some analyses list homogeneity instead of sizes. Any lot of malt that will crush reasonably well must have kernels that are at least 90 percent adjacent sizes, regardless of the plumpness. Brewers generally demand malt that is of 95 percent or greater homogeneity.

Malt is also rejected for containing more than 1 percent thin kernels or more than 2 percent of kernels smaller than 2.2 millimeters, because their presence indicates unmodified kernels.

Wort pH: Base malts should give a pH of 5.5 to 5.8, with ale malts giving the lower value and lager malts the higher. The pH value is used by the brewer to adjust liquor acidity for the particular lot of malt.

Viscosity, cP (centipoise units): The viscosity is a measure of the breakdown of beta-glucans (endosperm cell walls) during malting. A malt that gives a laboratory wort of high viscosity (more than 1.75) will not run off well during sparging. The higher the viscosity, the slower lautering and filtering will be, and the greater the need for a decoction program, or less effectively, a step mash. Boiling and a protein rest help break down beta-glucans to less viscous gums and polysaccharides.

Where given, the IOB 70-degree mash viscosity should be 6.3 to 6.8.

Odor of mash: This measure is primarily used to indicate off-odors, such as moldy, green-malt, or burnt. With colored malts, very aromatic should be expected.

Speed of filtration: The lower the modification or the higher the protein and beta-glucan content, the slower any malt will filter in the lab. Slow filtration with presumably well-converted malts indicates conversion problems.

Degree of clarity: Brewers generally accept slightly hazy as an acceptable degree of clarity, but it does indicate protein or starch conversion shortcomings. A review of the other parameters of the lot analysis should pinpoint changes in the brew-house program that can be made to improve the runoff from the mash.

Several other parameters may be given in a lot analysis. Some of these, and their usual values, are the following: 1,000-kernel weight (36 to 45) or bushel weight (42 to 44), DMS-P (DMS precursor, 5 to 15 parts per million for lager malts), and growth (acrospire 0 to 1/4, 1/4 to 1/2, 1/2 to 3/4, 3/4 to full, overgrown; 80 percent minimum of 3/4 to full growth for American and British/fully modified malts, and 1/2 to 3/4 for multirest lager malts). Other evaluation techniques may be performed by the brewer to judge the quality of any malt.

Ultimately, only experience with the particular barley type, its origin, season of growth, age, and malting permits finite procedural adjustments.

Evaluation

Good malt should be plump and firm, even in size and shape, and of a light, straw-colored hue. A sample handful should contain almost no straw, rootlets, dust, or debris. The malt kernel should be easily crushed between the fingers, and uniformly soft from end to end. When broken, the kernel should write like chalk and show no air pockets within the husk.

If no growth specifications are given in the lot analysis, it is advisable to check growth when the malt is received. The acrospire can be exposed by cutting or

Malt

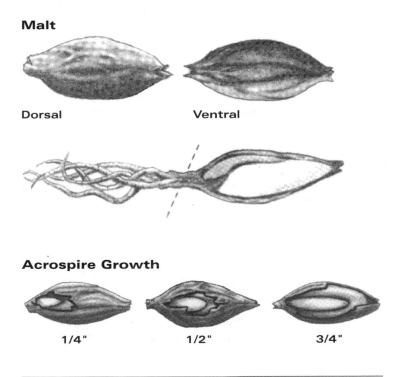

Dorsal   Ventral

Acrospire Growth

1/4"   1/2"   3/4"

rubbing away the husk over the acrospire of fifty kernels, or by boiling the kernels for an hour to turn the husks translucent. At least 80 percent of the kernels of any malt delivery must fall within a single size group for the malt to be uniformly crushed and mashed. Moreover, malt that is 5 percent or more ungerminated (zero to one-fourth growth) is unacceptable for decoction mashing; 2 percent or more is unacceptable for infusion mashing. Malt to be mashed by only one temperature rest must have been uniformly sprouted, and the acrospire growth should uniformly be from three-fourths to the full length of the kernel. Malt that has been kilned when the acrospire growth is only from one-half to three-fourths the length of the grain can yield a greater amount of extract than fully modified malt, but it should be step or decoction mashed. Malt of widely varying acrospire growth also should be step or decoction mashed. Brewing-quality malt should yield no appreciable number of kernels with acrospire growth less than one-half the length of the grain.

Acrospire growth should be considered in conjunction with examination of the endosperm. Thirty or so kernels are split lengthwise, and the starch is examined for steeliness/vitreosity; short acrospires and steely ends indicate insufficient sprouting, whereas steeliness irrespective of acrospire length indicates poor drying/kilning.

Another test of germination/modification is made by the "sinker" test. Fifty kernels are shaken into water, and then let rest for ten minutes. After ten minutes, the floaters and sinkers are counted. Ungerminated and under-modified kernels will sink. At the very least, thirty-five of the kernels (70 percent) should float; with good malt, 95 percent will float parallel to the surface of the water. Vertical floaters indicate poor modification.

The malt should yield 65 to 80 percent sugar by weight after mashing and test between 1.4 and 2.0 percent nitrogen. Malt of greater than 2 percent nitrogen should only be used when brewing with low-protein adjuncts.

Malt should be selected by its color and modification to suit the type of beer being brewed and the brewing method.

Avoid malt of very high protein content because it has correspondingly fewer carbohydrates. The protein can retard starch conversion during mashing and increases the likelihood of hazing in the beer. Finally, there is no substitute for tasting the malt. The better the flavor and aromatics of the malt, the better the malt complement of the finished beer will be.

Table 2

Grading by Size	
Grade	**Characteristic**
1	Remains on 7/64" screen, plump
2	Remains on 3/32" screen
3	Remains on 5/64" screen, "thin" European
4	Falls through 5/64" screen, "thin" American

The two larger sizes will mash well and produce high yields. The small kernels have greater husk content and will give lower extracts.

Grading Pale Malt by Character		
Mealy	(mellow, soft)	Will mash well
Half-glassy	(semihard)	Must employ a longer, more thorough mashing
Glassy	(hard, translucent, grayish white)	Unsuitable for brewing

Carbohydrates

Carbohydrates are compounds formed by molecules of carbon, hydrogen, and oxygen. They include simple sugars, chains of four or more sugars called oligosaccharides, and polysaccharides, formed by the union of ten or more monosaccharides. Barley and malt are largely made up of carbohydrates, as are 90 to 95 percent of the wort solids. The barley carbohydrate group is composed of insoluble cellulose (the membranes and casing of the barley corn) and soluble hemicellulose, starch, dextrins (alpha-glucans), and the simpler mono- , di- and trisaccharides that we call sugars.

Cellulose is an insoluble compound-sugar (50 to 5,000 molecules of $C_6H_{10}O_5$) that makes up the barley husk; it is irreducible by malt enzymes. It constitutes roughly 5 to 10 percent of the malt by weight. Although it is structurally similar to starch, cellulose does not contribute fermentable extract or desirable flavors to the malt extract. But as malt husks, cellulose is employed in the lauter-tun to form a filter bed through which the mash extract is strained. Extraction by high temperature and alkaline sparging leaches harsh tannins from the husk into the extract to the detriment of the beer.

Hemicellulose and soluble gums bind the aleurone layer of the barley kernel together, and are constituents of endosperm cell walls that encapsulate starch granules. They account for about 10 percent of the weight of the barley kernel. They are both polysaccharide mixtures complexed with protein. The malt gums are largely pentosans of xylose, arabinose, galactose, and complexed glucose, which may be dissolved at temperatures of 160 to 176 degrees F (71 to 80 degrees C). They compose about 20 percent of the endosperm cell walls. They can be fully reduced to simple sugars in a thorough mash cycle.

Table 3

Degree of Modification	
Acrospire Growth:	**Characteristic of:**
0"–1/4"	Cereal malt, unmodified
1/2"–2/3"	Steely lager malt
1/2"–3/4"	Lager malt
3/4"–Full	British malt, American brewers' malt

Malt Colors				
Malt	**Type**	**SRM**	**EBC**	**IOB**
Diastatic	Base malt	1.0–1.4	1.5–2.5	1.2–2.0
Pilsener	Base malt	1.2–1.6	2.0–3.0	1.6–2.4
Lager	Base malt	1.4–1.8	2.5–3.5	2.0–2.8
Brewers	Base malt	1.4–2.0	2.5–4.0	2.0–3.2
CaraPils	Vitreous	1.4–4.0	2.5–9.0	2.0–7.2
British pale	Base malt	2.0–2.7	4.0–6.0	3.2–4.8
Vienna	Base malt	3–5	7–12	5.6–9.6
Munich	Toasted	6–12	15–30	12–24
Light caramel/Carastan	Vitreous	5–45	12–120	10–96
Amber/Biscuit/Dunkles	Toasted	20–30	50–80	40–64
Crystal/Caramel 50	Vitreous	45–60	120–160	96–130
Brown	Roasted	45–60	120–160	96–130
Caramel 80	Vitreous	75–85	200–225	160–180
Caramel 120	Vitreous	100–122	265–325	210–260
Chocolate	Roasted	340–500	900–1325	720–1060
Roast barley	Roasted	270–650	725–1700	580–1400
Black/Roast	Roasted	550–650	1450–1700	1220–1400

Hemicelluloses are more complex and stubbornly resist hydrolysis. They give a purple-to-black color with iodine. Very viscous beta-glucan is the major constituent of barley hemicellulose, accounting for about 75 percent of the cell walls. In intermediate stages of cell-wall solubilization, the release of beta-glucan inhibits lautering and filtering and cause hazes. One consequence of forced malting is insufficient hydrolysis of beta-glucans to glucose by beta-glucanase enzymes, which are denatured above 140 degrees F (60 degrees C) and do not usually survive kilning. High wort viscosity indicates excessive beta-glucans in the malt. With reasonably well converted malt, manageable amounts of beta-glucans may be liberated from hemicellulose by proteolytic enzymes during a 95 to 113 degree F (35 to 45 degree C) mash rest and contribute to a beer's fermentability, body, and foam head.

Starch

Native starch (in malt, 20 to 400 molecules of $C_6H_{10}O_5$) occurs as granules that are insoluble in cold water, accounting for about 60 percent of the malt's weight. If the native starch granule is crushed to flour, it readily combines with moisture to form a pastelike gel. In warm water, amylose, the small fraction of a granule that is water soluble, can be diffused out of native starch. In hot water, the starch granule swells until it finally bursts, exposing insoluble amylopectin as well.

Amylose occurs as straight helical chains of glucose molecules joined by 1-4 links. Exposed to amylose, iodine becomes entrapped within the coils, giving an intense blue-black color. Amylose is reduced to maltose and mal-

Starch

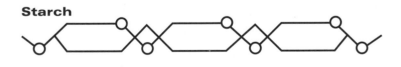

Cellulose

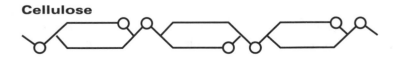

totriose from the nonreducing end of the chain by the beta-amylase enzyme. The alpha-amylase enzyme facilitates this process by randomly severing amylose chains, yielding glucose, maltose, and maltotriose, and exposing more chain ends to beta-amylase activity.

Amylopectin accounts for about 75 percent of the malt starch; consequently, its decomposition is central to mashing. It occurs as highly branched glucose chains that give a red color with iodine. The chain and branches are formed by 1-4-linked glucose molecules, but the glucose molecules at the branching points are joined in a 1-6 configuration.

Dextrins

Dextrins, or alpha-glucans $(C_6H_{10}O_5) \bullet H_2O$, are residual, unfermentable fractions of amylopectin of from four to thirty glucose molecules. Dextrins occur in brewing because neither alpha- nor beta-amylase can sever the 1-6

Amylose   **Amylopectin Fragments**

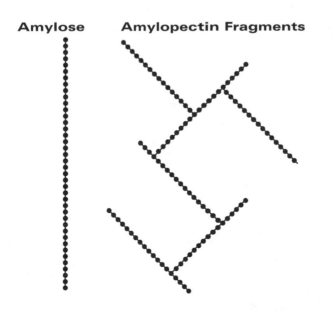

links of amylopectin or the 1-4 links near those branching points. In malting, limit dextrinase debranches amylopectin by separation of the 1-6 links, but this enzyme group does not survive malting and mash temperatures. In the mash, beta-amylase is only able to effect a slight reduction of amylopectin, liberating maltose only at the nonreducing

Starch

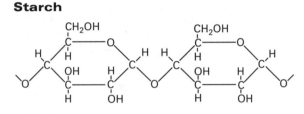

Maltose

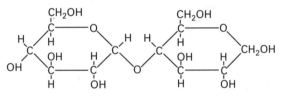

Isomaltose

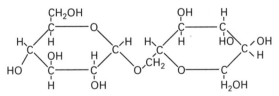

Sucrose

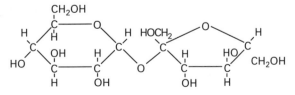

ends of the many branches. The large dextrins it leaves behind are called ß-limit dextrins. ß-limit dextrins give a mahogany (reddish-brown) color to iodine.

ß-limit dextrins are dismantled in the mash by alpha-amylase. It randomly breaks 1-4 glucose links in the amylopectin complex, exposing new nonreducing ends for

Melibiose

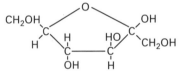

Fructose

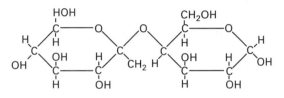

Mannose

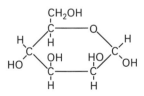

Galactose

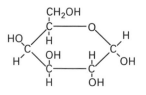

Glucose

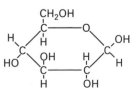

beta-amylase to convert to maltose. Acting together, the amylases reduce amylopectin to much smaller a-limit dextrins. Small a-limit dextrins give no color with iodine, while the largest give a faint red-to-violet color.

Sugars

Monosaccharides $(C_6H_{12}O_6)$ are single-molecule carbohydrates. Glucose, photosynthesized in the leaves of green plants from carbon dioxide and water, is the primary sugar associated with grains. However, it accounts for only 1 to 2 percent of the malt's weight. After mashing, it accounts for 7 to 10 percent of the wort extract. Fructose (an isomer, or molecular rearrangement, of glucose), galactose and mannose are other monosaccharides found in malt. They are all readily and wholly fermentable. Galactose is a constituent of many oligosaccharides and polysaccharides, occurring especially in gums and pectins.

The disaccharides are double sugars $(C_{12}H_{22}O_{11})$. Maltose, the sugar most closely associated with brewing, is the simplest compound sugar. It is formed by two molecules of glucose, joined together at their 1 and 4 carbon atoms by the removal of a water molecule $(C_6H_{12}O_6 + C_6H_{13}O_6 - H_2O = C_{12}H_{22}O_{11} \times H_2O)$. Although it makes up only 1 percent of malt's weight, it is the sugar that is primarily derived from the hydrolysis of starch, and accounts for 40 to 55 percent of the wort solubles. It is slowly but very surely fermentable.

Other disaccharides present in malt are sucrose (one molecule each of glucose and fructose), lactose (an isomer of sucrose), and melibiose (one molecule each of galactose and glucose). Sucrose is readily fermentable, lactose is unfermentable, and melibiose is fermentable only by *Saccharomayces uvarum*. Of these disaccharides, only sucrose is present in malt in any appreciable amount, composing 3 to 5 percent of the wort extract.

Trisaccharides are three-molecule sugars. In malt, they are maltotriose, glucodifructose, and fructosant; raffinose, which is present in barley, disappears during malting. Maltotriose (three molecules of glucose) is slowly fermentable by most strains of brewing yeast. It is the only significant trisaccharide in brewing, accounting for up to 15 percent of the wort solids.

Protein

Carbohydrates alone do not form a satisfactory brewing extract; malt protein is essential as a yeast nutrient and to give the beer body and head. In the barley kernel, protein serves as plant food for the embryo. During malting and mashing, it is reduced by protein-metabolizing enzymes to less-complex *albumins* (an outdated but useful term that groups together all coagulable and water soluble protein fractions) or even simpler amino acids. In solution with mineral salts, some of the protein forms acids, causing the pH of the mash to drop.

The term *protein* strictly defines very complex polymeric coils of amino acid chained together by peptide links (molecular weight 17,000 to 150,000), but in a wider sense, it also includes the products of their decomposition. This reference to protein on the one hand as an unwieldy malt constituent (e.g., high-molecular-weight albumin and less soluble globulin, glutelin, and hordein), and on the other as a source of a beer's body and head can be confusing. In fact, the brewer does not strive to eliminate the proteins but to simplify them to a range of colloidable and soluble fractions. Only when an excessive number of complex proteins (molecular weight 10,000 to 100,000, average 30,000) are carried into the beer will they result in chill haze, an irreversible cloudiness, or off-flavors caused by oxidation.

The large protein complexes of the malt must be largely reduced to intermediate albumins (molecular weight 5,000 to 12,000), such as proteoses and peptones, and peptides (molecular weight 400 to 1,500) during mashing, so that they are simple enough to dissolve, or colloid with hop resins, and be carried over into the finished beer. Considerable nitrogenous matter must be present: amino acids and peptides to sustain culture-yeast activity, and simple albumin to form the body of the beer. Three to 6 percent of the wort extract is usually nitrogen-based. A beer brewed so that it had little or no low-molecular-weight protein fractions (molecular weight 12,000 to 20,000) left in it would be unable to form or support a foam head. Generally, 25 to 50 percent of the malt protein is carried into the ferment as simple nitrogen complexes (amino acids, peptides, albumin).

Because enzymes are proteins, the protein content of any malt is an indication of its enzymatic strength. In general, protein-rich, six-row malts are more apt to cloud beer than are other malts, but they do produce stronger enzymatic activity. Low-protein malts are less apt to cause hazing, but as a consequence have less enzymatic power and must be carefully mashed.

Other Malt Fractions

Nonprotein nitrogen accounts for up to 10 percent of the total malt nitrogen. Peptides, although not true proteins, are intermediate forms between protein and amino acids. They are nitrogen based, as are vitamins and nucleic acids. Peptides, which enhance the beer's viscosity (palate fullness), may also oxidize to high-molecular-weight polypeptides. Polypeptides are unstable and contribute to nonbiological haze formation.

The vitamins in malt are principally of the B complex; they are necessary for yeast growth. Products of the decomposition of nucleic acids account for only .1 percent of the wort extract, but contribute to both yeast nutrition and flavor enhancement.

Polyphenols, phosphates, lipids, and fatty acids are other significant malt constituents. Polyphenols from the husk, pericarp, and aleurone layers of the malt kernel are acidic precursors of tannins and give beer an unpleasantly bitter, astringent taste and reddish hue. With highly kilned malt, oxidation of phenolic melanoids (pigments) to aldehydes, such as by hot-side aeration, contribute to stale flavors in beer. Complex polyphenol polymers are true tannins and counteract the solubility of otherwise stable proteins. They should be eliminated from the extract by a well-roused kettle boil; in the cooled wort and the ferment, the oxidative polymerization of polyphenols to tannins causes medicinal off-flavors, astringency, and haze formation.

Phosphates in the malt, principally organic phytin, are major factors in the acidulation of the mash. They give up phytic acid (phytate) at high kiln temperatures during malting, and by enzymatic reduction during an acidifying mash rest at below 128 degrees F (53 degrees C).

Lipids are fatlike substances composing roughly 3 percent of the malt; they range from straight-chain to complex branched-ring hydrocarbons, including neutral fats, fatty acids, alcohols, aldehydes, and waxes. About one-third of malt lipids occur as reserves in the embryo, and most of the rest are concentrated in the aleurone layer. Triacylglycerol and other triglycerides (triesters of glycerol and long-chain fatty acids) are the predominant neutral lipids in barley. They support respiration of the embryo during malting.

Fatty acids ($C_nH_{2n}O_2$), or vegetable oils, are fat-derived *(aliphatic)* hydrocarbon chains. In barley malt, these are the relatively long-chain linoleic ($C_{18}H_{32}O_2$), palmitic

$(C_6H_{32}O_2)$, and oleic $(C_{18}H_{34}O_2)$ acids. Proportionally more of these than other malt lipids are carried into the wort. Although they are essential in the yeast cell as reserves and they comprise only .05 percent of the malt extract, if excessive amounts of lipids are washed into the runoff by overzealous sparging they will reduce foam stability and give rise to "cardboardy," "goaty," and "soapy" stale flavors in beer.

Finally, considerable silica and inorganic phosphate are leached out of the malt, along with a wide range of trace minerals necessary for yeast metabolism.

CHAPTER **3**

Water

Water constitutes 85 to 90 percent of the volume of any beer, and therefore the mineral content of the brewing water has a marked effect on the flavor and appearance of the finished beer — and on the brewing process. Certain beer styles are suited to waters of very specific mineral composition, and an otherwise well-brewed example will always be diminished by the use of totally inappropriate brewing water.

By looking closely at the geology of any given area, it is often possible to find wells or springs that will perfectly suit a given brew. Local, regional, and state water departments and services can be very helpful in locating such sources. For most brewers, however, mineral treatment of the local supply is the more reasonable alternative.

Only brackish, polluted water and sea water are entirely unsuitable for brewing. Most potable fresh waters, whether too "hard," too carbonate, too "soft," or iron contaminated, may be boiled, aerated, sedimented, filtered, or treated with an appropriate mineral salt or acid to be made suitable for brewing almost any type of beer. Practically speaking, however, brewing water should be clear, bright, unpolluted, and have agreeable taste and reasonably uniform composition from day to day. It should not be corrosive, have a detectable odor, or throw an appreciable amount of sediment upon resting or boiling.

All naturally occurring waters are dilute solutions of minerals in which small quantities of gases and organic matter may be dissolved. Rainwater should be the purest natural source of water, but because it assimilates atmospheric gases and organic mineral particles wherever the air is the least bit polluted, most rainwater is absolutely unsuitable for use in brewing. Precipitation in areas far removed from large fossil-fuel burning plants more often than not is still polluted by highly corrosive sulfuric acid (H_2SO_4). Free hydrogen carbonates (HCO_3, usually referred to as *bicarbonates*) are also common in rainwater. They rob the calcium from the mash, wort, and ferment by forming bicarbonate salts that are precipitated from solution during boiling.

Surface waters, besides having the dissolved materials and gases found in rainwater, usually contain large amounts of organic matter, vegetable coloring, soil, silica, clay, and microflora. Especially in marshy terrains and industrial areas, surface water is likely to be heavily contaminated with organic acids and nitrates and is completely unsuitable for use in brewing.

Surface waters suitable for brewing are generally limited to clear-running, spring-fed brooks and streams that flow over gravel, sand, or rocky beds, and deep reservoirs with carefully protected watersheds. Water from old soft-bottomed streams, which flow sluggishly or carry topsoil and vegetation in suspension, and rivers, ponds, and lakes needs to be filtered, at the very least, before use, and is seldom a good choice for brewing. If the water tastes like it comes from a pond, so will the beer.

Municipal water supplies are usually gathered from several deep wells and reservoirs, and sometimes from rivers. They are invariably filtered and treated (most commonly with up to 0.5 parts per million chlorine) to inhibit microbial contamination. Such tap water is often perfectly suitable for use in brewing, after being filtered, rested, or boiled and aerated to drive off free chlorine and induce sedimentation of carbonates, silicates, and incrustants. Chlorine and organics may be removed by activated carbon filtration. Water departments often vary the inflows from several different sources, and water composition varies accordingly.

The quantity and composition of underground water at any given location and depth are contingent upon subsurface geological formation. Although the elementary minerals and metals dispersed in the earth's crust are relatively few (rock is largely silica with aluminum, iron, calcium, potassium, magnesium, manganese, zinc, and copper), the soluble components (mineral salts) they form yield water of varying composition from place to place. The mosaic geological structure of the earth's crust causes water to rise to different levels at different locations, and its level may be fairly constant or may fluctuate with changing patterns of precipitation, freezing, and thawing.

The value of a spring or well as a brewing source should first be judged by the seasonal consistency of its flow. There is less fluctuation in the composition of any ground water that has a reasonably constant flow year-round. Shallow wells and seasonal springs do not usually yield acceptable brewing water. Their composition varies widely, and they often carry soil and other surface contamination in suspension. They commonly yield unacceptable levels of bacterial contamination.

Deep wells originating in large subterranean aquifers, and mountain springs percolating up through fissures in

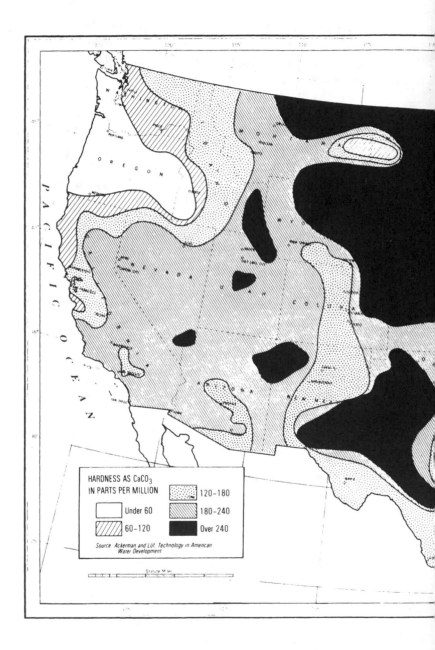

HARDNESS AS CaCO₃ IN PARTS PER MILLION

Under 60

60-120

120-180

180-240

Over 240

Source: Ackerman and Löf, Technology in American Water Development

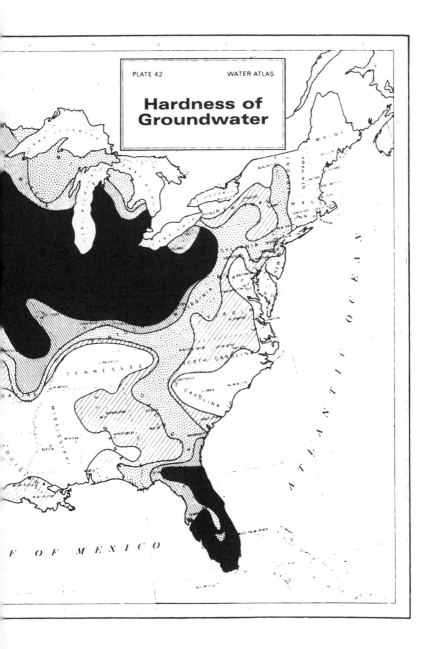

PLATE 42   WATER ATLAS

Hardness of Groundwater

bedrock formations without leaching through soil or disintegrated rock are usually of very stable composition and free from surface contamination. Subterranean springs (with the notable exception of mineral springs) emerging from inorganic rock complexes commonly yield water with less dissolved materials than does deep-well water. Deep wells usually tap water sources that have traveled farther than the water of springs, and having contacted more mineral-bearing substrata consequently have more minerals in solution than does spring water. Which minerals occur in ground water is dependent on the nature of the strata the water has contacted. Igneous and metamorphic rocks (granite, basalt, marble, gneiss, and quartz) are both very dense and compositionally very stable; they yield the fewest mineral ions to hydrolysis of any rock formations. Because they are hard, they do not filter the water passing over them as do most sedimentary formations. They are not likely to bear much water unless they are extensively fissured or enclose voids left by the dissolution of softer strata. Granite is the most common of the igneous rocks, composing the greatest part of the continental plates. It commonly yields very "soft" water of less than 100 ppm hardness (as $CaCO_3$), and water of less than 50 ppm hardness is not at all uncommon.

These rocks are eroded by freezing water, scaling, hydrolysis, or friction, and the particles are carried away by wind and water and ultimately deposited in topographical depressions. This alluvia forms unconsolidated sediments, often far from the parent rock.

Sand, which is largely silica dioxide split off from quartz, passes water freely while filtering out most suspended solids. Where it lies above impervious bedrock, it yields excellent water. Clay, on the other hand, is impervious and yields very little water, but water pools above it wherever it makes an unbroken sediment. Clay underlies many excellent aquifers. Clay is mostly hydrous silicates of aluminum, often colored red by iron oxide or dark by carbon-based impurities. Gravel (pebbles of 1/8 to 2 1/2 inches in diameter) is usually found with sand or clay, either on river terraces or as the residue of glacial retreat. It often serves to make clay subsoil pervious to penetration by some surface runoff.

Consolidated sediments are deposits of sand, clay, or gravel that have hardened under pressure or have been cemented by lime. They are typically deposits left on the floors of prehistoric seas and lakes. Sandstone is very common; it is porous and generally rather coarse. It filters water very effectively but also gives up its mineral ions to hydrolysis very readily. Sandstone formations yield predominantly "permanent" hardness, but the mineral composition and "total" hardness vary widely from place to place. (For an explanation of water hardness, see pages 61 through 65.)Water drawn from older sandstone may be soft but is usually moderately hard, averaging 50 to 300 ppm hardness. New red sandstone usually bears very hard water (150 to 400 ppm). Although the hardness is largely sulfate, water drawn from new red sandstone is often objectionably inundated by iron.

Formed from loose sediment, limestone (calcium carbonate) is not an extremely dense rock, but it is impervious and yields water only if it has been extensively fissured by seismic activity or eons of hydrolysis. The passage of water along joints and bedding plates has carved out huge subterranean caverns and labyrinths in some limestone formations, where abundant water may be tapped. Carbonic acid from the atmosphere readily dissolves calcium carbonate, forming very soluble calcium hydrogen-carbonate (bicarbonate) salts. Consequently aquifers and springs from limestone tend to yield water high in "temporary" hardness, with other minerals in solution. Some limestones are

Underground Water

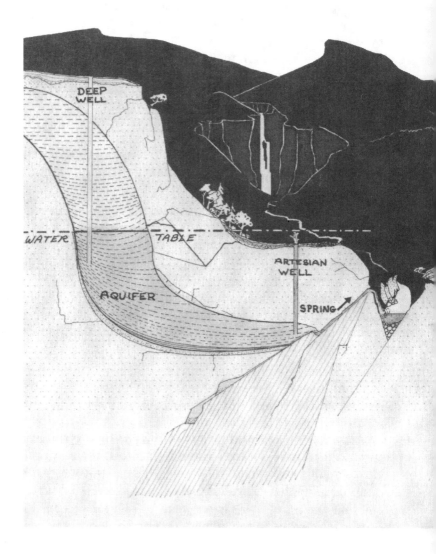

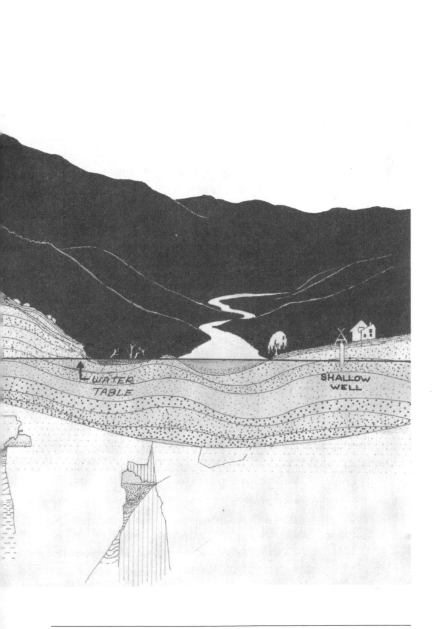

largely made up of magnesia and may yield considerable sulfate as well. Hardness of 150 to 350 ppm is common.

Chalk formations are very soft, fine-grained limestone from mudlike sea-bottom sediment. They yield from 150 to 375 ppm hardness, largely as calcium carbonate. Soapstone (talc) is insoluble hydrous magnesium silicate, often found with magnetite (iron oxide) and chlorite. Formed from consolidated clay, shale is impervious but may pass water along its bedding plates. Like other sedimentary rock, it commonly contains many minerals.

Marl is consolidated clay with sand, and most often calcium carbonate, potash, or phosphorus. It is commonly found stratified with sandstone or limestone. Marl generally yields little water, and of an undesirable mineral composition. Conglomerates are impervious, hard rocks from lime-cemented gravel and sand; they vary widely in composition but usually have little effect on the water coming in contact with them.

Using the Water Analysis

Any potential source of brewing water should be analyzed for organic and inorganic composition and biological purity. Because the composition of any water supply is likely to vary seasonally, and even within each season, it is advisable to make or obtain an analysis of it before brewing, or when changes in the brew may be due to changes in the water. Where periodic testing is not possible or practical, a simple pH test demonstrates changes in the mineral content and can indicate what the changes in the mineral distribution may be.

The standard water analysis identifies the amounts of the mineral ions present in the water and indicates the presence of organic pollution as well. A bacterial analysis may be included or made separately. Analyses for community water supplies are available upon request from local water departments; other sources are analyzed by private labs for a fee. Do-it-yourself kits are also available for identifying the pH, hardness, and alkalinity of water, and the presence of various mineral ions (calcium, magnesium, iron, chlorine, sulfate, nitrate, nitrite); they are easy to use, handy, and inexpensive over the long run if analyses would otherwise have to be made by a private lab.

Table 4

Water: Typical Analysis U.S. Public Health Service (U.S.P.H.S.) Units
Turbidity   Color   pH   Sediment   Odor Specific Conductivity (micromhos/cm) Hardness – Total ($CaCO_3$, in ppm [mg/L]) Alkalinity – Total ($CaCO_3$, in ppm)

Major Constituents 1–1000 ppm	
Calcium (Ca)	Sulfate (SO_4)
Magnesium (Mg)	Chloride (Cl)
Sodium (Na)	Silica (SiO_2)

Secondary Constituents .01–10 ppm	
Potassium (K)	Iron (Fe)
Nitrogen (Ammonia, NH_4)	Nitrogen (Nitrate, NO_3)
Nitrogen (Nitrite, NO_2)	

Minor Constituents .001–.1 ppm
Manganese (Mn) Copper (Cu)

Trace Constituents less than .001 ppm
Zinc (Zn) Coliform bacteria (colonies per 100 mL)

If testing by a lab is necessary, certain procedures for obtaining the specimen are advisable. Rinse a clean quart jar several times with the water to be tested; fill the jar and immerse it nearly to its neck in a kettle of water. Heat and boil for twenty minutes. Decant the water from the jar and invert the jar on a clean paper towel to drain. When cool, fill it with the water to be tested. If it is tap water, allow the cold water to run for a minute before taking the sample to flush clear any mineral deposits jarred loose by the initial release of water from the tap. Cap the jar tightly and rush it to the lab where you have made arrangements to take it. The longer the sample sits, the less accurate the analysis will be. Where pollution is suspected, the water must be tested within twelve hours of collection, and in all other cases, within seventy-two hours.

When the brewing water is to be treated with mineral salts or boiled to precipitate carbonates, an analysis after treatment will pinpoint the resultant mineral distribution, but it is hardly necessary. The carefully weighed addition of salts and a simple pH test after treatment usually adequately indicates the subsequent mineral distribution.

Brewing with an untreated natural water supply is possible in almost all cases by manipulating the brewing procedure. A water analysis should be made before brewing to determine the formulation and procedure that best suits the particular water composition.

Turbidity, Sediment, Color, and Odor

Turbidity and sediment may be caused by suspended clay and other inorganic soil, organic topsoil or waste, colloidal ferrous and aluminum oxides, or manganese and silicon dioxide.

Color is usually due to colloidal vegetable pigments, although a yellow-to-brown hue may be from suspended clay or silt. This sediments out upon resting; particles in colloidal suspension may be eliminated only by filtering. Odor may be from dissolved gases or organic decay.

Overall character may be improved by activated-carbon filtration. Where this is not satisfactory, a clearer water should be found to brew with.

U.S. Public Health Service Drinking Water Standards suggest as limits that should not be exceeded: turbidity — five units; color — fifteen units; odor — threshold number three. For brewing, it is recommended that these all be less than one.

pH

The pH indicates acid to alkalinity ratios and the mineral composition of water as well, both of utmost importance to the brewer. Appropriate acidity is a prerequisite of a successful brewing cycle. Enzyme activity, kettle break, and yeast performance rely upon conducive acidity in the mash, wort, and beer. The acidity of the brewing water source is therefore of concern to the brewer.

pH is the measure of the acidity or alkalinity of a solution. Acid solutions taste sour; alkaline solutions taste bitter and flat. In other terms, acidity is expressed as a greater number of positively charged particles in solution than negatively charged ones; conversely, alkalinity marks an excess of dissociated negative particles.

Ions

All elements are reducible to single atoms. Atoms are made up of an equal number of positive and negative charges, respectively termed protons and electrons. The atoms of each element are distinguished from those of every other element by the number of protons in their nuclei and the number and arrangement of electrons they have in orbit. Atoms are chemically inactive because the charges of their protons and electrons neutralize each other. They may, however, be unstable. Only atoms having two electrons in their first orbit and eight electrons in their outermost orbit are stable; only these elements occur in their true atomic form.

Atoms

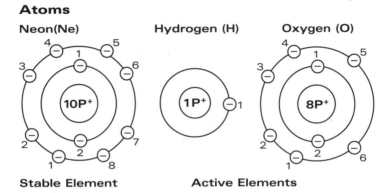

Neon(Ne)   Hydrogen (H)   Oxygen (O)

Stable Element   Active Elements

An unstable atom either gives electrons to or receives electrons from another unstable atom, each thereby forming an ion of the element that has a stable electron configuration.

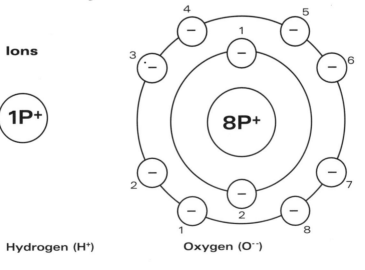

Ions

Hydrogen (H⁺)   Oxygen (O⁻⁻)

Ionic Compounds

Unstable Elements Sodium and Chloride

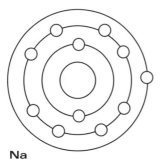

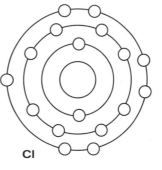

Na   Cl

Electron Transfer

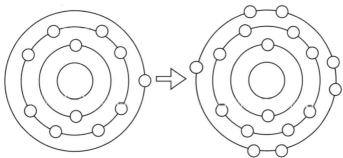

Ionic Compound, Sodium Chloride

Na⁺   Cl⁻

Because this results in an imbalance in the number of positively charged protons and negatively charged electrons, all ions have an electromagnetic charge. Ions that have a positive attraction are cations; negatively charged ions are anions.

Cations and anions combine to form ionic compounds; the strength of their bond and the charge of the compound itself are dictated by the relative electromagnetic attraction of the ions involved. The greater the difference in their charges, the stronger the ionic bond, and the more acid or alkaline their compound.

Ionic compounds are formed by the exchange of electrons. Other compounds are formed by sharing electrons; these are termed covalent. Most organic compounds (compounds containing carbon) are covalent.

The water molecule, H_2O, is covalent. Only a single electron orbits the nucleus of a hydrogen atom; the outer orbit of an oxygen atom contains only six electrons. Both atoms are unstable, hydrogen needing to give up an electron and oxygen needing to receive two. In the covalent compound of the water molecule, the hydrogen atoms achieve stable single orbits by sharing their electrons with the oxygen atom, which then has a stable outer orbit of eight. Since no electrons are exchanged, the bond is nonionic, and the molecule is electromagnetically neutral. The negative valence (-2) of the oxygen atom (O^{--}, or lacking two electrons) is precisely neutralized by the combined positive valence (+2) of the two hydrogen atoms (H_2^{++}).

Although neutral, the water molecule retains a strongly polar character, because the eight protons of its oxygen molecule have slightly more attraction for the negatively charged electrons of the shared orbits than do the single protons of the two hydrogen atoms. The oxygen side of the water molecule is thus slightly negatively charged and the hydrogen side equally positively charged; it is even polar enough to disrupt the ionic bonds of many inorganic compounds, causing them to dissolve into their component ions. When all of the water present is absorbed in the reaction with an ionic compound, that compound is said to be hydrated by water of crystallization. For example, gypsum ($CaSO_4 \bullet 2H_2O$) is a hydrated salt. Like other compounds, it can be dissolved into its component ions by the introduction of more water. In fact, water is the most universal solvent known, and it is able to react chemically with most inorganic acids and bases, and to dissolve many salts.

Although pure water is characterized as being covalent, a certain number of its molecules react in pairs to form hydroxide ions (OH^-) and hydronium ions (H_3O^+, most often expressed as simply H^+). This is an equilibrium

Water Molecule

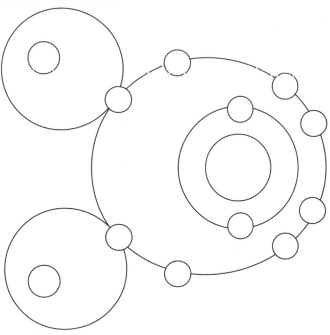

reaction, and the combined number of hydroxide and hydronium ions always remains constant; in pure water at 77 degrees F (25 degrees C), the concentration of electropositive hydronium ions and electronegative hydroxide ions are each .000,000,1 moles per liter. When mineral compounds dissolve in water, their positive mineral ions bond to the oxygen side of the water molecule, freeing hydronium (H^+) ions, and their negative ions react with the electropositive hydrogen side, releasing hydroxide (OH^-) ions.

When an excess of either hydroxide or hydronium ions is released, the ionic equilibrium of pure water is disturbed. Because the combined value of hydroxide and hydronium ions always remains constant, an increase in either always results in a proportional decrease in the other.

Measuring pH

The pH scale represents the relative molar concentration of hydrogen and hydroxide ions present in any solution by measuring the activity of the free hydronium ions in solution. If the hydronium ion concentration exceeds .000,000,1 moles per liter, the solution is acidic; if it is less than .000,000,1 moles per liter, the solution is alkaline and will neutralize acids and liberate CO_2.

The reaction that the hydrogen ion concentration represents causes a color change in litmus paper and other pH indicators. The degree of color change is gauged against a standard scale to identify the pH of any solution. For a more detailed analysis, electromagnetic equipment is employed.

The pH, however, is not expressed as the molar concentration of hydrogen and hydroxide ions. The pH scale uses the exponent of 10 in the logarithm (see table 5) to identify the acidity of a solution. Because it is a logarithmic scale, a solution at pH 4 is 10 times more acidic than a solution at pH 5, 100 times more acidic than a solution at pH 6, and 1,000 times more acidic than a solution at pH 7.

Table 5: pH

Part A.				
Moles Per Liter, H$^+$		**pH**	**Moles Per Liter, OH$^-$**	
.1	$1 \bullet 10^{-1}$	1	$1 \bullet 10^{-13}$	.000 000 000 000 1
.000 1	$1 \bullet 10^{-4}$	4	$1 \bullet 10^{-10}$	.000 000 000 1
.000 01	$1 \bullet 10^{-5}$	5	$1 \bullet 10^{-9}$	.000 000 001
.000 000 1	$1 \bullet 10^{-7}$	7	$1 \bullet 10^{-7}$	.000 000 1
.000 000 001	$1 \bullet 10^{-9}$	9	1.10^{-5}	.000 01

Part B. Hydrogen Ion Concentration in the pH Scale				
pH	**4**	**5**	**6**	**7**
H$^+$, moles/L	.000 1	.000 01	.000 001	.000 000 1

pH Adjustment

All changes in the pH of the brewing liquor, the mash, the wort, or the beer, whether induced or consequential, are due to the formation, addition, or precipitation of mineral ions or organic acids. The pH of the brewing water may be adjusted by precipitating out alkaline carbonate salts or by adding organic acids or mineral salts. Salts are added when additional mineral character is also desired. As an alternative to water treatment, the mash may be made more acidic by the metabolism of certain bacteria, which causes the formation of organic acids.

The pH of the mash affects the level of enzyme activity within it, and the acidity of the wort and beer. The pH significantly affects hop extraction and protein precipitation in the kettle, and yeast performance and clarification in the ferment. Because ideal pH levels often cannot be attained, or because the pH at one stage conflicts with the pH optimum of a more critical reaction, concessions are sometimes made; shortcomings can usually be overcome by time and temperature manipulation. For example, in the mash the enzymatic reduction of proteins to soluble nitrogen is most efficient at pH 5 or below, a level of acidity that conflicts with starch reduction optimums during mashing. Therefore, it is necessary to make a longer rest at temperatures conducive to protein degradation, especially when the mash begins at above pH 5.5.

At above pH 6, any mash suffers from sluggish enzyme activity, and in the lauter-tun, troublesome tannins and silicates are leached into the extract. With "soft" water and pale malt, the few acid ions cannot overcome ("invert") buffers leached from the malt, which results in a strong resistance to further acidulation of the mash.

pH 5.2 to 5.5 should be the target acidity of the saccharification rest for all mashes. This is the range at which enzyme activity, filtering, color, and clarity are best. A mash at pH 5.2 to 5.5 can be expected to yield a sweet wort of 5.5 or slightly above, which best serves hop extraction and flocculation of protein in the kettle.

Total Dissolved Solids/Specific Conductivity

The *total dissolved solids* are the mineral ions in solution. Total dissolved solids are measured by passing water through a filter fine enough to screen out all sediments and colloids, then weighing the residue left after the filtered water has been evaporated.

The specific conductivity of water measures the mineral ions in solution by gauging the solution's ability to conduct an electric current at 77 degrees F (25 degrees C). Most inorganic acids, bases, and salts are good conductors of an electric current because ions are by definition electrovalent, or charged, particles, whereas organic compounds conduct current very poorly, if at all. Specific conductance, therefore, is a measure of the total dissolved solids in any water.

The specific conductance in micromhos per centimeter (*mho* is the opposite of the basic unit of electrical resistance, the *ohm*) is roughly equatable to the total dissolved solids in solution in parts per million (ppm is the same measurement as milligrams per liter [mg/L]) by multiplying the specific conductance by a factor that ranges from .55 (for water of pH less than 7.2 or more than 8) up to .90 (for saline water). For most natural waters, multiplying the specific conductance by a factor between .55 and .70 gives a reasonable assessment of the total dissolved solids.

Hardness/Alkalinity

The *hardness* of water is gauged by measuring the dissolved cations of the alkaline-earth elements, most significantly calcium (Ca^{++}) and magnesium (Mg^{++}). These common minerals inhibit the sudsing of sodium-based soap in "hard" water and are precipitated as an insoluble, furry residue.

Alkaline-earth ions are weakly electropositive and give water slight acidity. The polar bonds they form with water molecules are weak and readily broken by strongly basic anions, causing them to precipitate as insoluble salts. Calcium exhibits a fragile solubility. Magnesium is more electropositive than calcium but is not correspondingly less soluble; it is actually more stable in solution. The cations of the larger, less electropositive alkali metals sodium (Na^+) and potassium (K^+) are even more weakly acidic. They are much more stable in water, give an essentially neutral pH reaction, and do not contribute to water hardness.

Calcium is the most widely occurring "metal" found in water, followed by magnesium, sodium, and then iron. Potassium and manganese are much less common; when considering their effects, potassium is often grouped with sodium, and manganese with iron.

The metal cations all occur out of solution bonded to acid anions in crystalline-structured ionic compounds called *mineral salts*. The bicarbonate, sulfate, chloride, nitrate, borate, and phosphate ions are all classified as acids because they are derived from carbonic, sulfuric, hydrochloric, nitric, boric, and phosphoric acids; their effects, however, are decidedly alkaline.

The several salts that may be formed by the acid anions with any given metal vary in solubility and acid or alkaline reaction according to the electronegative valence of the particular anion involved. A weak metal and a weakly alkaline anion in solution have very little attraction for each other and stay in solution. The same metal with a moderately alkaline anion may be precipitated out of solution under certain conditions. With a strong base, the metal may even be insoluble. Thus, calcium chloride is freely soluble, calcium sulfate is of limited solubility, and calcium carbonate is nearly insoluble. Sodium and potassium, because they are only slightly electropositive at best, are freely soluble not only with both chloride and sulfate ions but also with the carbonate ion.

Similarly, the pH of a solution is determined by the relative electrovalence of the several cations and anions dissolved together. Since soluble metals are all only weakly acidic and acid anions range from very weakly alkaline to extremely alkaline, their solution in water may be slightly acidic (calcium and the sulfate ion), neutral (sodium and chloride ions), or very alkaline (calcium and carbonate ions). Mild alkalinity is usually indicative of solutions containing more than one anion (calcium with the sulfate and carbonate ions, for instance).

The anions found in water are almost exclusively sulfates (SO_4^{--}), chlorides (Cl^-), and bicarbonates (HCO_3^-). The sulfate ion is weakly basic, and the chloride ion only slightly more so, whereas the unstable bicarbonate ion is a very strong buffer, because in its formation from the carbonate ion (CO_3^{--}), it pulls a hydronium ion off a water molecule, freeing hydroxide ions into solution.

Far less common than the sulfates, chlorides, and bicarbonates are the weakly basic nitrate, borate, phosphate, and silicate ions; few of their salts are even soluble. In fact, only six salts commonly dissolve in ground water: calcium bicarbonate, magnesium bicarbonate, calcium sulfate, magnesium sulfate, sodium sulfate, and sodium chloride. Only three other salts are occasionally present in significant amounts: calcium chloride, magnesium chloride, and sodium bicarbonate. Potassium compounds are rarely present in any quantity.

Calcium and magnesium significantly affect the brewing process. When calcium and magnesium occur primarily with the bicarbonate ion, calcium precipitates out of solution during boiling, potentially robbing the yeast of a necessary element of its composition and causing high mash pHs that may react sluggishly to acidification. On the other hand, calcium in solution with the sulfate ion provides a very stable vehicle for the transmission of calcium into the ferment, and aids rather than retards mash acidulation.

The hardness of water expresses the calcium and magnesium in solution. The hardness of any water is determined by titration, as with EDTA, after addition of a dye, to an end point. It is expressed as "hardness as $CaCO_3$," although it represents all of the calcium and magnesium ions in solution, arbitrarily combined with carbonate ions.

Bicarbonates, and to a lesser extent, carbonates, constitute most of the alkalinity of natural waters. Combined with calcium, they are expressed as the temporary or carbonate hardness of water, or that part of the hardness that will precipitate out of solution by boiling or with the addition of lime.

After boiling, calcium and magnesium ions remain in solution with noncarbonate ions. These are expressed as the permanent or noncarbonate hardness. In fact, some carbonate ions remain, bonded to water molecules; calcium carbonate is soluble to 20 ppm, and with magnesium in solution, magnesium carbonate may remain at up to 300 ppm.

The alkalinity of water measures the buffering capacity of dissolved anions, especially the bicarbonate (HCO_3; the carbonate ion CO_3 is only a significant factor in waters of pH 8.3 and above). By titrating the alkalinity, the temporary hardness can be assessed more readily than by boiling the water and can be used to precisely indicate treatment. An indicator dye, such as Bromcresol Green-Methyl Red, whose color in neutral and alkaline solutions is known, is added to a measured volume of water. The number of drops of a strong mineral-acid solution, such as .035N sulfuric acid, it takes to neutralize the water (overcome its alkalinity) is indicated by the color change of the dye, from blue-green to methyl-orange end point. When multiplied by a factor based upon the sample size, the number of drops it takes to reach end point expresses the bicarbonate alkalinity as parts per million of calcium carbonate. For more alkaline waters with a pH above 8.3, phenolphthalein is used as an indicator dye, and the carbonate alkalinity is titrated before the bicarbonate is measured.

Hardness actually measures calcium and magnesium in solution, and alkalinity measures all the alkaline ions. By expressing hardness and alkalinity in the same terms, as $CaCO_3$ (calcium carbonate), the two values are readily compared; "as $CaCO_3$" is the accepted standard because its cation is the primary mineral of hardness and its anion is the principal cause of alkalinity in most waters. This convention also simplifies water treatment.

Hardness and alkalinity nicely define the permanent and temporary hardness of water. *When the alkalinity as*

$CaCO_3$ exceeds the hardness, then the hardness is largely temporary. When the hardness value exceeds the alkalinity, the difference is indicative of permanent sulfate hardness. Especially where hardness greatly exceeds alkalinity, the water is eminently suitable for brewing and responds well to acidulation during mashing.

Where alkalinity as $CaCO_3$ is unknown, the hardness before and after boiling must be measured to define permanent and temporary hardness. This method is at least as satisfactory an indicator as is the alkalinity reading of a water analysis, but a great deal more difficult to make.

Temporary hardness is always strongly alkaline; permanent hardness is usually only slightly acidic, so only soft waters or waters where hardness well exceeds alkalinity yield a proper mash pH with pale malt.

Most water supplies are slightly alkaline, due to the buffering of any calcium and magnesium in solution by the strongly basic reaction of even a small amount of bicarbonate. At over 50 ppm alkalinity as $CaCO_3$, water reacts sluggishly to acidulation in the mash and kettle. This water becomes weakly acidic upon precipitation of its carbonate salts. The carbonates can be sedimented out by boiling or the addition of slaked lime, or overcome by the addition or formation of organic acids, and to some extent by adding calcium or magnesium as sulfate or chloride salts to the mash or the mash liquor.

The larger of the two readings, hardness or alkalinity, can also indicate how much of the total dissolved solids are sodium, potassium, and chloride, which contribute to neither the hardness nor the alkalinity, by subtracting it from total dissolved solids.

Where calcium and magnesium measurements are not given in an analysis, dividing the hardness reading by 1.25 and by 5.0 roughly indicates the calcium and magnesium in solution (assuming a four-to-one Ca/Mg ratio).

Molarity, Equivalence, and Normality

The chemist's tools molarity, normality, and equivalence, as described by Dr. George Fix in *Principles of Brewing Science* (Brewers Publications, 1989), are of significance to brewers, especially for understanding liquor acidification.

Molarity is a method for quantitative analysis of a substance in solution. Molarity employs the mole (mol, gram-molecular weight, gmw, gram mole, combining weight) as its unit of measure. Molecular weight is the sum of the atomic weights of the elements that compose any given substance; a mole is the molecular weight in grams. A molar solution (**M**) of any given substance is equal to one mole in a liter of solution.

The atomic weights of the elements sulfur and oxygen are 32.066 and 15.9994. The sulphate molecule, SO_4, is composed of one atom of sulfur and four atoms of oxygen. The molecular weight of the sulphate ion is 96.0636, because 32.066 + (4 x 15.9994) = 96.0636. A mole of the sulphate ion, then, is 96.0636 grams, and a molar solution of sulphate is equal to 96.0636 grams in one liter of solution.

A molar solution of sulfuric acid (H_2SO_4) is 98.08 grams, of phosphoric acid (H_3PO_4) 97.995 grams, citric acid ($C_6H_8O_7$) 192.13 grams, and lactic acid ($C_3H_6O_3$) 90.08 grams in one liter of solution.

Molarity is generally given as a decimal percentage; .01**M** sulfuric acid means that the solution contains .01 moles of lactic acid per liter, or .9808 grams per liter.

The concentration in parts per million (milligrams/liter) of a molar solution can be derived by the formula ppm = molarity x mole x 1000. So for sulfuric acid, .01**M**: .01 x 98.08 x 1000 = 9.808 ppm.

Equivalence measures the number of moles of hydrogen or hydroxyl ion that a substance can liberate. The moles and equivalency of some common ions are:

Ion	Mole weight	Equivalent Weight
H^+	1.00794	1.00794
Ca^{++}	40.078	20.039
Mg^{++}	24.3050	12.1525
Na^+	22.989768	22.989768
K^+	39.0983	39.0983
SO_4^-	96.0636	96.0636
CO_3^{--}	60.0092	30.0046
HCO_3^-	61.01714	61.01714
Cl^-	35.4527	35.4527

The strength of an acid is measured by its ability to release H^+ ions, lowering pH. Sulfuric acid (H_2SO_4) disassociates when it is added to water, releasing two hydrogen ions into solution: $2H^{++} + SO_4^{--}$. It has an equivalency, then, of 2. In a solution containing the carbonate ion (CO_3^{--}), the two hydrogen ions released by sulfuric acid exert a strong enough attraction on the unstable atoms of the carbonate ion to pull it apart:

$$H_2SO_4 + CaCO_3 \rightarrow H_2CO_3 + Ca^{++} + SO_4^{--}$$
$$\rightarrow H_2O + CO_2 + Ca^{++} + SO_4^{--}$$

The alkaline carbonate ion is thus eliminated, because one mole of sulfuric acid neutralizes one mole of carbonate.

Phosphoric acid (H_3PO_4) is another mineral acid. Each molecule of phosphoric acid contains three hydrogen ions, but still only has an equivalence of 2, because it only partially disassociates in water and releases only two of its three hydrogen ions:

$$H_3PO_4 + CaCO_3 \rightarrow H_2CO_3 + CaHPO_4, \text{ precipitated}$$

Two organic acids commonly used by brewers are citric and DL-lactic acid. Citric acid ($2C_6H_8O_7$) partially disassociates and releases three hydrogen ions in solution, giving an equivalence of 3. Lactic acid ($2C_3H_6O_3$) has an equivalence of 1, because it releases only one hydrogen ion. Only two-thirds of a mole of citric acid is needed to neutralize a mole of carbonate, but two moles of lactic acid are needed to neutralize a mole of carbonate:

$$2C_6H_8O_7 + 3CaCO_3 \rightarrow 3H_2CO_3 + 3Ca^{++} + 2C_6H_5O_7^{---}$$
$$2C_3H_6O_3 + CaCO_3 \rightarrow H_2CO_3 + Ca^{++} + 2C_3H_5O_3^{-}$$

Normality *(N)* is how the strength of an acid is expressed. It may be given as a decimal or fraction: .02*N* or *N*/50. One mole of a 1*N* compound releases one mole of hydrogen (H^+) or hydroxyl (OH^-) ion. A .02*N* acid solution releases .02 or one-fiftieth of a mole of hydrogen, and a 5*N* acid solution releases five moles of hydrogen. Normality is equal to the molarity of the acid times the equivalence of the acid. So the normality of one mole of the four acids are:

Lactic acid, with an equivalence of 1: 1 x 1**M** = 1*N*
Sulfuric acid, with an equivalence of 2: 2 x 1**M** = 2*N*
Phosphoric acid, with an equivalence of 2: 2 x 1**M**=2*N*
Citric acid, with an equivalence of 3: 3 x 1**M** = 3*N*

Reversing the equation, 1*N* solutions of these acids give:

Lactic acid, 1*N*: gram mole 90.08/equivalence 1= 90.08 grams $C_3H_6O_3$/liter of solution
Phosphoric acid, 1*N*: gram mole 97.995/equivalence 2 = 48.998 grams H_3PO_4/liter of solution
Sulfuric acid, 1*N*: gram mole 98.08/equivalence 2 = 49.04 grams H_2SO_4/liter of solution
Citric acid, 1*N*: gram mole 192.13/equivalence 3 = 64.043 grams $C_6H_8O_7$/liter of solution

These values allow for ease of calculations for alkalinity adjustments, since they represent milligrams per milliliter as well as grams per liter, and multiplied by 1,000 they give milligrams per liter, or ppm, the measurement by which alkalinity as $CaCO_3$ is expressed. Alkalinity reductions require acid additions that are equivalent to the molarity of the alkaline cations, and the equivalence of acids is measured by normality.

Mineral Ions Common in Water

Cations — Earths

Calcium (Ca^{++}, atomic weight 40.08). Calcium is the principal mineral of hardness. It comes from the water's passage over limestone, dolomite, gypsum, or calcified gypsiferous shale. Calcium increases mash acidity and inverts malt phosphate to precipitated alkaline phosphate by the following reaction:

$$CaH_4(PO_4)_2 \bullet H_2O \text{ Calcium Phosphate (Organic)}$$

+

CA
Calcium

+

$3H_2O$

$\downarrow$

2H
Hydrogen Ions
-
$2CaHPO_4 \bullet 2H_2O$
Calcium Phosphate (Secondary, Precipitated)

In appropriate amounts, calcium is advantageous to the brew. Calcium stimulates enzyme activity and improves protein digestion, stabilizes the alpha-amylase, helps gelatinize starch, and improves lauter runoff. It also extracts fine bittering principles of the hop and reduces wort color. A calcium precipitate formed with potassium phosphate improves hot-break flocculation. It is also an essential part of yeast-cell composition. Small amounts of calcium neutralize substances toxic to yeast, such as peptone and lecithin. It improves clarification during aging, as well as the stability and flavor of the finished beer.

Precipitation of Calcium Carbonate

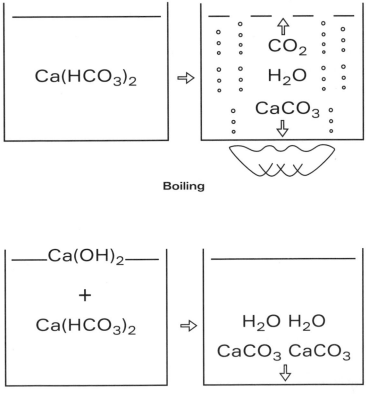

Boiling

Adding Slaked Lime

In excess, however, calcium precipitation with organic phosphates interferes with runoff filtering and robs the wort of phosphate, a necessary yeast nutrient. Calcium levels are usually 5 to 200 ppm; its solubility is greatly affected by anions in solution with it.

Magnesium (Mg^{++}, atomic weight 24.32). Magnesium is the secondary mineral of hardness. It is essential as a cofactor for some enzymes, and as a yeast nutrient. In concentrations of 10 to 30 ppm, magnesium accentuates the beer's flavor, but it imparts an astringent bitterness when it is present in excess. At levels higher than 125 ppm it is cathartic and diuretic. Usually found at levels of 2 to 50 ppm, its solubility is less affected by carbonate anions in solution than is calcium.

Cations — Metals

Sodium (Na^+, atomic weight 22.991). The sour, salty taste of sodium can accentuate beer's flavor when it is found in reasonable concentrations, but it is harsh and unpleasant in excess. It is poisonous to yeast, and brewers generally avoid water that contains sodium in excess of 50 ppm, especially where softness is characteristic of the beer flavor. Usually found at levels of 2 to 100 ppm, it is very soluble.

Potassium (K^+, atomic weight 39.1). Potassium imparts a salty taste. In excess of 10 ppm, it inhibits enzyme activity and acts as a laxative. It is difficult to measure and is usually grouped with sodium. Levels seldom exceed 20 ppm, although potassium is very soluble.

Iron (Fe^{++}, atomic weight 55.85, Fe^{+++}). Common in ground water, iron gives an unpleasant, inky taste detectable at levels as low as .05 ppm. Above 1 ppm, iron weakens yeast and increases haze and oxidation of tannins. It blackens porcelain and spots fabrics at .02 ppm, causes white turbidity in water, and corrodes metal. Levels should be less than .3 ppm. Reduce iron content to .1 ppm by aerating and filtering the water through sand.

Manganese (Mn^{++}, atomic weight 54.94). Trace amounts of manganese are found in most ground and surface waters. It imparts an unpleasant taste and streaks porcelain at .05 ppm. The manganese level should be less than 2 ppm and optimally below .05 ppm. It can be reduced to .02 ppm by aeration.

Ammonia (NH_4^+, atomic weight 18.04). Ammonia is a corrosive ion from microbial organic decomposition. Most volatile of the nitrates, it is reduced by oxidation to the corrosive alkaline gases NH_3 and NH_2. Always indicative of pollution, ammonia is never present in unpolluted water. Levels of ammonia are normally .00 to .03 ppm and should never exceed .05 ppm.

Copper (Cu^{++}, atomic weight 63.54). Elevated levels of copper cause yeast mutation and haze formation. Copper in a water supply is evidenced by blue-green stains on porcelain. Levels of copper should be less than 1 ppm.

Zinc (Zn^{++}, atomic weight 65.38). Zinc is a yeast nutrient when it is found at .1 to .2 ppm, but toxic to yeast and inhibiting to enzymes above 1 ppm.

Anions

Carbonate (CO_3^{--}, atomic weight 60.0092). Carbonate is a strongly alkaline buffer formed by the reaction of atmospheric carbon dioxide with hydroxides of alkaline-earth and alkali metals. Carbonates go into solution as hydrogen carbonates (HCO_3^-, "bicarbonates"), which are strong buffers. Bicarbonates form by the reaction of a carbonate ion with a molecule each of carbon dioxide and water.

Bicarbonate resists increases in the mash acidity by neutralizing acids as they are formed. It also hinders gelatinization of starch by alpha-amylase, impedes trub flocculation during the cold break, and increases risk of contamination in the ferment. It contributes a harsh, bitter flavor that is overwhelming in delicate lagers. Carbonate in excess of 200 ppm is tolerable only when dark-roasted malts are employed to buffer its excessive alkalinity. Carbonates in the brewing liquor should be less than 50 ppm if the mash is from only pale malts and no liquor acidulation is employed. Where carbonates exceed 50 ppm, water treatment is generally in order.

Sulfate (SO_4^{--}, atomic weight 96.0576). Sulfate is weakly basic, and its alkalinity is overcome by most acids. It is fairly soluble. It gives beer a dry, fuller flavor, although the taste can be objectionably sharp. With sodium and magnesium it is cathartic. Above 500 ppm it is strongly bitter, and levels are generally kept at less than 150 ppm unless the beer is very highly hopped. With intensely bitter beers, sulfate at 150 to 350 ppm gives a cleaner, more piquant bitterness.

Chloride (Cl^-, atomic weight 35.453). Chloride is very weakly basic, and readily neutralized. It accentuates bitterness, but also increases mellowness; it increases the stability of any solution and improves clarity. The "salt" taste of chloride generally enhances beer flavor and palate fullness, but the salt flavor is reduced by the presence of calcium and magnesium. Usually found at levels of 1 to 100 ppm, chloride levels in the brewing liquor may be as high as 250 ppm for British mild ales.

Silica (SiO_2, atomic weight 60.0843), silicon dioxide. Originating from sand or quartz, silica is insoluble. As a colloid, it interferes with the filtering of the mash. Under certain conditions, silica forms silicate ($HSiO_3^-$), which causes hazes, precipitating out of the boil as scale with calcium and magnesium. Silica levels are usually less than 10 ppm but may be as high as 60 ppm.

Nitrate (NO_3^-, atomic weight 62.0049). Nitrate is the most highly oxidized naturally occurring form of nitrogen.

It may be from geological strata or originate from contact with sewage or oxidized organic matter. Above 10 ppm, it is indicative of pollution by sewage. It is alkaline, and during fermentation in the presence of chlorides, it forms nitrites, which are more strongly alkaline yet.

Nitrite (NO_2^-, atomic weight 46.0055). Strongly basic, nitrite originates from nitrates during decomposition of organic matter by coliform bacteria. It rarely exceeds .1 ppm, and is always indicative of pollution. Nitrite is toxic to yeast in minute concentrations; as little as .1 ppm may retard or terminate yeast growth.

Table 6: Water Composition Indicators

Hardness and Mineral Content of Water	
Nature	**Hardness as CaCO$_3$, ppm**
Very soft	Less than 50
Soft	50–100
Slightly hard	100–150
Moderately hard	150–250
Hard	250–350
Very hard	350 and above

Multiplying the ions below by the corresponding factors yields hardness as $CaCO_3$.
Ca–2.497 Mg–4.116 Fe–1.792 Mn–1.822 Zn–1.531

Total Dissolved Solids/Specific Conductivity		
	Total Dissolved Solids	**Specific Conductivity**
Water low in ionized matter	Below 50 ppm	Below 90 micromhos/cm
Range of average water supplies	30–275 ppm	50–500 micromhos/cm
Very highly mineralized water	Above 275 ppm	Above 500 micromhos/cm

Table 6, continued

pH and Hardness as a Treatment Indicator		
pH	**Hardness, ppm**	**Character**
Below 7	0–100	Soft and acidic, little bicarbonate alkalinity to overcome. May need to treat with acid to correct mash pH for light-colored worts. Add calcium salts to correct deficiency, and as appropriate to style.
Above 7	0–100	Soft, but largely bicarbonate alkaline hardness, treat with acid to correct mash pH; add calcium salts as appropriate to style.
Up to 7.6	100–150	Slightly hard, bicarbonate alkalinity is easily overcome by acid liquor treatment.
7.0–7.2	150 and up	Moderately hard, predominately sulphate hardness. Excellent water for all but Bohemian Pilseners.
7.2 and up	150–250	Moderately hard, largely bicarbonate hardness. For Dortmund lagers and Burton ales, treat with gypsum; for most other beer styles, precipitate carbonates or adjust pH with acid.
7.2 and up	250–1000	Hard to very hard water, predominately bicarbonates. Appropriate for Dortmund/Vienna lagers and British ales. For other styles, precipitate carbonates and/or adjust pH with acids.

pH as an Alkalinity and Treatment Indicator			
pH	**Alkalinity, as $CaCO_3$**		
	% HCO_3	**% CO_3**	**% H_2CO_3**
10	68	32	0
9	95	5	0
8	97	0	3
7	81	0	19
6	30	0	70
5	4	0	96

From table A–1, *Principles of Brewing Science,* by George Fix.

Other

Coliform bacteria. Measures the amount of any fecal bacteria, such as *Escherichia coli, Streptococcus faecalis,* pathogenic *Salmonella* strains, *Shigella dysenteriae,* and *Vibrio cholerae.* The U.S.P.H.S. standard for drinking water is that there should be less than 2.2 colonies per 100 milliliters. For brewing water, it is recommended that this be zero.

Where bacterial population is not given in an analysis, nitrate, nitrite, and ammonia values suffice to indicate water pollution.

Water Treatment

Brewing water sources should be chosen first for their purity and second for their mineral composition. In fact, treatment is only necessary when the mineral distribution of any water is unsatisfactory, or when accentuation of bitterness or saltiness is desired.

The most common correction of brewing water is the reduction of bicarbonate to yield a satisfactory mash acidity/pH. The bicarbonate is alkaline, and if it is reduced, so is the alkalinity.

Where liquor of less than 50 ppm of alkalinity is mashed with pale malt, proper mash acidity is usually realized without liquor treatment, because phosphates dissolved from the malt react with calcium bicarbonate, precipitating calcium phosphate and releasing CO_2. With more alkaline water, an excess of carbonate remains in solution, and the mash pH will be too high. Decomposition of the carbonates may be accomplished in several ways.

The most basic is by bringing water to a boil and aerating it thoroughly to decompose bicarbonates to carbonates, which are precipitated as calcium or magnesium carbonate salts, and to decompose carbonic acid to CO_2, which is driven off. After a reasonable rest to allow the carbonates to sediment the water should be decanted off the sediment, so that gradual dissolution of atmospheric CO_2 back into the water does not result in bicarbonates re-forming from the precipitate.

The use of naturally acidic toasted malt, or a portion of dark-roasted malt, is a time-honored manner of water treatment. The acidity released by intensive kilning can overcome the alkalinity of even moderately alkaline waters.

Where only pale malts are being mashed with soft to moderately alkaline waters (less than 250 ppm alkalinity or 150 ppm HCO_3), proper mash acidity is most often achieved by the formation or addition of mild acid. Mixing a portion of sourmalt or lactic-acid mash into the main mash reduces alkalinity and contributes flavor nuances that help round out a beer's flavor. Sourmalt is made by allowing limited lactic-acid bacterial activity prior to the malt's being kilned. In the brew house, formation of lactic acid may be accomplished by *Lactobacillus delbruckii* activity in a partial mash, held closely covered at 95 to 120 degrees F (35 to 50 degrees C) for forty-eight to seventy-two hours, until its pH drops below 4

Where acids (most commonly lactic, phosphoric, sulphuric, or citric) are used to reduce alkalinity, carbonates are decomposed with the formation of carbonic acid and lactate, phosphate, sulphate, or citrate anions, but the reactions are to some extent reversible. Moreover, if the water is more than moderately alkaline, the excessive amounts of acid required give the beer a noticeable sourness and characteristic taste. Generally, DL-lactic acid is preferred by brewers, but orthophosphoric, monohydrate citric, and sulfuric acids are also commonly used.

Approximate carbonate reduction can be made by gradual acid addition, checking the pH of the liquor after each dose, until it drops below 7. For moderately modified pale malt that won't undergo acid or protein rests, the pH reduction of the liquor may need to be as low as pH 6.

Carbonate and alkalinity reduction of a water can be more accurately made, where the parts per million of alkalinity as $CaCO_3$ is known, by calculating the treatment beforehand. Some difficulty arises because various dilutions of the acids are offered, and may be expressed as percentage solutions or percentage-of-normality solutions (N). Normality is discussed below. The following quantities of the commonly used acids are equivalent to $1N$:

> Lactic acid, $1N$ = 90.08 milligrams $C_3H_6O_3$ per milliliter of solution
> Phosphoric acid, $1N$ = 48.998 milligrams H_3PO_4 per milliliter of solution
> Sulfuric acid, $1N$ = 49.04 milligrams H_2SO_4 per milliliter of solution
> Citric acid, $1N$ = 64.043 milligrams $C_6H_8O_7$ per milliliter of solution

And as percentage solutions, common dilutions give:

> Lactic acid 85 to 90% w/w: 1,020 milligrams per milliliter of solution
> Phosphoric acid 85 to 88% w/w: 1,445 milligrams per milliliter of solution
> Sulfuric acid 95 to 98% w/w: 1,766 milligrams per milliliter of solution

Citric acid is generally available as the monohydrate, in granular or powder form, and so can be weighed out, each milligram of the monohydrate giving .9143 milligrams of citric acid.

These values allow ease of calculations for alkalinity adjustments. Given a water with alkalinity as $CaCO_3$ of 220 ppm and pH 7, the brewer wants to reduce the alkalinity to below 50 ppm; to, say, 35 ppm: 220 - 35 = 185 ppm. 185

ppm of alkalinity should be removed. Reference to table 6 shows that at pH 7, 81 percent of that alkalinity is bicarbonates, and the remainder is harmless carbonic acid. 185 x .81 = 150 ppm of alkalinity as $CaCO_3$ (at this pH, actually bicarbonate, HCO_3) needs to be disassociated. The acid treatment required to accomplish this is predicted by calculating the total alkalinity to be removed; that is, the ppm of alkalinity as $CaCO_3$ times the total volume of liquor.

Where the brewer is using liters as a measure, this is simply done by multiplying the alkalinity as $CaCO_3$ times the number of liters of liquor needed for the brew. Where the brewer is working with gallons, the conversion factor of liters in a gallon (3.7854) needs to be included in the formula:

Alkalinity as $CaCO_3$ x 3.7854 x number of gallons of liquor

Divided by the milligrams per milliliter that the particular acid solution on hand bears, the formula gives the milliliters of acid needed to disassociate the carbonate/bicarbonate alkalinity. For example, for 185 ppm of alkalinity to be disassociated, and 7.5 gallons of water to be treated:

185 x 3.7854 x 7.5 = 5,250 ppm of alkalinity as $CaCO_3$ to be disassociated.

Using 85 percent lactic acid, which bears 1,020 milligrams of lactic acid per milliliter:

5,250/1,020 = 5.2 milliliters of 85 to 90 percent lactic acid will reduce the alkalinity as $CaCO_3$ of 7.5 gallons of water by approximately 185 ppm.

Mineral Salt Treatment

Ion-exchange water softeners should never be used to reduce hardness. They do not remove the carbonate ion from solution, but precipitate calcium and magnesium by exchanging them for more soluble sodium ions, correspondingly increasing the sodium concentration.

Table 7

	Ca	Mg	K	Na	SO$_4$	HCO$_3$	Cl	Hardness	Total Dissolved Solids
Pilsen	7	2		2	5	15	5	30	35
Munich	75	18		2	10	150	2	250	275
Vienna	200	60		8	125	120	12	750	850
Dortmund	225	40		60	120	180	60	750	1000
London	90	5		15	40	125	20	235	300
Dublin	120	5		12	55	125	20	300	350
Yorkshire	100	15		25	65	150	30	275	400
Edinburgh	120	25		55	140	225	65	350	650
Burton	275	40		25	450	260	35	875	1100

Estimated Characters of the Classic Brewing Waters

Iron, manganese, and colloids that cause hazes are best removed by aeration, followed by filtration or sedimentation.

Mineral salts may be added to the brewing water when additional hardness or other mineral character is desired, or to precipitate carbonates. All salts should be carefully weighed (on a gram scale for small batches) before they are added to the brewing water. Mineral salts cannot be accurately dispensed by volume. One level teaspoon of finely powdered gypsum might weigh 3.65 grams. Tightly packed, it weighs 5 grams. A teaspoon of more crystalline magnesium sulfate weighs 4.55 grams, finely granular potassium chloride 5.05 grams, and sodium chloride 6.45 grams. For accuracy, salts need to be measured by weight.

It is advisable to first mix salts into a small quantity of boiling water before introducing them to the brewing water. Salts should never be added directly to the mash because uniform dispersal is unlikely.

Table 8

Mineral Salt Treatment

One gram of a freely soluble mineral salt in one U.S. gallon of water at 68 degrees F (20 degrees C) can be expected to increase the total dissolved solids by 264.2 ppm. The amount of any ion in the salt being added may be estimated from the salt composition percentages given; for instance, one gram of gypsum (calcium sulfate dihydrate) yields 264.2 x .2328 = 61.5 ppm of calcium and 264.2 x .5579 = 147.4 ppm of the sulfate ion. Brewing water profiles in table 7 and the analysis of your water supply may be used to guide salt additions.

Calcium Sulfate (Gypsum), $CaSO_4 \bullet 2H_2O$

Ca 23.28%, SO_4 55.79%, H_2O 20.93% . Mol. wt. 172.172 ($CaSO_4$ 136.142). Increases calcium content and lowers pH. Improves the quality of hop bitterness, gives drier and fuller flavor. Soluble to 2,650 ppm in cold water, to 2,000 ppm upon heating. Apparently most beneficial at 150 to 350 ppm. In excess, precipitates with calcium phosphate in the kettle. One gram in one gallon yields 61.5 ppm Ca, 147.4 ppm SO_4. The anhydrous salt $CaSO_4$ (plaster of Paris), mol. wt. 136.14, gives 77.8 ppm Ca, 186.5 ppm SO_4.

Magnesium Sulfate (Epsom Salts), $MgSO_4 \bullet 7H_2O$

Mg 14%, SO_4 55%, H_2O 31%. Mol. wt. 246.475 ($MgSO_4$ 120.369). Increases magnesium content. Freely soluble. Most satisfactory at 150 to 300 ppm; reduce when adding with calcium sulfate. Very bitter in excess. Generally avoided in pale lagers. One gram in one gallon gives 37 ppm Mg, 145.3 ppm SO_4.

Calcium Hydroxide (Slaked Lime, Hydrated Lime), $Ca(OH)_2$

Mol. wt. 74.093. Reacts with calcium bicarbonate, causing both to precipitate as carbonates $[Ca(OH)_2 + Ca(HCO_3)_2 \rightarrow 2CaCO_3 + 2H_2O]$. Also precipitates magnesium bicarbonate. Its calcium ion may

Table 8, continued

replace any magnesium that is in solution with the chloride ion. Addition of slaked lime should not exceed the ppm of alkalinity as $CaCO_3$ given in the water analysis. One gram in one gallon yields 264.2 ppm of the salt.

Calcium Carbonate (Precipitated Chalk), $CaCO_3$

Ca 40.04%, CO_3 59.96%. Mol. wt. 100.087. Strongly buffers mash acidity. Partially precipitates in the wort boil. One gram in one gallon gives 106 ppm Ca.

Sodium Chloride (Common Table Salt), NaCl

Na 39.34%, Cl 60.66%. Mol. wt. 58.443. Accentuates bitterness and enhances flavor and fullness of beer. Also promotes diastatic enzyme activity and the release of acid malt phosphates. Usually less than .75 grams per U.S. gallon (198 ppm) as treatment, or so that neither sodium nor chloride contents exceed 100 ppm (250 ppm of each for very dark and full beers). Objectionable in excess. Inhibits or even kills yeast over 850 ppm. One gram in one gallon equals 104 ppm Na, 160.25 Cl.

Potassium Chloride, KCl

K 52.44%, Cl 47.56%. Mol. wt. 74.551. A substitute for part of sodium chloride treatment. In excess of 150 ppm inhibits enzyme activity. One gram in one gallon yields 138.6 ppm K, 125.6 ppm Cl.

Calcium Chloride, $CaCl_2$

$CaCl_2$•$2H_2O$•Ca 27.26%, Cl 48.23%. Mol. wt. 147.014 ($CaCl_2$ 110.983). Adjusts calcium and adds saltiness. Commonly used. One gram in one gallon gives 72 ppm calcium, 127.4 ppm chloride. The anhydrous salt $CaCl_2$, mol. wt. 110.99, gives 161.4 ppm Ca, 168.8 ppm Cl_2.

Sodium Sulfate, $NaSO_4$

$NaSO_4$•Na 14.27%, SO_4 29.89%. Mol. wt. 119.053. Rarely used. One gram in one gallon gives 37.7 ppm Na, 79 ppm SO_4.

Potassium Metabisulfite, $K_2S_2O_5$

K 35.2%, S 28.8%, O 36%. Mol. wt. 222.33. Removes chloride from solution; in excess antifermentative. Not commonly used, and not usually more than 1 to 2 ppm added.

Hops

Hops are the conelike female "flowers," *strobiles,* of the vining *Humulus lupulus.* The strobiles are formed by a cluster of petallike, yellowish-green bracts and bracteoles emerging from a central stem. Each bract bears many tiny glandular sacs (trichomes) of *lupulin* at its base. Lupulin accounts for as much as 15 percent of the weight of the hop. The yellow lupulin is composed of essential oils, resins/bittering principles, polyphenols, nitrogen, sugars, pectin, lipids, and wax.

The resins may be classed alpha acids, beta acids, and gamma resins. The alpha and beta acids are "soft," whereas the gamma resin is hard, and contributes nothing to the brewing.

The alpha resin group is the most important hop fraction, and the most stable. Alpha acids have no aroma but are intensely bitter. They are responsible for the hops' bacteriostatic contribution to the brew. Alpha acids (humulone, cohumulone, and adhumulone) may be are *isomerized* during boiling (their atoms are rearranged) to somewhat soluble and even more bitter iso-alpha acids.

In contrast, the beta acids (lupulone, colupulone, and adlupulone) are far less stable than alpha acids, are extremely subject to oxidation, and are only slightly soluble. They become even less soluble as the hot wort cools, and are deposited in the trub as an amorphous yellow precipitate. Very little of their antibiotic, aromatic, and bittering properties are carried into finished beer unless they are oxidized, in which case they are extremely bitter, but the hops may taint the beer with an unpleasant spoiled-vegetable taste.

Varieties of hops that are high in alpha acids are generally preferred for bittering beer, because less hops are thereby required to achieve target bitterness levels. Because the amount of alpha acid that is isomerized by boiling is in large part time-dependent, hops for bittering are generally boiled in wort for thirty to ninety minutes. Boiling, however, drives off hop flavor and aromatics. Where hop flavor is desired, some isomerization efficiency is given up, and "flavor" hops are only boiled for five to thirty minutes.

Hop aromatics are even more fugitive; although some aromatics survive boiling for as long as twenty to thirty minutes, the full, fresh aroma of hops is only captured by "dry-hopping," or adding whole hops or their extract to the conditioning beer after fermentation. Hop-oil esters and floral ketones are generally evaporated more quickly than the terpene and sequiterpene oxides and alcohols that give beer a spicy flavor/aroma and greater mouthfeel.

The other major contribution of hops to the finished beer is the *tannins* they dissolve into the boiling wort. Tannins are complex, generally oxidized polyphenol polymers. When proteins and proteoses come into contact with the astringent-tasting amorphous flakes, they adhere to them and, by virtue of their increased mass, are precipitated out of solution. Because there are generally fewer hop tannins than proteins, they do not usually carry over into the finished beer and significantly affect flavor.

Although the bitter flavor and tangy aroma of the hop is now considered an essential complement to the malt sweetness of beer, hops were first employed in brewing as a preservative. Beer made with hops stored better than beer brewed without them, although the reason why was not understood. Only toward the end of the nineteenth century did brewers discover that hops prevented the growth of many waterborne and airborne bacteria. The role that hop polyphenols play in precipitating unstable proteins in the kettle, thereby reducing the potential for chill haze in the beer, also began to be understood.

On the Vine

Hops are grown on perennial vines that trail along wires strung on trellises fifteen to twenty-five feet above ground level. Each year new stems twine clockwise around the wire strands supporting the strobiles. When the strobiles are mature, the plant is cut loose from the trellis, and the clusters of hop cones are stripped from the stems of the plant.

Hops that are of brewing quality must be harvested during the five to ten days of their prime. Immature hops are very green and have a haylike aroma; overripe cones have rusty-colored petals, tend to shatter easily, and have a harsh smell.

The cones, which contain 70 to 80 percent moisture at harvesting, are dried to 8 to 10 percent moisture (usually at 140 to 150 degrees F [60 to 65 degrees C] but sometimes below 130 degrees F [55 degrees C] when a very strong aroma is characteristic) over a period of eight to twelve hours. They are sometimes fumed with sulfur to lighten their color and give them a softer, silkier, more appealing feel. Dried hops are cured in cooling bins for five to ten days to equalize their moisture content, improve their aroma and appearance, and make the cones more

Hops on the Vine

NOONAN

resilient against shattering. They are compressed and baled, each bale measuring approximately twenty by thirty by fifty-four inches and weighing between 185 and 205 pounds. They are traditionally stitched in burlap hopsack, but modern foil-mylar laminate vacuum-packaging under nitrogen or CO_2 atmosphere is gradually replacing burlap.

The harvest is purchased by hop merchants, who hold the hops in cold storage until they are sold to the brewer. If the hops have been properly dried and baled, protected from direct sunlight, and stored at low humidity and low temperatures (33 degrees F [1 degree C] is ideal), little destructive oxidation occurs; hops that have a beta-acid content equal to their alpha acids store better than hops with a low percentage of beta acids. Under ideal conditions hops will keep for up to two years. Under adverse storage conditions, however, the essential oils are driven off, and many of the alpha-acid resins are oxidized to uncharacterized bitter substances or to useless hard resins. Such hops may have an "off" cheesy, soapy, or other disagreeable aroma and may be yellow or brown. At this point, their bittering strength has been greatly diminished and their flavor contribution to beer is abnormal.

In the Brewery

Brewing hops should be whole cones of a light yellowish-green color, not mottled or spotted, roundish or slightly elongated in shape, and of less than 6 percent stem and leaf content. They should have a pleasant aroma; it is this bouquet that indicates the condition of the essential oils. The hop cones should be silky, glossy, and springy to the touch. Small hops tend to be of finer quality than large hops.

Two or three small cones should be rubbed in the palm of the hand and sniffed to assess the aroma. The lupulin quality and content can be judged by the stickiness left on the hand. Several cones should be broken lengthwise and the quantity and color of the lupulin assessed. It should be lemon colored and plentiful. Old, deteriorated hops have powdery, light-brown lupulin and range in color from green or greenish-yellow to yellow or brownish-green. Usually the discoloration is obvious. Old, dry, and powdery hop cones should be avoided, as the alpha-acid content will be considerably reduced. The deterioration of old or mishandled bales may account for a 50 percent or greater loss of alpha acids. This is also true in the case of lots containing an excessive number of broken cones. Improved oxygen-barrier packaging is becoming an important factor to brewers, since it can cut alpha-acid losses to a fraction of what can be expected with burlap-baled hops.

An alpha-acid analysis is usually made of samples taken from each hop bale. Alpha acidity is given as a percentage of the sample, by weight. This is stated by the dealer and is used by the brewer to adjust bittering-hop rates.

Alpha acids go into solution only after boiling has isomerized them to iso-alpha acids. Their bittering contribution is dependent upon isomerization efficiency in the kettle and the quantity and alpha-acid content of the hops used. Several methods for the quantitative analysis of iso-alpha acids make it possible to estimate the hop bitterness in beer; the internationally agreed upon standard is bitterness units (IBU). One IBU equals .0001335 of an ounce (avoirdupois) of iso-alpha acid per gallon of solution, or one milligram per liter.

Where stated in a beer profile, bitterness units are used to target bittering-hop rates, adjusting the amount to reflect the widely varying alpha-acid content of hops from lot to lot and season to season.

Dave Line (*The Big Book of Brewing*) devised the alpha acid unit (AAU) to simplify these adjustments; his method was adopted by the American Homebrewers Association as the homebrew bitterness unit, or HBU. One AAU/HBU equals one ounce of a 1 percent alpha-acid hop. Using this system, two ounces of a 5 percent alpa-acid hop gives 10 HBU, and so on.

Assuming 30 percent isomerization/utilization of the alpha resins by a 90- to 120-minute rolling boil, each HBU will contribute 22.472 IBUs to a gallon of wort, or 85 IBUs

Hop Cross-section

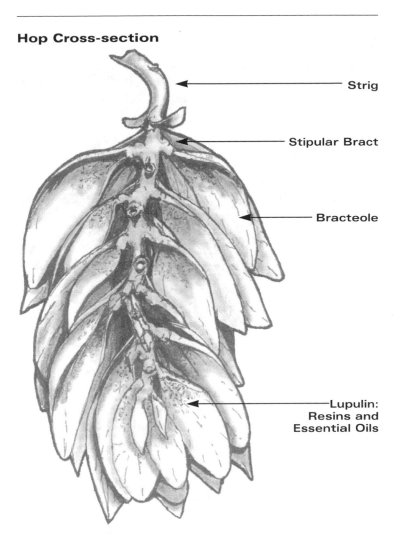

Strig

Stipular Bract

Bracteole

Lupulin:
Resins and
Essential Oils

per liter. Where utilization is high, dividing the IBU given for any beer by 22.472 can approximate the HBUs required per gallon of wort. Likewise, where bitterness units aren't given in a recipe, they can be roughly figured by multiplying the AAUs given by 22.472 (per gallon of wort). More accurate predictions of bitterness can be made using table

Table 9: Hops

Color Range		
Low-quality hops	**High-quality hops**	**Deteriorated hops**
Dark green	Yellowish-green	Yellow
Olive green	Greenish-yellow	Brownish-yellow
Mottled brown-green		Brown
		Brownish-green

Cone Size		
Large	**Medium**	**Small**
2 1/4–3" long	1 1/4–2" long	3/4–1" long

Analysis			
MC	8–13%	Essential oils	.2–3%
Resins	7–20%	Tannins	2–5%
Alpha acid	4–15%	Nitrogen	2–4%
Cohumulone %	20–40%	Fats and waxes	2–5%
Alpha:beta ratio	.8–3.5	Hop storage index	50–85%

18. In any case, bitterness units can only be accurately matched if fresh, properly stored hops are used; with oxidized hops, alpha acidity is diminished and the proper hop rate becomes guesswork.

Varietal and lot analyses of hops include several commonly quoted parameters; only the percentage of alpha acid, the alpha:beta ratio, the percentage of cohumulone, and the percentage of total oils seem to be of definite significance. Other indicators are much more subjective; the hop storage index (percent alpha acid after six months storage at 68 degrees F [20 degrees C]), for instance, is a guideline only, since merchants and brewers store hops under varying temperature and packaging conditions. Percentages of the significant hydrocarbon fractions, taken into consideration with the percentage of total oils, may to some extent indicate the aroma that a hop will give, but the compounds actually responsible for the flavors and aromatics that brewers prize have not been defined. Furthermore, although it is known that oxygenated hydrocarbons, especially terpenes and sesquiterpenes, are less volatile and contribute a major part of hop flavor and aroma to wort and beer, synergic relationships between them and their esters, alcohols, and acids are not understood. Consequently, aroma and flavor characteristics cannot be defined from laboratory data.

The ratio of alpha to beta acid and the percentage of cohumulone do seem to have some significance regarding the fineness of wort bitterness, but there are exceptions to the brewer's rule that the best hops have a high beta-acid ratio and a low percentage of cohumulone.

Hop bitterness is accentuated by magnesium, carbonate, and chloride ions, and hop rates must generally be reduced as these increase; historically, brewers have employed carbonate and chloride waters only for malty, low-hopped beers. Increasing amounts of sulfate, on the other hand, give a cleaner hop flavor. Well-hopped beers brewed with gypsiferous liquor commonly exhibit a finer, less coarse bitterness than is obtained with other liquor profiles.

Hop pellets have gained in popularity with brewers in recent years because they are less susceptible to oxidation during storage, especially under adverse conditions. Pellets stored under the same conditions as whole hops will lose only about one-third the alpha acids that whole hops will lose. They are compressed from fresh hops and foil-packaged in an oxygen-free environment. Because pellets are almost invariably less deteriorated than whole hops, utilization is usually 3 to 10 percent better (5 to 35 percent; as opposed to 3 to 30 percent for whole hops).

Table 10

Part A: Hop Varieties

Hop Varieties	% Alpha Acid	% Beta Acid	Cohumulone, % of AA
Czech Saaz	2.5–4.5	2.5–4.0	22–28
Polish Lublin	3.0–4.5	2.5–3.5	25–30
Spalt	4.0–5.5	4.0–5.5	23–28
U.S. Spalt	3.0–6.0	3.0–5.0	20–25
Tettnang	3.5–5.5	3.5–5.0	23–29
U.S. Tettnang	3.0–5.0	2.5–4.5	20–25
H Hersbruck	2.0–5.5	3.0–5.5	19–25
U.S. Hersbruck	3.5–5.5	5.5–7.0	20–30
H Hallertau	2.5–5.5	2.5–5.5	18–24
U.S. Hallertau	3.0–5.5	3.0–5.5	18–24
U.S. Perle	5.5–9.5	3.5–5.0	27–32
Mt Hood	3.0–6.5	3.0–5.5	24–30
Liberty	3.0–5.5	3.0–4.5	24–30
Crystal	2.0–4.5	4.5–6.5	20–26
Cascade	4.5–8.0	4.0–8.0	30–40
Bav N Brewer	6.0–10.	3.0–5.0	28–33
U.S. N Brewer	6.5–10.	1.5–5.0	20–30
Nugget	12.0–16.	4.0–8.0	24–30
Eroica	9.5–14.	2.5–5.0	36–42
Centennial	8.5–12.	2.5–5.0	29–30
Galena	12.0–15.	7.0–9.5	38–42
Brewers Gold	7.0–10.	3.0–4.5	40–45
Chinook	10.0–14	2.5–4.0	29–34
Styrian Gldng	4.0–6.0	2.0–3.0	26–30
Willamette	4.0–7.0	3.0–4.5	26–35
U.S. Fuggle	4.0–6.0	1.5–3.0	25–32
UK Fuggle	4.0–5.5	2.0–3.0	25–30
BC Goldings	4.0–6.5	1.5–2.5	22–28
UK Goldings	4.5–6.5	2.5–3.5	22–32
Pride Rngwd	6.0–10.	3.0–6.0	33–39
Cluster	5.5–10.	4.5–8.0	36–42
UK Challenger	6.5–8.5	3.0–4.5	22–28
UK Northdown	7.0–9.0	4.5–7.0	28–32

Chart compiled from references provided by Morris Hanbury and HopUnion.

Notes: % alpha acid and % total oils vary widely year to year.

M=Myrcene, H=Humulene, C=Caryophyllene, F=Farnesene. These are significant hop oil hydrocarbons; their respective amounts help define aroma characteristics.

Total Oils mL/100g	M % of each:	H	C	F	%AA after 6 mo. @ 20°C	Origin
.4–.7	23	43	11	13	50	
.7–1.2	30	38	10	11	50	
.5–1.1	20	22	13	13	55	
.5–1.0	45	15	5	13	50	
.6–1.1	23	23	8	14	60	
.4–.8	41	21	7	7	60	
.7–1.3	20	20	10	<1	60	
.6–1.2	45	25	8	<1	50	
.6–1.2	20	33	12	<1	55	
.6–1.0	40	34	11	<1	55	
.7–.9	50	31	11	<1	85	NBrwr+
.6–1.2	38	38	11	<1	50	Hal+
.6–1.2	38	38	11	<1	45	Mtlfh+
1.0–1.5	52	21	6	<1	50	Hal+
.8–1.5	53	13	4	6	50	Fug+
1.6–2.1	33	28	9	<1	75	BGold+
1.5–2.0	55	25	8	<1	80	
1.7–2.3	55	18	9	<1	75	BGold+
.8–1.3	60	1	10	<1	60	BGold+
1.5–2.3	50	14	7	<1	65	BGold+
.9–1.2	58	13	4	<1	65	BGold+
1.8–2.5	63	15	8	<1	55	
1.5–2.5	38	23	10	<1	70	Fugl+
.5–1.3	30	36	10	3	65	Fugl+
1.0–1.5	50	25	8	6	65	Fugl+
.7–1.2	45	23	8	5	65	
.7–1.1	26	37	12	9	60	
.8–1.1	26	41	13	<1	60	
.8–1.0	24	45	14	<1	55	Kent+
1.0–2.0	38	6	8	<1	55	
.4–.8	50	17	7	<1	85	BGold+
1.0–1.5	31	29	9	2	55	Chal+
1.2–2.2	25	43	15	<1	60	

Percent alpha to beta acids, % cohumulone, total oil, and percentages of M, H, C, F are all factors that indicate relative values of individual hops. A low percentage of cohumulone, for instance (below 30%), indicates hops with desirable "noble" aromatics.

Table 10, continued

Part B: Hop Producing Districts		
Country of Origin	Hop Type	Grown
Czech Republic	Saaz/Zatec Red	Zatec, Auscha, Raudnitz, Dauba
Germany	Hallertauer/Mittlefrueh Tettnanger Spalt Hersbrucker/Gebirg	Hallertau, Baden Wurtenburg Spalt Hersbruck
Yugoslavia	Savinja/Styrian Goldings	Wojwodina, Slovenia
Belgium	Hallertau/Saaz	Alost, Poperinghe
United States	Various	Yakima Valley (Washington) Willamette Valley (Oregon) Boise and Snake River Valleys (Idaho)
Australia	Pride of Ringwood	Victoria, Tasmania

The most highly prized hops in the world are the mild southern-English and central-European varieties. Although these and similar types are being more widely cultivated in the western United States, they are not frequently used by large domestic commercial breweries. New disease-resistant, high-alpha-acid varieties are emerging that also have desirable aromatic qualities, giving better kettle utilization and economy without forsaking fine hop character, as has been the case with high-alpha-acid-percentage strains previously developed for economical use.

CHAPTER 5

Yeast

Yeast are nonphotosynthetic, relatively sophisticated, living, unicellular fungi, considerably larger than
bacteria. Brewers' yeast are of the genus *Saccharomyces*. In
an aciduric aqueous solution, they absorb dissolved vitamins, minerals, and simple nitrogenous matter (amino
acids and very simple peptides) through their hemicellulose cell membranes. Then they employ a structured series
of reactions known as *metabolic pathways* to break down
these substances into nutrients, mainly amino acids to
nitrogen and sugars to carbon. They obtain oxygen for
metabolism from what is dissolved in the solution, or they
split it off of molecular compounds.

Yeast, although living organisms, are actually highly
organized enzyme collectives, each and every reaction of
the yeast cell being controlled by a separate enzyme. In
one reaction, simple sugars are reduced to alcohol and carbonic gas in the presence of a constitutive intracellular
enzyme group called *zymase* and a phosphoric coenzyme.
This process is known as *fermentation.* Yeast metabolism

directly determines the degree of attenuation of any wort, and its character greatly affects the flavor of the finished beer. In fact, just as every living organism varies from every other, every yeast strain, and even every fermentation, has qualities distinctly its own. These depend on a number of factors. Particular strains of yeast produce different flavor characteristics; variations in the pH, temperature, or composition of each ferment result in slight to significant changes in the metabolic products.

Although brewing dates back to prehistory, it was not until 1841 that Mitcherlich discovered that yeast were essential to fermentation. Further research by Pasteur and Buchner revealed that yeast produced alcohol only as a by-product of carbon metabolism, and that it was in fact the nonliving zymase enzyme that was responsible for the fermentation of sugar.

Bottom fermenting began with Gabriel Sedlmayer in Munich and Anton Dreher in Vienna in 1841, using mixed strains of yeast that were not purely bottom fermenting. Emil Hanson, working at Jacob Christian's Carlsberg brewery in Copenhagen, set the stage for modern lager brewing by isolating two distinctly different *pure-culture* yeasts, that is, strains propagated from a single cell and therefore all exhibiting the same characteristics. These were a top-fermenting *Saccharomyces cerevisiae* and the bottom-fermenting *Saccharomyces carlsbergensis (S. uvarum)*. Pure-culture, bottom-fermenting yeast were first employed at Carlsberg in 1883; within the decade, lager culture yeast were being employed in refrigerated fermentation throughout Europe and America.

Besides their visually different flocculating characteristics, the yeast operate at different temperatures and ferment different sugars. The top-fermenting yeast strains are generally only effective at 55 to 75 degrees F (13 to 24 degrees C). They form colonies that are supported by the

Yeasts

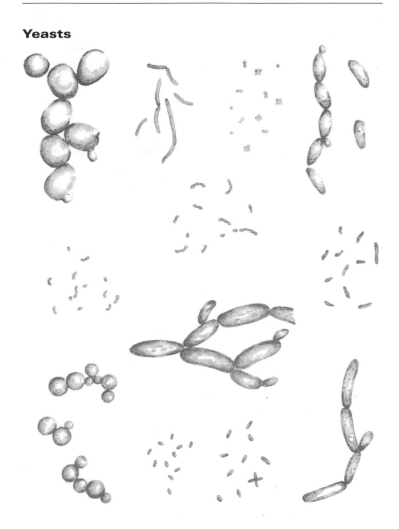

Top, left to right: *Saccharomyces carlsbergensis, Lactobacillus, Pediococcus, Exiguus*

Middle: *Acetobacter, Acetomonas, Hafnia*

Center: *Pichia membranaefaciens* (wild yeast)

Bottom: *Torulopsis* (wild yeast), *Klebsiella, Zymomonas, Mycoderma*

surface tension of the beer and create a very thick, rich yeast head; in general, they ferment glucose, fructose, mannose, galactose, maltose, sucrose, xylulose, and maltotriose, and partially ferment the trisaccharide raffinose. (*S. cerevisiae* splits off and ferments the fructose molecule from raffinose, leaving the disaccharide melibiose.) "Bottom-fermenting" lager yeasts, which don't have as great an ability to chain and cling together, form smaller colonies that make a thinner, less tenuous head and that sediment out on the bottom of the fermenter more rapidly. They operate best at temperatures below 50 to 55 degrees F (10 to 13 degrees C). They ferment glucose, fructose, mannose, galactose, maltose, sucrose, melibiose, xylulose, and maltotriose, and fully ferment raffinose. Neither yeast ferments lactose, and all but the monosaccharide sugars need to be reduced by specific yeast enzymes before they can be fermented; sucrose must be split into glucose and fructose by invertase (sucrase), and maltose and maltotriose must be reduced to glucose by maltase (a-glucosidase). Maltose is able to be absorbed into the yeast cell before being hydrolyzed, but all the other disaccharides need to be reduced to monosaccharides by excreted enzymes before they can be transported into the yeast cell; this is the basis of maltose's ready fermentability.

There are two distinctive subdivisions of the bottom-fermenting yeast *S. carlsbergensis*. The Frohberg type (F.U., dusty or "powdery" yeasts) ferment very strongly, and attenuation is very rapid. Because they do not clump well, they remain in suspension longer and consequently have a greater effect upon wort attenuation. They ferment isomaltose as well as maltose. The Saaz type (S.U., or "break" yeasts) settle out of the ferment more satisfactorily than do the powdery yeast strains. Consequently, they are very weak fermenters and reduce the extract very slowly. They do not ferment isomaltose.

Different yeast strains span the spectrum between these two major classifications, producing very different aspects of taste, mouthfeel, alcohol, and clarity in the finished beer; the yeasts that ferment the quickest and most completely are not often the yeasts that produce the best beer. Yeast strains are selected for the character of their fermentation, their ability to form colonies, their ability to ferment with or without forming esters, and their viability rather than their ability to attenuate the wort rapidly.

Chemically, yeasts are constituted of proteins (especially *volutin*, a nucleoprotein visible as small, shiny bodies in the vacuoles and cell plasma), glycogen (a starchlike reserve not usually found in older or stressed cells), minerals, enzymes, and vitamins (especially those of the beta complex).

Yeasts require various nutrients to renew these elements of their cellular structure. They absorb simple protein from hydrolytic solution, which they refine to a very high quality amino-acid group that composes roughly half of the yeast cell. Another 10 percent of the cell is calcium based and requires renewal, as do the minerals and trace elements that account for up to 5 percent of its structure. The minerals, besides calcium, are mostly the inorganic salts of phosphorus and potassium, with some magnesium, sodium, and sulfur. Yeast obtain these from mineral compounds in the ferment. The trace elements, especially zinc, boron, and manganese, are almost always available in small amounts from the malt, hops, or water. Yeast cells also require readily available oxygen for membrane synthesis; this is particularly important during the reproductive phase.

Yeasts reproduce by cell division, known as *binary fission* or budding. They reproduce only in a nutrient-rich environment; one daughter cell emerges and grows to the size of the mother cell in two to six hours in a suitable solution.

There are numerous strains of yeast, and each operates successfully within a very narrow pH and temperature range. It is necessary to carefully control these factors during brewing because the metabolic reactions and the reproduction rate of the yeast greatly influence the nature and flavor of the beer being brewed.

Yeast operate in suspension in a sugar solution, until they clump together and are brought to the surface by attached CO_2 or are sedimented by virtue of their increased mass. They cease to have a considerable effect on attenuation once they have clumped.

As yeast cells age, their previously colorless, homogeneous plasma (protoplasm) becomes bubbly, then separates into solids and liquid substances by forming vacuoles that envelop the liquid plasma secretion; later they become granulated, and gradually the plasma turns to fat (visible as round bodies of varying sizes within the cell walls). Although they are incapable of sporulation, yeast can be sustained in an unsuitable environment for long periods by these fatty bodies.

In solutions lacking obtainable nutrients, the culture yeast will cease reproducing. When they can no longer sustain their own metabolic functions, albumin-, hemicellulose-, and vitamin-dissolving enzymes are activated, which reduce the yeast cell to amino acids and other simple substances. This autolization releases typical organic decomposition flavors into beer that is not racked off its sediment.

Because a ferment lacks nutrients needed by the culture yeast, or because the temperature or the pH of the ferment does not suit the particular yeast strain does not mean that wild yeast strains, mutations, or other microbes will not find the conditions ideal. Under normal conditions, one in a million yeast cells spontaneously mutates; under hostile conditions mutations increase dramatically. Either a

wild yeast strain or one of these genetically altered mutations may become the dominant fermentation organism, to
the detriment or ruin of the finished beer.

Wild yeast cause spoilage, including clove, sour,
vinegar, sulphuric, phenolic/medicinal, fusely, and diacetyl
flavors, and create film formation on the beer surface.
Because wild yeast do not tend to cling together as well as
culture yeast, and consequently remain in suspension
longer, they almost invariably cloud the beer. The offending
yeast may even be a wild strain of *S. uvarum (S. carlsbergensis)* or *S. cerevisiae,* but this does not make their presence any
more desirable. Other common spoilage yeasts are
Torulopsis, Candida, Dekkera, and *Pichia* species. It is essential
to ferment with solely the culture yeast alone, maintaining
its purity, ensuring its adequate nutrition, and carefully controlling its metabolic functions through manipulation of the
nutrient spectrum, pH, and temperature of the ferment.

Culturing Pure Yeast Strains

Pure-culture yeasts are strains propagated from a
single cell. Yeast from a successful primary fermentation
that has exhibited good brewing characteristics are collected and mixed into a small amount of distilled water
until the solution just becomes cloudy (approximately
100,000 cells/milliliter). One drop of the yeast solution is
then mixed into one fluid ounce of diluted wort gelatin
(beer wort diluted with sterile water at 4 to 8 °Plato [SG
1016 to 1032] mixed with 5 to 10 percent pure vegetable
gelatin). The yeast is distributed by thorough agitation
before the mixture is thinly spread over a clean cover glass,
allowed to congeal, and placed in a sterile, moist container.
The glass is then fixed to a graduated stage and microscopically examined at powers of 400 to 1,000 magnification,
and the location of isolated, healthy-looking (white, hemi-
spherical, nonreflective, uniformly sized) cells marked.

Pure Yeast Culture Growth

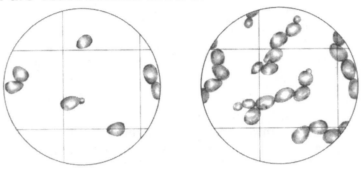

After twenty-four hours at 68 degrees F (20 degrees C), the glass is reexamined. Colonies should have formed. If they appear healthy, sample yeast cells from several isolated chains that are known to have grown from a single cell are removed with a flame-sterilized platinum or stainless-steel wire loop. Where a microscope is unavailable, the loop can be used to take a sample directly from a cloudy yeast solution, and an isolated colony can be chosen from the petri dish in the next step.

Each sample is streaked onto the surface of a sterile, staining nutrient agar (WL nutrient agar) in a petri dish. The inoculating streak is cross-hatched to isolate individual cells from it. When visible colonies have formed, an isolated clump ("rosette") is microscopically examined, and if it is uncontaminated, it is used to inoculate an agar wort slant (eight fluid ounces of wort diluted to 4 to 8 °Plato [SG 1016 to 1032] with sterile water, mixed into five grams of prepared agar or vegetable gelatin, at room temperature, heated to boiling after fifteen minutes, and boiled [or autoclaved at 15 psi] for fifteen minutes). This is poured into sterile twenty-milliliter test tubes tilted fifteen degrees from the horizontal, that are then capped or plugged with cotton and allowed to cool.

The temperature is maintained at 50 to 68 degrees F (10 to 20 degrees C), until fermentation is apparent (usually two to four days); then the culture may be refrigerated for three months at 39 degrees F (4 degrees C) for lager yeast, or at above 50 degrees F (10 degrees C) for ale yeast. The medium can be covered with a layer of sterile mineral oil to maintain an anaerobic environment.

The slants may be recultured by adding one-half inch of wort to each of the older tubes, and after fermentation begins, using that mixture to inoculate four freshly prepared slants. All culturing must be done under strictly sanitary conditions using sterile labware.

For the brewer who does not have the laboratory equipment necessary to isolate and incubate pure cultures (basically, a microscope, wire loop, and the several items of glassware mentioned), purchase of commercially prepared vials or slants is the best source of a yeast culture. Frozen yeast is a reasonable alternative, as are properly handled liquid cultures. Granulated dry yeasts are the least-desirable alternative, as they are likely to contain many dead cells and be contaminated by bacteria during the drying process.

Slants are activated by covering the culture with one-half inch of wort. After forty-eight hours, that pure liquid-culture is used to inoculate a sterile, narrow-necked eight- or twelve-ounce vessel (or Erlenmeyer flask) filled with four fluid ounces of (sterile) aerated wort; this volume can be successfully inoculated directly from the cover glass if slant culturing must be omitted. The bottle must be capped or covered with a fermentation lock.

After twenty-four hours at 82 degrees F (28 degrees C), each four fluid ounces of wort should yield two to four grams of pure culture yeast. Cooler temperatures, however, are generally employed to retard the yeast's reproduction rate; for lager yeasts, 50 to 68 degrees F (10 to 20 degrees C) for two to three days is usual. If capped, the lid must periodically be loosened to release pressure. When strongly fermenting, the culture may be roused into one quart of wort at a slightly warmer temperature than is usual for the brewery fermentation. It may be cooled to as low as 39 degrees F (4 degrees C) if the culture is not needed immediately. It is ready to pitch when it comes into active kraeusen. Each quart of starter should yield sixteen grams or more of pure culture yeast.

Aerate starter cultures often and well, so that the increase in available oxygen will stimulate greater yeast growth. In professional practice, a swab of yeast from the starter is cultured on a slide and microscopically examined for contamination before the parent culture is pitched.

Storing Yeast

Starters may be held at 39 degrees F (4 degrees C) for up to three weeks, or until fermentation subsides. The beer above the yeast can then be decanted, and the yeast covered with cold wort before it is refrigerated again.

For longer storage, after one week at 50 degrees F (10 degrees C), the yeast may be forced to sediment by lowering the temperature. The liquid above the yeast is decanted, and the yeast sediment pressed to remove at least all of the free liquid. The yeast mass is formed into a ball, tightly covered with plastic wrap, placed in chipped ice, and frozen.

Yeast prepared in this manner may be stored for several months. When reactivation is desired, it is crumbled into a quart of well-aerated wort.

Yeast may be collected from each brewing and successively subcultured until undesirable changes occur in the beer flavor or the strain's fermentation profile. Most breweries repitch yeast only three to fifteen times before going back to the pure culture.

Washing Yeast

Usually yeast requires only rinsing before reuse, but periodically cultures should be washed to destroy bacterial contaminants. (This will not, however, destroy wild yeast; they can only be eliminated by reculturing.)

To wash, chill the vessel to sediment the yeast, then decant off the liquid above the yeast cake. Rinse the yeast by covering with, and then decanting off, distilled or biologically sterile water. Cover again with a solution of sodium metabisulfite, phosphoric or tartaric (winemakers) acid at pH 2.8, or a .75 percent solution of acidified ammonium persulfate (one teaspoon of tartaric acid with two teaspoons of ammonium persulfate in one quart of water, at pH 2.8) in water or sterile beer, equal in volume to the amount of yeast being washed. Agitate the yeast into temporary suspension. When the yeast have completely settled, or within two hours, decant off the liquid above the yeast, rinse several times, and cover with sterile wort. Some yeast may display abnormal characteristics in the first fermentation cycle following an acid wash; they should be cultured through at least one fermentation cycle before being pitched. The above precautions notwithstanding, many breweries wash their yeast regularly, often pitching the yeast, still in the acid solution at pH 2 to 2.5, after two hours.

CHAPTER

Bacteria

Some bacteria are almost invariably present during brewing, having been transported into the brew by air, water, or the yeast culture. Certain bacteria may be present in small quantities without noticeably affecting the finished beer, but small concentrations of other bacteria can quickly ruin it. In some beer styles, bacteria in the ferment give a beer its particular character, but on the whole, bacterial contamination and growth need to be discouraged by strict sanitation. Bacteria are only tolerated in a lager brewery where they are cultured to reduce the mash acidity.

The countless types of bacteria oxidize or ferment a wide variety of organic substances. Fortunately, only a relatively few types of bacteria are encountered during brewing, and no pathogenic bacteria can survive in beer. Bacteria grow on sugar, wort, beer, protein, and hop residues, and even on the yeast. By careful control and strict sanitation, flavor and stability problems caused by bacterial contamination of beer can be kept in check. The brewer must work to eliminate any contaminant, or reduce it to a level where its growth will not appreciably affect the finished beer.

Because bacteria adapt and mutate so readily (far more readily than yeast), they can emerge as the dominant fermentation microbe from a relatively small number of cells. It is also because they mutate so readily that bacteria are so difficult to classify. Although they have a host of characteristics, they are initially categorized by whether or not they are stained by gentian violet (the Gram stain).

Gram-Positive Bacteria

The gram-positive bacteria encountered during brewing are the Peptococcaceae (family) *Pediococcus* (genus) and the Lactobacillaceae *Lactobacillus*. These are grouped together as *lactic acid* bacteria, and were formerly referred to as "beer sarcina" (a term more specifically applied to *Pediococcus*). Both operate anaerobically and ferment simple sugars to lactic acid; they have little effect upon protein.

The several species of *Pediococci* are strictly anaerobic, globular ("cocci") bacteria occurring singly, paired, or in cubicle groups called *tetrads*. They form diacetyl and inactive lactic acid from dextrins and glucose. Heterofermentive strains also ferment maltose, fructose, and sucrose, producing acetic acid as well. In general, the *Pediococci* produce a disagreeable taste, odor, and turbidity (cloudiness). Contamination is most often from calcified trub deposits on poorly cleaned equipment; it is *Pediococcus's* ability to survive even rigorous cleaning, sheltered by "beerstone" deposits that make them the most pernicious brewery contaminants.

The *Lactobacillus* are the single genus of their family. These long, thin, curved rods occur singly or paired at obtuse angles. Microaerophiles, they form lactic acid by the fermentation of carbohydrates in even oxygen-poor solutions. Although they do not cause odor, they may produce a sour taste and turbidity. Several species of *Lactobacillus* and *Pediococcus* also cause a *ropy* or gelatinous fermentation, or a silky turbulence, formed by the excretion of an extracellular slime. It disappears briefly during stirring, but reforms as chains upon the beer surface.

Lactobacillus delbruckii (pH 5.6 to 5.8, active below 131 degrees F [55 degrees C]) is a heat-tolerant or *thermophilic* homofermentive species that grows on malt. It is especially well suited to the acidulation of the mash, without producing undesirable flavors or turbidity. It metabolizes glucose and yields only lactic acid. Because it is favored by anaerobic conditions, its growth is encouraged by holding a tight, saccharified mash, closely covered, at above 95 to 120 degrees F (35 to 49 degrees C). This inhibits both aerobic and nonthermophilic bacteria.

When lactic acid bacteria, and especially thermophilic heterofermentive strains, are active in the mash or its extract, they may spoil it by acidification and souring, turbidity, or the formation of off-flavors, most notably a rancid-butter taste from the diacetyl diketone. The same symptoms in cooled wort, in young beer, and sometimes in aged beer are more likely due to contamination by *Pediococcus cerevisiae* (pH 5.5, active over a wide temperature range, most active at 70 to 77 degrees F [21 to 25 degrees C]) and other nonthermophilic strains.

The thermophilic gram-positive bacteria are inhibited by isohumulones from the hops and usually will not survive in bitter wort or in beer. Lactic-acid bacteria are often contaminants from pitching yeast or from air. They may be the most significant infectious organism in the fermentation.

The gram-positive bacteria are rarely a problem in the aged beer because they have highly complex nutritional requirements and are inhibited by hops. During fermentation, the yeast will have absorbed many of the essential amino acids, making them unavailable to the lactic acid bacteria. Only when the proteolysis and precipitation of protein has been poor, when aging beer is not separated from deteriorating yeast sediment, or when temperature shock to the yeast causes it to autolyze will the bacteria be able to obtain enough amino acids to support reproduction.

Gram-Negative Bacteria

The most significant gram-negative bacteria commonly affecting the lactic-acid mash is the coliform *Clostridium butyricum* (butyric acid bacteria). These are thick, principally anaerobic rods that putrefy the mash by forming rancid-smelling ethylacetic acid (butyric or butatonic acid). They are inactive above 112 degrees F (45 degrees C) and very active below 104 degrees F (40 degrees C). This spore-forming bacteria may also occur in beer.

Acetic-acid bacteria sometimes taint mashes that come in contact with the air below 122 degrees F (50 degrees C) (they are quite active below 95 degrees F [35 degrees C]), but they present a far greater danger to fermenting beer. The acetic-acid bacteria are active over the entire pH range of the brewing cycle and are not inhibited by isohumulone from the hops. They are strong oxidizers and are usually responsible for any overwhelming sour-fruit or vinegary taste and odor, and oftentimes turbidity. The surface contamination they cause is often apparent as an oily or moldy (pellicle) film. They are usually introduced to the ferment during racking; aeration of the beer by rousing or splashing provides them with sufficient oxygen for respiration. Active yeast in kraeusen beer, when added during racking, can consume the dissolved oxygen quickly enough to prevent their growth, but in racking "quiet" beer, it is imperative that all aeration be avoided. Dispensing equipment should be given frequent and complete sterilization, as it is also a point of contamination. Sour-tasting or -smelling draft beer has almost

certainly been contaminated by these bacteria. The lactophilic Achromobacteraceae *Acetobacter* (significantly *A.
aceti* and *A. suboxydans*) oxidize ethanol to acetic acid. They
are short, chain-forming, ellipsoidal-to-rod-shaped aerobic
bacteria. The glucophilic Pseudomonodaceae *Acetomonas
(Gluconobacter)* excrete vinegar and gluconic acid. They are
short, rod-shaped-to-ovoid, polarly flaggelated aerobic
bacteria occurring singly, paired, or in chains.
Achromobacter and *Pseudomonas* are infrequently encountered, and then only in sweet wort, because they are acid
intolerant and inhibited by alcohol.

The coliform bacteria (termobacteria) commonly
taint the wort by adding a dimethyl-suphide-related
cooked- or spoiled-vegetable odor, caused by very rapid
metabolism of wort sugars. They are waterborne, non-
sporulating aerobes and faculative anaerobes most active at
98.6 degrees F (37 degrees C). Enterobacteriaceae
Escherechia are straight rods occurring singly or in pairs.
Enterobacteriaceae *Klebsiella (Aerobacter)* are nonmotile,
encapsulated rods occurring singly, paired, or in chains.
The cooled wort is an ideal medium for their growth.
Aerobacter aerogenes is a commonly encountered source of
pungent, vegetable, or sulfuric taste and ropy fermentation
in both wort and green beer. They adapt and reproduce far
more quickly than culture yeast. It is essential that the
starter or kraeusen beer used to inoculate the wort be
strongly fermenting and of similar temperature and composition to the wort into which it will be pitched.
Otherwise coliform bacteria may become strongly established in the lag phase.

The source of these coliform bacteria is most commonly rinsing water. Although they are active over a wide
temperature range and are unaffected by hop resins, most
are inhibited below pH 4.4 and are not commonly encountered during the later stages of brewing.

Table 11

Brewing Contaminants			
Brewing Stage	**Symptoms**	**Bacteria Responsible**	**Solution**
Mash, at below 140°F (60°C)	Acidity, sourness, turbidity	Thermophilic lactic acid bacteria	Raise temp. to above 131°F (55°C)
	Rancid odor	Butyric acid bacteria	Raise temp. to above 112°F (45°C)
	Sour, vinegar taste and odor	Acetic acid bacteria	Raise temp. to above 122°F (50°C)
Cooled Wort	Fruity or vegetable odor	Coliform bacteria	Pitch quickly
Primary Fermentation	Celery odor	*Hafnia protea*	Go to new yeast culture
Secondary Fermentation	Sour taste, silky turbidity	Lactic acid bacteria	Lower temp.
	Sour taste, odor and turbidity	Lactic acid bacteria	Lower temp.
Aging/conditioning	As above	Acetic acid bacteria	None
	As above	Lactic acid bacteria	None
	Stench	*Zymomonas*	None

Enterobacteriaceae *Hafnia (Obesumbacterium)* are short, nonmotile, straight rods of variable shape that commonly taint the early stages of fermentation. *Hafnia protea*

(O. proteus) are fat rods (pH optimum 6.0) that, when present, are almost always in the yeast culture and only rarely in the wort (other *Hafnia* strains, as well as acetic and lactic-acid bacteria, may also contaminate pitching yeast). They produce sourness, diacetyl, and a dimethyl-sulphide smell like parsnips or celery. Like others of their family, they are intolerant of very acidic solutions and do not usually affect the aging beer.

Acetic and especially lactic-acid bacteria are the most prevalent contaminants of aging and bottled or kegged beer, but Pseudomonaceae *Aeromonas* is also encountered. The plump rods of Pseudomonaceae *Zymomonas (Achromobacter anaerobium*, pH 3.5 to 7.5, temperature optimum 86 degrees F [30 degrees C], active as low as 40 degrees F [5 degrees C]) are relatively uncommon, but when they are present, they produce an objectionable acetaldehyde and rotten-egg stench in a very short time. *Zymomonas anaerobia* or *Z. mobilis* are then the usual contaminants, fermenting fructose and glucose to ethanol, hydrogen sulfide, and acetaldehyde. Ground water or soiled equipment are the usual inoculants.

Bacterial contamination can be assessed both by perceptory analysis of the wort or beer (accentuated by "forcing" closed samples at 85 degrees F [30 degrees C]) and by culturing the wort or beer on a staining or yeast-inhibiting nutrient agar in a petri dish and estimating the microbial population after several days.

Enzymes

Enzymes are complex, protein-based biological cata-lysts that induce reactions between substances without being changed by the reaction or appearing in its end product. Enzymes may be *constitutive,* that is, normally present within the cell, or *inducible,* formed only in the presence of a particular substrate. They may be *intracellular,* operating only within the cell, or *extracellular,* excreted by the cell into solution.

During the malting and brewing cycle, the barley kernel is decomposed to soluble simple sugars and albu-minoids by diastatic and proteolytic enzymes. These sugars are in turn fermented to carbon dioxide and ethyl alcohol by the zymase enzyme group, while other enzymes form organic acids, aldehydes, fusel alcohols, and esters.

The traditional decoction mash is constructed largely upon a series of conditions that reactivate enzyme activity that was prematurely checked by kilning the green malt. It completes the reduction of the native barley proteins and carbohydrates to a soluble extract. In the decoction mash, proteolytic enzymes associated with malting are employed to overcome flaws in the malt.

The proteolytic (peptonizing) group reduces proteins of high molecular complexity to simpler peptides and amino-acid constituents through a structured series of interdependent reactions that sever the peptide links (CO–NH) between protein coils and replace them with a water molecule. This restores the amine (NH_2) and carboxyl (COOH) groups of the amino acid

$$(NH_2 \cdot \underset{H}{CH} \cdot CO\text{-} NH \cdot \underset{H}{CH} \cdot COOH + H_2O \rightarrow \text{Proteinase} \rightarrow$$

$$NH_2 \cdot \underset{H}{CH} \cdot COOH \quad NH_2 \cdot \underset{H}{CH} \cdot COOH)$$

Protease and proteinase (optimum range 122 to 140 degrees F [50 to 60 degrees C] pH 4.6 to 5.0), and then peptase and peptidase (optimum range 113 to 122 degrees F [45 to 50 degrees C] pH below 5.3) solubilize protein and sequentially reduce it to proteose, peptones, polypetides, peptides, and amino acids.

Phytase and phosphatase acidify the malt by forming phytic acid, and they are primarily responsible for the acidulation of the mash at 95 to 122 degrees F (35 to 50 degrees C). They also increase the soluble mineral content of the wort. Cellulase, hemicellulase, collagenase, and pectinase are active within the same temperature range, dissolving the cell walls, endosperm case, gelatin, and pectins.

The diastatic enzymes reduce starch to fractions. Primarily, these are the amylolytic enzymes — alpha- and beta-amylase. The alpha-amylase liquefies native starch and reduces amylose and amylopectin to a stew of carbohydrate fractions. By randomly separating 1-4 linked glucose molecules within the length of polysaccharide chains, it liberates

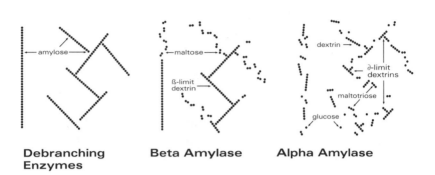

Debranching Enzymes   **Beta Amylase**   **Alpha Amylase**

glucose, maltose, maltotriose, and dextrins, leaving "a-limit" dextrins wherever it is stopped by 1-6 link branching points in amylopectin. It reduces complex starch to a-limit dextrins very rapidly and completely, so that its solution gives only a faint-red reaction with iodine. Yet it further generates a predominance of maltose only very slowly and ineffectively. It is present in the unmalted barley.

Beta-amylase, on the other hand, does not appear until malting. It has no effect on the native starch. In solution it detaches glucose molecules from the nonreducing ends of amylose and amylopectin chains, rejoining them with a water molecule to produce maltose. Alone, it breaks down amylose very slowly and amylopectin very incompletely, because it proceeds in a linear fashion and only from one chain end. It is ineffective within two or three glucose molecules of amylopectin's outermost branching points, leaving a very large "ß-limit" dextrin that gives a deep mahogany color reaction with iodine. Where alpha-amylase activity splits soluble starch into smaller fractions, beta-amylase operates more efficiently, capitalizing upon the increased number of exposed chain ends.

Both amylases are made more effective by the activity of debranching enzymes. A-glucosidase (maltase), limit dextrinase, and pullulanase reduce amylopectin and limit dextrins to amylose by cleaving the linkages at their branching points. The debranching enzymes are most active during malting, and very few survive kilning, even with low-color Pilsen malt. At low mash temperatures they may dismantle some amylopectin, but not at hotter saccharification temperatures in the mash.

During fermentation, the zymase enzymes and a phosphoric coenzyme convert glucose to alcohol and carbonic gas; other enzymes are formed during fermentation that split and invert the more complex sugars present in the ferment. Intracellular maltase and glucase reduce maltose to two molecules of glucose; extracellular invertase splits sucrose into glucose and fructose. Finally, proteolytic enzymes within the yeast cell, triggered by a decline in the yeast's metabolism, autolyze the cell contents to other enzymes, minerals, and vitamins that are slowly released into solution.

It is the enzymatic composition of the yeast cell that determines the nature and vigor of fermentation. Various yeast strains have widely varying enzymatic capability. When the yeast cells do not contain the specific enzymes to reduce the sugars in a wort, they synthesize them. Fermentation lag times, however, are dangerously extended.

THE BREWING PROCESS

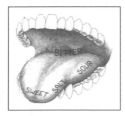

Malting

Barley must be malted before it is mashed. The starch of unmalted barley is too complex to be readily converted to sugars, so the grain must pass through a series of steps to activate its constitute enzymes. The first is steeping.

During *steeping,* or soaking, many enzymes in the grains are either formed or activated, and the starchy endosperm mass is solubilized to gummy *polysaccharides.* During *sprouting,* the hydrolytic enzymes inside the developing plant embryo increase and penetrate the endosperm, reducing proteins and hemicellulose to soluble fractions. Polysaccharides and protein are reduced nearly proportional to the degree of the acrospire growth until both are arrested by kilning.

The *acrospire,* or germinal stem of the barley plant, is grown to the full length of the kernel in British malts, almost fully modifying the endosperm to readily saccharified polysaccharides. American "brewers'" malts are less completely modified, and traditional continental malts modified the least of all. The acrospire growth of continental

malt may be stopped when it is only one-half the length of
the grain, in order to minimize the loss of starch by the
digestion of the endosperm by the germinating embryo.
The lesser degree of conversion is responsible for the lower
enzyme strength and greater nitrogen complexity of continental malt. Haze-forming proteins that remain in continental malt must be decomposed during a low-tempera-
ture mash that is unnecessary when using British malt and
most modern malts.

American malts are sprouted more fully than traditional continental malts. Acrospire growth is usually two-
thirds to three-fourths the length of the kernel, but because
American barley, especially six-row, is of much higher nitrogen content than traditional lager malt, its enzyme strength
is correspondingly greater. High kiln temperatures can be
held longer than with continental malt without risking a
serious depletion of the malt's enzyme strength. Traditional
continental malts require a protein rest to degrade large proteins, and albumin in excess of the amount required for
body, head, and yeast nutrients. Although American malt
can usually be infusion mashed, it is more often given a
protein rest to reduce the potential for chill haze.

Steeping

The barley to be malted is examined, and if it is
judged suitable, steeped to thoroughly wet the endosperm
mass and float off dust, debris, and lightweight, unmaltable
grains. The kernels are stirred in an aerating fashion into
water at 50 to 65 degrees F (10 to 18 degrees C), which is
allowed to overflow the steeper to carry off the debris,
then soaked for two to four days (preferably in alkaline
water) to 35 percent moisture content. The water is
drained, and the moist grains are turned several times
during steeping to increase oxygen uptake by the respiring
barley. The barley may be aerated for up to twelve hours

before it is re-covered with water. Kernels are periodically removed and the extent of the moisture penetration is determined (wet endosperm is off-white). The grains will have swollen 1 1/3 times their original size. Before sprouting, the malt should be of 45 percent moisture content.

Steely or nitrogenous barley must be wetted even more completely. The moisture content is verified by weighing a sample of the moist grain, drying it completely at a low oven temperature, and reweighing the dried grain; the weight loss should generally be 40 to 45 percent.

The white tips of the rootlets may be just emerging (chitting) when steeping is complete.

Germination

Barley may be sprouted in many different ways, but the traditional floor malting produces the most uniform growth as well as the mellowest possible malt. The grain is laid eight to twelve inches thick (thirty-inch maximum) on waterproof concrete, at an ambient temperature of 45 to 60 degrees F (7 to 15 degrees C), for six to ten days. It is wetted and turned periodically to aerate it and to keep the temperature at an even 50 to 70 degrees F (10 to 21 degrees C).

Cooler temperatures encourage greater enzyme production and soluble-carbohydrate yield by impeding acrospire and rootlet growth. Reducing the initial sprouting temperature to below 55 degrees F (13 degrees C) produces the mellowest and most enzyme rich malt. Temperature control is achieved by lowering room temperature and reducing the depth of the sprouting grain to allow the heat being produced by the respiring grain to dissipate.

Growth should start during the first day, as the embryo internally forms immature rootlets; during the second day, the grains are wetted, then aerated by lifting and turning. This is done regularly thereafter. Growth speeds up, and by the fourth day rootlets usually have appeared.

Generally, the acrospire will have grown to one-half the length of the kernel by the sixth day of germination.

The degree of modification can be judged with some degree of accuracy by comparing the length to which the rootlets have grown against the length of the kernel, and by cutting through the hull and examining the endosperm and the length of the acrospire.

Table 12

Rootlet Growth as an Acrospire-Length Indicator	
Rootlet Length	**Acrospire Length**
½– ¾ the length of the kernel	½
1–1½ times the length of the kernel	¾
1½–2 times the length of the kernel	Full

The modification of the endosperm proceeds in the same direction and at approximately the same rate as the growth of the acrospire, although modification tends to exceed acrospire growth in grain malted at lower temperatures.

The green malt should have a clean, wholesome smell and appear plump, with healthy, unwithered rootlets. The endosperm mass should feel chalky when it is rubbed between two fingers. Hard, watery, or gummy malt endosperm is poorly modified.

The objectives of malting for lager malt are even modification, reduction of beta-glucan cell-walls, gums, and protein matrixes, reduction of native starch to "mash-able" fractions, and the development of proteolytic and diastatic enzymes. For malts for infusion mashing, the reduction of the sprouted kernel needs to be carried even further. British pale malt must be partially "mashed" as part of the malting program by a longer sprouting cycle and by saccharification at the start of the kilning cycle.

Kilning

Kilning dries the malt, facilitates removal of the rootlets, and gives malt its character. It also reduces the pH in the mash.

The temperature of green lager malt is generally raised to 90 degrees F (32 degrees C) over twenty-four hours to allow the enzymes to continue starch modification and proteolysis. The lumps of tangled grain are gently broken up after drying has begun but while the green malt is still moist. The temperature is slowly raised to 120 degrees F (49 degrees C) and held for twelve hours to dry the malt, then raised to roasting temperature. It is essential that the malt be bone dry before it is heated above 120 degrees F (49 degrees C) so that enzyme destruction is minimized.

Domestic lager malt may be kilned-off at 130 to 180 degrees F (55 to 82 degrees C), while British pale-ale malt is dried to 2 to 3 percent moisture content and kilned, usually at 200 to 220 degrees F (94 to 105 degrees C). Temperatures for Czechoslovakian and Bohemian malts are raised very slowly from 120 to 153 degrees F (49 to 67 degrees C) to completely dry the malt before it is roasted at 178 degrees F (81 degrees C). Dortmund is roasted at 195 to 205 degrees F (90 to 95 degrees C). Enzymatic malts are slowly germinated at cooler than usual temperatures for six-row, high-nitrogen malts. They are slowly dried to 6 to 8 percent moisture content and cured at below 145 degrees F (63 degrees C). Vienna malt is dried to near 5 percent moisture content before kilning for about an hour at 210 to 230 degrees F (99 to 110 degrees C), while Munich malts are brought up to 210 to 220 degrees F (99 to 105 degrees C) for light, and up to 244 degrees F (118 degrees C) for darker Munich (dunkles).

Vienna and Munich malts give richer, maltier flavor and slightly fuller color to beer. Melanoids developed during kilning, especially those that are amino-acid derived, give these malts their characteristic flavor. Melanoids act as antioxidants (reductones), improving a beer's storage stability. Historically, Vienna and Munich malts were kilned from well-modified malt to ensure good color and flavor development. In modern practice they are likely to be kilned from overmodified barley so that they will be less problematic in an infusion mash. Just as often, however, these malts are made from inferior or high-protein barley, because maltsters expect them to be used only in small (5 to 15 percent) portions of the malt bill. Where they will compose a larger percentage of the grist, the brewer needs to review typical analyses provided by the maltsters and choose high-quality malt suited to the mash program being employed.

Amber malt is made from very well modified grain (slightly overmodified by British standards; similar to mild ale malt) that is dried to 2 to 3 percent moisture content and heated from 122 degrees F (50 degrees C) to 340 degrees F (171 degrees C) over the span of one hour. Some maltsters use lower temperatures, in the range of 280 to 300 degrees F (138 to 149 degrees C), for a longer time.

"Aromatic" and biscuit malts are very similar but employ different kiln temperatures; 240 degrees F (115 degrees C) for a longer time for aromatic, and 430 to 460 degrees F (221 to 238 degrees C) for biscuit. Amber, aromatic, and biscuit malts give intensifying degrees of a coppery color, dry, "biscuity" flavors, and toasty aromatics to beer.

Brown malt is dried before kilning at up to 355 degrees F (180 degrees C) for twenty minutes. It gives a deeper color and a more bitter/burnt flavor to beer.

Amber and brown malts contribute considerable fermentable extract to a brew, but the darker-roasted and crystal/caramel malts contribute very little. Caramel and crystal malts give a red to red-brown color to beer. They also increase the sweetness, fullness, foam retention and storage stability of beers; pound for pound, the fully crystallized versions impart these characteristics more than the caramel ones do.

Crystal and caramel (caramalt, carastan) malts are similar products, but they should not be considered interchangeable. Caramel malts have a higher moisture content, are not completely saccharified, and are not kilned to the point that the endosperm is entirely vitrified/glassy. Both are commonly kilned in drums. Both are surface dried at temperatures rising to 150 degrees F (65 degrees C) over an hour's time, during which period a significant amount of proteolysis occurs. "Caramel" versions of CaraPils (CaramelPils, CaraPilsen) malt are generally raised to 212 degrees F (100 degrees C) within five to ten minutes, then held there for thirty to forty-five minutes without ventilation to "caramelize" the endosperm. After kilning, the temperature is reduced to 175 degrees F (80 degrees C) to cure for forty-five minutes; "crystal" versions of the malt are completely saccharified during kilning. They both increase the sweetness, fullness, foam retention, and storage stability of beers without appreciably increasing the color.

Other caramel malts are treated similarly but are colored at higher kiln temperatures — 240 to 275 degrees F (116 to 135 degrees C). Caramel malts as 5 to 15 percent of the grain bill give a caramel, often raisinlike flavor and "chewy" character to beers. As caramel malt color increases, bitterness and roastiness increase accordingly.

Caramel malts were traditionally used by continental lager brewers, whereas crystal malts were favored by British ale brewers. The distinctive, complex flavors of caramel malts have their place in brewing, but unfortunately, modern maltsters are eschewing the production of crisper-flavored crystal malts in favor of the easier-to-process caramel malts. In fact, most modern maltings no longer make a distinction between caramel and crystal malts.

True crystal malts are completely saccharified in a moisture-saturated environment at 158 degrees F (70 degrees C) for 1 1/2 to 2 hours. This stewing of the malt liquefies and completely saccharifies it before it is brought up to kilning-off temperatures. Crystal malts are drum kilned at 250 to 275 degrees F (120 to 135 degrees C) for 1 1/2 to 2 hours, depending on the color desired. They give flavors that are crisper and cleaner than caramel malts; the lighter-colored crystal malts especially give less bitterness and pungency than caramel malts.

Undermodified ("lager") malts are used to produce chocolate and black malts. They are generally dried to 5 percent moisture content, loaded in the kiln at 158 degrees F (70 degrees C), and roasted for up to two hours, to 420 degrees F (215 degrees C) for chocolate malt and to 435 to 480 degrees F (224 to 249 degrees C) for black malt, before being quenched by spraying water over the roasted grain.

When using specialty malts, the brewer needs to adjust the amounts lot to lot to keep beer color consistent. Moreover, a chocolate malt, for instance, at 350 °Lovibond, gives vastly different character to a beer than does a "chocolate" malt at 600 °Lovibond. At 2 to 5 percent of the grist bill, roasted malts richen color and contribute a burnt or nutty flavor to beer. They are used at 10 to 15 percent of the grist bill for porters and stouts.

Malts that are kilned over open hardwood (beech wood, fruit woods) or peat fires have special "smoked" flavors (from phenols released from the wood), which are characteristic of certain beers. These malts may be sold as mild, medium, or heavily smoked as measured by the phenol content. For peat malts, lightly peated malt gives 3 to 6 ppm phenols, moderately peated 7 to 11 ppm, and heavily peated 12 to 15 ppm.

In kilning, the maximum temperature is usually held only until the grains are evenly roasted; then the malt is cooled to below 100 degrees F (38 degrees C) and cleaned to remove rootlets and debris. Rootlets are easily screened from the dried grain, but care must be taken that the malt is not injured and the husk not broken during cleaning.

Weight loss during malting and kilning should be roughly 7 to 15 percent. Losses are more extreme where the rootlet growth is excessive or the malt has been caramelized during kilning.

Before being mashed, the malt must be binned for twenty to thirty days in a cool, dry place to mellow it and improve wort clarity.

CHAPTER **9**

Crushing the Malt

Barley malt should be milled so that the husk is not shredded; ideally it should be split along its length. In this manner, the contents of the crushed kernel is released, and the maximum surface area of starch grits is exposed to enzyme activity without tearing the hulls. Only reasonably intact husks will form a suitably porous filter bed in the lauter-tun. Shredded hulls also contribute to a rough, harsh palate in the finished beer.

The best grist is obtained from six-roll malt mills, which crush the malt by running it between three successive pairs of rolls ten to twelve inches in diameter, each pair being set closer together and turning faster than the previous pair. Screens are placed between each set of rolls to allow the fine grits to fall through, so they are not pulverized into flour by further crushing. More than 75 percent of the malt may be reduced to grits in this manner — the remaining part being hulls and flour. More than 10

Mills

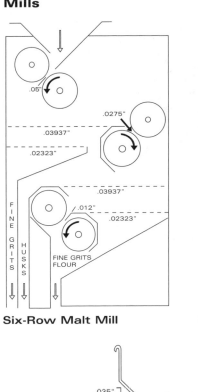

Six-Row Malt Mill

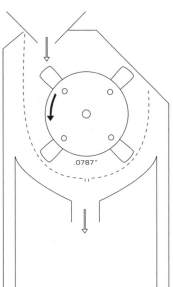

Hammer Mill

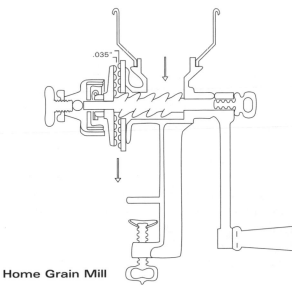

Home Grain Mill

Crushed Malt

Well-Crushed

Poorly-Crushed

percent flour is undesirable because it balls or cakes readily. Balled flour is inaccessible to enzymes and results in unconverted starch, some of which washes into the wort during sparging, causing an irreversible haze in the beer.

Milling equipment other than a six-roll mill is employed, but none yields as good a grind. Only mills equipped with blades that cut the grain are entirely unsuitable, however. Hammer mills and the more commonplace grain mills that employ radially grooved, opposing-face grinding wheels are used, although they tend either to grind grain too finely and shred the husks, or to leave large chunks of the kernel intact.

Coarsely ground malt also does not yield the extract that it should. Heavy, gummy, insufficiently modified starch particles interfere with mash filtering. The hard ends of poorly malted grain are particularly subject to being left uncrushed. In general, it is better to crush the malt too finely (at the risk of a set mash), taking extra care doughing-in, and sparge very slowly than not to mill it finely enough. Only well-modified malts give up their extract when very coarsely ground; poorly modified malts especially require adequate milling. If the iodine test after a sufficient mash saccharification rest shows significant blue-black starch particles and grain ends (not husk fragments, which always deeply discolor iodine), and the spent malt gives any sweet taste, then crushing was probably insufficient.

Milling for lauter-tun brewing should yield predominantly fine grits.

Table 13

Lauter-Tun Grist Profile			
U.S. Standard Mesh	Mesh Width	Characteristics	Lauter-Tun Grist Composition
10	.0787 inches	husks held	
14	.05512	husks held	15%
18	.03937	husks held	
30	.02323	coarse grits held	25%
60	.00984	fine grits held	30%
100	.00587	flour held	20%
100	.00587	fine flour falls through	10%

CHAPTER 10

Mashing

During mashing, the reduction of complex sugars and of insoluble proteins to simpler amino acid chains is entirely an enzymatic process. Before mashing, the malt is only 15 to 25 percent soluble (CWE). Mashing should yield an extract equal to 65 to 80 percent of the weight of the dry malt. Not all of this extract is fermentable; in fact, the varying percentages of unfermented "rest extract," i.e., dextrins, proteins, and peptides, give each beer its malt character. The part of any extract that is unfermentable dextrins (sweetness and flavor) and proteins and peptides (body) is controlled by manipulation of the times and temperatures of the mash.

Doughing-In

Enzymes act on the malt only in an aqueous solution; water induces the enzymes, encased in the aleurone layer of the malt kernel, to go into extracellular solution with soluble starch and hemicellulose. Because crushed malt, and especially floury malt, tends to "ball" into a dry

Time/Temperature Graph

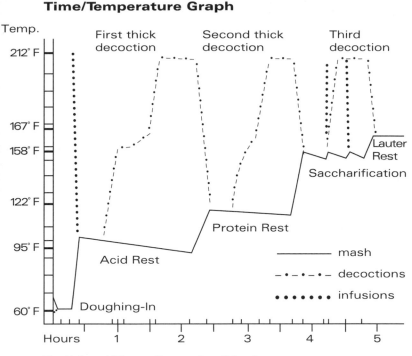

Traditional Three-Decoction Mash

mass that isolates it from enzyme activity, it is essential to mix the grains with liquor in a way that does not saturate any part of the mash while another part is still dry. The intention is to create conditions conducive to dissolving all of the endosperm, including the enzyme-rich particles of the aleurone layer, and not to induce enzymatic activity just yet. Even moistening prevents the starch from balling and entirely solubilizes the enzymes.

A successful mixture is most readily accomplished by the gradual addition of liquid to the grain. Small amounts of liquor are sprinkled onto and then kneaded into the whole of the grain mass until the crushed malt can absorb no more. When a mash is doughed-in cold,

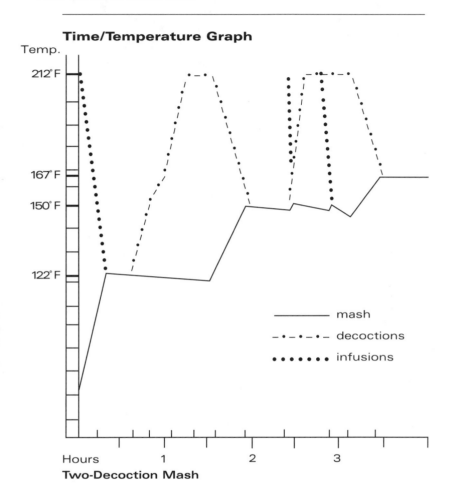

Time/Temperature Graph

Temp.

212° F

167° F

150° F

122° F

——— mash

– · – · – · – decoctions

•••••• infusions

Hours   1   2   3

Two-Decoction Mash

only a small amount of liquor should be standing free at the bottom of the well-kneaded mash.

Using the least possible amount of liquor to form a very thick mash improves enzyme effectiveness early in the mash and simplifies rest-temperature maintenance later on. Liberal infusions of boiling-hot liquor may then be made to hold the saccharification temperature without overly thinning the mash. In decoction mashing, this is best accomplished by doughing-in the malt with twenty-four to forty fluid ounces of cold liquor at a deep-well water temperature of about 58 degrees F (14 degrees C) per pound of crushed grain, the higher end of the range being for larger brew lengths and mechanized systems.

The doughed-in mash is allowed to stand for fifteen to thirty minutes, the longer time being for malts that are dark, weakly enzymatic, hard tipped, or poorly malted. At the same time, roughly half the volume of liquor used to dough-in the malt is brought to boiling. It is infused into the mash to raise the temperature of the whole from 60 degrees F (16 degrees C) or so up to 95 to 105 degrees F (35 to 41 degrees C).

Where the grist is not doughed-in cold, even more attention needs to be paid to evenly hydrating it. Even with well-modified British malts, balling is a problem as the temperature at doughing-in increases.

Mash pH

The correct initial pH of any mash depends on the type and color of the malts employed and the planned mashing technique. It must never be begun at above pH 6.2, or below 4.7. When the mash is from enzyme-poor malt that will be fully decoction mashed, the mash cycle may begin at a pH as high as 5.5 to 5.8 (as measured at the reference temperature, usually 68 degrees F (20 degrees C).

"Acid" sourmalt is used to lower the alkalinity of the mash. Sourmalt has been treated with lactic acid or lactic-acid bacteria to a percentage-lactic-acid of 3.5 to 4.0 percent, giving a wort pH of 4.0 to 5.0. It is employed as 5 to 10 percent of the grist to give an initial mash pH of 5.2 to 5.8. Colored malts also have a significant effect on wort pH; the darker-roasted the malt, the greater its effect on wort acidity. While lager malts generally give a wort pH of 5.7 to 6.0 in a laboratory mash from distilled water, more highly kilned Vienna and Munich give pH 5.5 to 5.7, better-modified pale pH 5.3 to 5.7, the darker brown and caramel/crystal-50 pH 4.5 to 4.8, chocolate 4.3 to 4.5, and black malt 4.0 to 4.2.

Depending on their proportion in the grist and the alkalinity of the liquor, colored malts may be enough to give proper mash acidity. Until the proper initial mash acidity is approximated (within pH 0.2), however, the mash cycle should not be begun.

Acid Rest

The pH of calcium-bearing liquor always drops as it is mashed with malt because phosphates in the malt react with calcium and carbonate, precipitating alkaline calcium phosphate and lowering the mash pH. Where malt color and calcium content of the liquor are low, however, this reaction is insufficient to give an acceptable mash acidity.

The *acid rest* is made solely to correct the initial mash pH. Significant phytase activity in conjunction with very limited bacterial fermentation of glucose to lactic acid acidifies the mash without imparting a harsh flavor to its extract. The rest is most successfully employed when mashing with reasonably soft or sulfate water; it cannot overcome the alkalinity of strongly carbonate waters. Excessive carbonate salts present in the brewing water must first be precipitated by boiling or adding slaked lime, or overcome by the inherent acidity of dark-roasted malt, or by adding lactic, phosphoric, sulfuric, or citric acid to the brewing liquor or sourmalt or lactic-acid mash to the mash itself.

Acidulation of the mash is primarily by the enzyme phytase, active at 86 to 128 degrees F (30 to 53 degrees C), which dismantles insoluble *phytin,* a salt in which most of the malt phosphate is bound up, to significantly acidic phytic acid. Generally referred to as an enzyme of malting, reactivation of phytase by the acidic hydrolysis at 95 degrees F (35 degrees C) accounts for a twofold or three-fold increase in the phytic acid in a decoction mash from lager malt. It benefits the mash not only by lowering its pH but by increasing the mineral content of its liquid extract and producing a rich and accessible source of yeast nutrients, especially myoinositol, a B-vitamin necessary for yeast growth.

$$Ca_5Mg(C_6H_{12}O_{24}P_6 \bullet 3H_2O)_2$$
Phytin

$$+$$

$$7H_2O$$

Phytase

releases into solution:
$$C_6H_6 \, [OPO \, (OH)_2]_6$$
Phytic Acid

$$C_6H_{12}O_6$$
Myoinositol

and precipitates:
$$5CaHPO_4 \bullet 2H_2O$$
Calcium Phosphate (Secondary)

$$MgHPO_4 \bullet 3H_2O$$
Magnesium Phosphate (Secondary)

Phytase activity is most dramatic when mashing undermodified malt, since less of the malt phosphate has been inverted during malting. Mashes made from highly kilned malts show little pH reduction during an acid rest because phytase is destroyed by the high kiln temperatures. The natural acidity of these malts, however, can be sufficient for establishing a proper mash pH.

During the rest, the pH of a mash from low-modified lager malt generally drops from 5.5 to 5.8 to pH 5.2 to 5.3. A mash sequence employing an acid rest thus needs to rely less on the brewing water being naturally acidic or calcium rich, or on using colored malts, or acid malt, mash, or treatment, and begins at a higher pH than an infusion mash.

The rest is not usually held for longer than it takes to boil the first decoction. When the acidulation occurring within this period is inadequate, some manner of acidifying treatment must be made.

Traditionally, where at mashing-in the pH would be above 5.8, a separate "lactic-acid mash" is made prior to the main mashing. A 5 to 15 percent fraction of the mash volume is doughed-in and saccharified, cooled to below 130 degrees F (55 degrees C), inoculated with crushed malt, and then rested, closely covered, at 95 to 122 degrees F (35 to 50 degrees C) for up to several days. The saccharified mash at 95 to 122 degrees F (35 to 50 degrees C) creates an ideal environment for the fermentation of glucose to lactic acid by *Lactobacillus delbruckii* (temperature range 86 to 131 degrees F [30 to 55 degrees C], most active at 107 to 111 degrees F [41 to 44 degrees C]; pH optimum 5.6 to 5.8). The closely covered lactic acid mash is held until its pH drops below 4.0. It is then intermixed into the main mash to correct its pH.

If the lactic-acid mash begins to smell the least bit solventy or rancid, if turbulence or ropiness develops on its surface, or if it is "off" in any way, it should be skimmed and its temperature raised to above 122 degrees F (50 degrees C) to destroy the spoiling mold, aerobic butyric or acetic-acid bacteria. Where thermophilic anaerobes (*L. bulgaris, L. brevis,* or any of the thermophilic strains of *Bacillus)* are the source of the spoilage, temperatures may have to go above 140 degrees F (60 degrees C) to terminate the activity. The most common contaminant is the putrefying

Clostridium butyricum, which turns the mash rancid and renders it unusable. Anaerobic conditions prevent the growth of most organisms that might otherwise spoil a lactic-acid mash, so elimination of air space between the mash and its cover is of primary importance.

Why Decoction Mash?

Although decoction mashing serves to raise the temperature of the mash to the protein, saccharification, and lauter-rest temperatures, its more important function is to cause several significant changes in the boiled portions.

Not even the most thorough infusion mash can eke out the quantity or quality of extract that is obtained by decoction mashing. There are several reasons for this. During decoction mashing, the thick part of the mash passes through the diastatic-enzyme temperature range two to three times. Boiling also reduces the size and complexity of malt starch and protein — a process that is absolutely essential when mashing-in difficult malts. Malts such as dark Munich, having only one third the enzyme strength of pale malt, cannot otherwise be satisfactorily mashed.

Since boiling destroys enzymes, the enzymes in the unboiled mash portion must be preserved. In a mash that is satisfactorily solubilized during doughing-in, the enzymes are washed into the free liquid when the mash is flooded to raise its temperature to 95 degrees F (35 degrees C). The thickest part of the mash — containing the heaviest and least accessible concentration of native starch and protein — can then be boiled without decimating the enzyme population.

The heavy decoction is quickly heated to 150 to 158 degrees F (65 to 70 degrees C), without resting at 122 degrees F (50 degrees C), so that no further enzymatic acidulation of the mash occurs.

There are two good reasons for passing by this rest, and both are based on the pH sensitivity of the diastatic enzymes. First, the dextrinization of native starch by alpha-amylase (pH optimum 5.7) is far more effective at the higher pH of this first decoction than later when the whole mash comes into the saccharification/dextrinization range at a far lower pH. Second, the same high pH that stimulates alpha-amylase activity retards beta-amylase activity (pH optimum 4.7). Because native starch is far too complex to be successfully reduced by beta-amylase until alpha-amylase has reduced it to shorter amylose chains and smaller amylopectin fragments, resting the decoction at saccharifying temperatures is not productive. It is quite enough that the manageable small dextrins replace the native starch, even when mashing for a high-maltose extract.

Regardless of the diastatic power of the malt, unconverted starch is invariably entrapped within poorly solubilized malt particles. As the decoction is heated above 167 degrees F (75 degrees C), the particles burst, and their contents are absorbed into the liquid extract. This makes them accessible to alpha-amylase activity during the diastatic-enzyme rest of the main mash. This otherwise lost extract increases both the quality and the quantity of the extract yield.

The acidity of worts generally decrease after mashing, as they are heated to boiling (the more so with rising liquor alkalinity), because heat disassociates carbonic acid in solution to H_2O and CO_2, causing the pH to rise. This phenomenon is of less concern to the decoction-mash brewer because the mash is stirred and portions of the mash are boiled, both of which actions decompose HCO_3, and because the acid and protein rests lower the mash acidity. Boiling the decotions also precipitates more inorganic calcium phosphate than is otherwise achieved.

Boiling also dissolves protein gum. At lower temperatures, protein gum is unaffected by enzyme activity and passes through mashing largely unconverted. Only when thick mash is boiled can the proteolytic enzymes successfully degrade dissolved gum to albuminous fractions; instead of clouding the beer, the smaller proteins enhance its body and head. Protein trub precipitated during wort cooling is also dramatically decreased.

Boiling also deoxygenates the mash, reducing hot-side aeration and allowing it to settle in well-defined layers in the lauter-tun. Only the absence of residual protein gum makes this effective filter bed possible; when an infusion mash is employed, such a dense filter bed likely results in a set mash.

In mashing techniques that do not use a decoction sequence, the proteolytic and diastatic enzymes are destroyed before the mash achieves optimum temperatures for the dissolution of starch particles and protein gum. The extract content, clarity, character, fullness, maltiness, and body of the finished beer are negatively affected. Where the malt is reasonably well modified and evenly crushed, however, the traditional three decoctions may not be necessary; even a single-decoction (or step) mash is never advisable with British ale or brewers' malts that have been thoroughly modified during malting and would be "overmodified" by exposure to low temperature rests.

Doughing-in with boiling water to 95 degrees F (35 degrees C), followed by a second infusion to 122 or 131 degrees F (50 or 55 degrees C), only a limited protein rest, and a single, thick decoction before saccharification is sufficient for all but the most undermodified malts, and doughing-in at 122 or 131 degrees F (50 or 55 degrees C) is sufficient for most modern lager malts.

During decoction mashing, the brewer is at his busiest, because two mashes must be handled at the same time, with great care. The brewer must be thoroughly organized before plunging into the sometimes hectic decoction mash cycle.

Decoction mashing is often met with open skepticism by brewers who have no experience with it. The fact remains that the beguiling maltiness of European lagers is only achieved by boiling undermodified malt. Extract yield is increased. Moreover, hot-side aeration is reduced, because the boiling and mixing of the mash deaerates it. Boiling of the mash does not lead to astringent harshness in the brew, probably because the density and pH of the decoction prevents phenols from being leached out of the husks.

There are two widely accepted programs for decoction mashing. The first, described here, employs a protein rest at 122 degrees F (50 degrees C) and saccharification/dextrinizing at 149 to 158 degrees F (65 to 70 degrees C). It is best suited to malts of below 37 percent soluble nitrogen.

The second program is better suited to higher-protein modern malts with a soluble nitrogen ratio of 37 to 40 percent. A combined proteolysis/saccharification rest is made at 131 degrees F (55 degrees C), allowing proteases to reduce large proteins to body- and head-building polypeptides and beta-amylase (temperature optimum 126 to 149 degrees F [52 to 65 degrees C], pH 5.4) to reduce amylose to maltose and glucose, and amylopectin to ß-limit dextrins. Dextrinization is then accomplished separately, usually at 158 to 162 degrees F (70 to 72 degrees C).

Three-Decoction Mash

First Decoction

The volume of thick mash to be boiled, relative to the volume of the whole mash, is dependent upon mash thickness. A very thick mash requires that only its heaviest one-third part (mostly grain mass, with only enough liquid to fill the spaces between the grain particles) be boiled, along with very little of the mash liquid. Thinner mashes require that proportionally more of the mash be boiled, along with more liquid, because even if most of the malt is removed and boiled, in a thin mash it would not contribute enough heat to the resting mash to sufficiently raise its temperature to the next rest. One pound of crushed malt contributes about the same amount of heat to the mash as does one pint of water, yet displaces only as much volume as six fluid ounces of water. In a thick mash, the favorable heat-to-volume ratio of the malt is such that the heaviest one-third part can raise the temperature of the whole mash to the next rest. In a thin mash, however, the heat value of the malt is not enough to overcome the far greater amount of water. A greater percentage of the mash must therefore be boiled — but usually not more than 40 percent.

After the decoction has been pulled, the rest mash (cold settlement) is closely covered and held undisturbed, except for occasional mixing to disperse temperature and enzyme activity. At the end of each decoction cycle, the mashes are remixed to raise the temperature of the whole to the next rest.

Protein Rest (First Thick Mash)

With traditional lager malts, the character of the finished beer — its body, clarity, lack of chill haze, stability, and resistance to spoilage — is largely established during the protein or "albumin" rest. This "softens" poorly modified malt and improves mash runoff by decomposing heavy, gummy, insufficiently modified malt particles. During the rest, complex protein globules are decomposed by proteolytic enzymes to less troublesome fractions. With relatively unmodified lager malts, proteases, peptases, and proteinases progressively dissolve the peptide links within the protein coils to liberate coagulable albuminous fractions, peptides, and amino acids. It is albumin (proteoses, peptones, and polypeptides), not protein, that gives beer its body and enables it to raise and support a frothy foam head.

The protein-rest temperature should be 122 to 131 degrees F (50 to 55 degrees C), although temperatures from 113 to 140 degrees F (45 to 60 degrees C) support proteolytic enzyme activity. It should be kept in mind, however, that at the lower end of the temperature range, head-and-body polypeptides may be denatured to peptides and amino acids, reducing the body of the beer. Proteinase (temperature range 104 to 140 degrees F (40 to 60 degrees C), optimum 122 to 140 degrees F (50 to 60 degrees C), pH 4.6 to 5.0, solubilizes and breaks down simple proteins to peptones, polypeptides, and peptides. Peptidase (optimum range 113 to 122 degrees F [45 to 50 degrees C] pH below 5.3) dissolves polypeptides and peptides to individual amino acids, which fuel yeast growth in the early stages of fermentation. In any all-malt beer, however, there are generally sufficient amino acids to support fermentation.

Extract efficiency is also enhanced by the protein rest. Extract is exposed by the dissolution of membranous proteins, and complex amylopectin may to some extent be dismantled by debranching enzymes (maltase, dextrinase).

Phytase continues its activity during the rest, reducing phytin from the aleurone layer and embryo of the malt to phytic acid. Other acids also rapidly form during the rest, further lowering the pH toward the optimum values for saccharification, the clarification of the wort during boiling, and subsequent yeast fermentation. During this rest, the pH should drop again to below 5.4.

Other nonproteolytic enzymes (most notably cytase, temperature range 113 to 131 degrees F [45 to 55 degrees C], pH 5.0, and beta-glucanase, range 95 to 131 degrees F [35 to 55 degrees C]) actively dissolve pectins and other constituents of the malt hemicellulose during the protein rest.

A thick mash improves enzyme performance. In a thin mash, proteolytic and other heat-labile enzymes are destroyed in the course of the rest; in a thick mash, they may survive into the saccharification range.

The protein digestion can be overdone, however. Devoid of proteoses and peptides, the beer would lack body and a froth head. It would be very stable, but very empty-tasting. Without any coagulable proteins to adhere to, hop tannin would not precipitate from the boil, and the beer would taste "rough." Reducing nitrogen complexes too far would result in the presence of an excessive amount of simple nutrients in early fermentation, which would encourage bacterial contamination.

The degree of protein degradation achieved during this rest may be fairly judged later on by the thickness and slickness of the protein sludge covering the settled grist in the lauter-tun. It should be moderately thick and powdery rather than gummy.

The rest temperature must be reached by effective mixing, accomplished by lifting the mash from the bottom of the tun. It is essential that the return of the decoction be competently handled so that temperature dispersal is absolutely even. Attempting to correct wide temperature fluctuations within the remixed mash is never easy.

In the event that the strike temperature is reached before all the decoction has been returned, the remainder of the boiled mash is force-cooled to 122 degrees F (50 degrees C) before it is returned to the main mash.

The objectives of the albumin rest should be accomplished in less than two hours, or the malt is entirely unsuitable for use in brewing. Usually after five to twenty minutes at 122 to 131 degrees F (50 to 55 degrees C), the heaviest part of the mash is again drawn off, to begin the second decoction. Up to 30 percent of the malt nitrogen can be expected to have gone into solution at its conclusion.

Saccharification Rest

Malt starch occurs as long straight or complex-branched chains of linked glucose, $C_6H_{10}O_5$. During the saccharification rest, alpha- and beta-amylase reduce that starch to simpler fractions. This yields flavorful dextrins and fermentable sugars.

Alpha-amylase very rapidly reduces insoluble native starch to smaller polysaccharide fractions (a mix of some glucose, maltose, maltotriose, and straight-chain dextrins with a predominance of branched "a-limit" dextrins). Given long enough, the alpha-amylase continues to sever 1-4 glucose links, producing more glucose, maltose, and maltotriose, but starch-chain fragments are more effectively saccharified to fermentable sugars by the faster-acting beta-amylase. Beta-amylase has no effect on native starch, but in hydrolytic solution, it reduces soluble starch by cleaving glucose molecules from one end of starch chain fragments and rejoining them in pairs with a water molecule to create maltose, $C_{12}H_{22}O_{11}$.

It is inadvisable to reduce all starch to fully fermentable maltose. Significant quantities of more complex polysaccharides must be carried over into the ferment for the beer to have a sweet flavor and sense of fullness. Partially fermentable dextrins, oligosaccharides, and especially maltotriose support the yeast during the long, cold aging period.

The temperature of the rest may be from 149 to 160 degrees F (65 to 71 degrees C), depending on the nature of the beer being brewed. Precisely hitting the appropriate rest temperature is essential, as a variation of two or three degrees for even five minutes will dramatically alter the maltose/dextrin ratio of the extract.

Mash thickness also affects the fermentability of the wort. A thick mash (less than three-tenths of a gallon of water per pound of malt) induces the greatest overall extraction. A much thinner mash increases the proportion of maltose, and thus wort attenuation.

The reduction of the large starch chains in a thick mash at 155 to 158 degrees F (68 to 70 degrees C), almost excludes any maltose formation whatsoever. The richly dextrinous wort produces a fullness and sweetness complementary to Munich-style lagers and darker beer with a contrasting burnt-malt bitterness. It is seldom suitable for light-colored beers.

Above 160 degrees F (71 degrees C), strong enzyme action ceases; temperatures below 149 degrees F (65 degrees C), on the other hand, seriously limit dextrin formation (by alpha-amylase, temperature optimum 149 to 158 degrees F [65 to 70 degrees C], pH 5.1 to 5.9) while favoring the formation of maltose by beta-amylase. Because starch granules are not gelatinized or dispersed below 149 degrees F (65 degrees C), beta-amylase activity at lower temperatures serves only to eliminate the straight-chain dextrins formed in the decoction, without further significant starch reduction.

For very light beers, the release of ungelatinized starch into solution at 149 degrees F (65 degrees C) is capitalized upon by raising the temperature of the mash from 131 to 149 degrees F (55 to 65 degrees C) over fifteen to thirty minutes; this largely eliminates the amylose liberated during the decoction. The mash is brought to rest at 149 to 151 degrees F (65 to 66 degrees C) to gelatinize and further dextrinize the starch, and to produce a maltose/dextrin ratio that favors lightness on the palate and rapid maturation.

For rather more usual palate fullness and fermentability, the recombination of the mashes requires even more careful handling. The decoction must be returned to the rest mash as quickly as possible, but without creating wide temperature variations within it.

The rest temperature should be evenly attained within less than ten minutes.

Most of the amber and gold lagers, and even the pale Pilsener/Dortmunder types, rely on the heavier, richer dextrin complement formed at 152 to 155 degrees F (67 to 68 degrees C). This is the strike temperature of most "character" beers brewed with undermodified malts and a protein rest at 122 degrees F (50 degrees C). Saccharification in this temperature range encourages an alpha-/beta-amylase activity ratio greater than five to one; as a result, the dextrin content of the wort is 25 percent or greater, and the alcohol content by weight of the finished beer is roughly one-third the value of the wort density (°Plato). Where a combined protein/saccharification rest at 131 degrees F (55 degrees C) has been made, similar results are acheived by a dextrinizing rest at 158 to 160 degrees F (70 to 71 degrees C).

As the mash saccharifies, it becomes thicker, brighter, and browner. The brewer may decide to add brewing liquor to thin an overly thick mash and to speed up saccharification (beta-amylase is more effective in the looser mash). Caution must be used, however; as mash temperatures rise above 149 degrees F (65 degrees C), enzymes are rapidly destroyed in a thin mash. Even in a thick mash, beta-amylase is destroyed in less than an hour at above 149 degrees F (65 degrees C), and alpha-amylase is destroyed within two hours at above 154 degrees F (68 degrees C) in a mash below pH 5.5. This fact must be remembered when mashing to yield a dextrinous wort; a satisfactory dextrinous wort cannot be formed at below 153 degrees F (67 degrees C).

As opposed to British infusion mashes, which are entrained with air and "float," a decoction mash is stirred regularly, in a nonaerating fashion, to break up any pockets of unmodified starch and ensure uniform conversion. After fifteen minutes at the rest temperature, testing for saccharification with iodine should begin.

Iodine Starch-Conversion Test

Place a small sample of the extract in a porcelain dish. Float common iodine (.02N solution; 1.27 grams iodine and 2.5 grams potassium iodide in 500 milliliters water) onto the extract, drop by drop, until a distinct layer of iodine is formed. Note any color change in the iodine at its interface with the mash liquid. Also observe the intensity of the color: is it trace, faint, or strong? Blue-black indicates the presence of native starch (amylose); deep mahogany/red-brown evidences gelatinized starch (amylose fragments and large a-limit dextrins), faint red simple a-limit dextrins. A faint mahogany to violet-reddish reaction denotes a mix of small dextrins. Total mash saccharification (a solution of some small a-limit dextrins with maltotriose, maltose, and simple sugars) causes no change in the yellow color of iodine.

Iodine is a poison. DISCARD ALL TESTS. Ensure that there is no iodine contamination by washing any article that comes into contact with it. Conduct iodine tests some distance from the mash so that no iodine will inadvertently contaminate the mash.

Most of the starch should be reduced to at least small a-limit dextrins by alpha-amylase. Even for sweet, less-fermented beers, the reaction with iodine should be no more than faintly mahogany-to-red. There should never be a strong color reaction with the iodine; neither, however, should rich beers be saccharified to the point that a negative iodine reaction occurs. A faint mahogany-to-reddish reaction indicates an acceptable extract composition for these beers.

The mash should be held at the strike temperature until saccharification is complete. Infusions of boiling water may be made with less regard to enzyme viability as conversion nears completion. The looser mash improves filter bed formation.

(Note: Koji or other diastatic enzyme preparations should not be used to increase enzyme activity. Although they convert hundreds of times their weight in soluble starch to simple sugar, they do not form dextrins.)

If the mash does not saccharify within one hour, it should be stirred, restored to temperature, verified for proper pH (5.2 to 5.5), and held for thirty minutes more. If the iodine color is not further reduced, addition of diastatic malt or extract may be required.

The efficiency of the malt crushing can be gauged by pressing a sample of the goods until all of the kernel ends and malt particles have been crushed, then separating the liquid from the particulate matter. Repeat the iodine test on the liquid, as above. If the color at the iodine-mash interface is intensely black or blue, then crushing was insufficient or the malt was poorly doughed-in. (Some isolated color from insignificant amounts of exposed starch is to be expected; husk particles themselves will always turn intensely black). Suspicions regarding the efficiency of milling may be verified either by a wort density that is less than predicted or by tasting the dried spent mash. If extract efficiency is below 65 percent or the spent grains taste sweet, the malt has probably been insufficiently crushed.

Final Decoction

When the starch end point has been verified, the very thinnest part of the mash is removed to be boiled. The decoction is usually 40 percent of the volume, although a very thin mash may require boiling half of the mash. Because there are fewer starch and albuminous particles in the thinner portion, there is less risk of these being decomposed during the boiling of the runoff. These remain with the rest mash. On the other hand, enzymatic reduction of the dextrins in the thin part of the mash is more quickly terminated, preventing oversimplification of the extract.

The lauter decoction is brought to boiling, while being stirred, in ten to fifteen minutes and may be held at a strong boil for a further fifteen to forty-five minutes, although in modern practice it is uncommon to boil the mash for more than five or ten minutes. The temperature of the rest mash is held at or slightly above the strike temperature during boiler-mash processing.

The boiled extract must be well mixed with the rest mash. Care should be taken that the strike temperature of the final rest, 167 to 170 degrees F (75 to 77 degrees C), is not exceeded. Temperature adjustments may be made by the infusion of either cold or boiling brewing liquor, as required.

Exact temperature maintenance is, as before, critically important. Lower temperatures do not terminate enzyme activity or expand particles of intermediate starch degradation enough to keep them in temporary suspension, up and away from the bottom of the mash filter bed. At higher temperatures, the starch granules burst, and insufficiently modified carbohydrate and albuminous matter becomes dissolved and unfilterable. Because the diastatic and proteolytic enzymes have been destroyed by the high temperatures, the starch and protein gum have no opportunity to be reduced to manageable fractions. High temperatures also induce the extraction of tannins from the husk.

The mash-out temperature may be maintained for up to one-half hour while the mash is roused up. Thorough mixing allows the mash to settle very slowly and form a well-delineated filter bed.

The lauter mash should be very thin and thoroughly intermixed to encourage the absorption of the malt extract into solution and to temporarily force small starches and proteins into suspension, allowing the husks to freely settle.

Wort Separation

The purpose of sparging/filtering is to rinse the soluble extract free from the malt husks and to trap insoluble, poorly modified starch, protein, lipids, and silicates within the husks. Without adequate filtering, extract is lost, while the mash runoff is clouded by starch, proteins, tannins, and husk particles. This produces beer likely to be cloudy, astringent, and unstable.

The mash may be transferred to a lauter-tun for filtering. The diameter of the vessel should allow the filter bed to form to a depth of twelve to eighteen inches. A filter bed of six-row barley, however, may need to be only six inches thick; the greater percentage of husks in six-row barley increases its filtering efficiency. The mash filter bed when brewing with infusion-mashed British ale malts is more commonly twenty-four inches deep at the start of the runoff.

The husks accumulate on a false bottom, or filter plate, that fits one-eighth to two inches above the real bottom of the lauter-tun. Slots or perforations in the plate allow the sparge water to slowly and evenly filter through the husks. The lauter-tun itself is equipped with a spigot located below the level of the false bottom to draw the extract-rich sweet wort off from below the grain mass.

Setting the Lauter Bed

The lauter-tun should be filled to one-half inch above the false bottom with water of 175 to 212 degrees F (80 to 100 degrees C). This preheats the lauter-tun and reduces the amount of debris that is otherwise carried into the space below the false bottom. This practice largely eliminates the need for flushing the space prior to filtering and improves the clarity of the runoff. The thin lauter mash is quickly transferred to the tun, given a last thorough stirring, and allowed to settle.

Mash Filter Bed

An infusion mash, on the other hand, is handled gently. Stirring is avoided. An unstirred infusion mash does not settle in as well-defined stratification as does a decoction mash, and tends to "float." The suspended particulate matter somewhat offsets the lack of a clearly defined filter bed, as it entraps less extract. However, it never yields so clear a runoff as does a decoction-mash filter bed. Commercially, false bottoms for infusion mashes generally have larger slots than those used for decoction mashes.

Within ten to twenty minutes, the liquid displaced by the settling mash should show clear and "black" above a nebulous cloud of trub. If it doesn't clear, then filtering efficiency can be expected to be poor. The temperature of the mash is likely to drop during the setting of the filter bed; every effort, however, should be made to limit its heat loss.

In an ideal stirred-mash filter bed, the heavy hulls that settle onto the false bottom are covered by a deeper layer of lighter hull fragments and endosperm particles. Until this porous filter-mass has formed, tiny, gelatinized particles of starch and protein remain suspended in the liquid; after it has formed, they should settle out, creating the pasty "protein-sludge" or upper dough.

If this trub precipitates too early and settles within the hulls in any appreciable quantity, some will wash into the sweet wort runoff. It may also cake within the filter bed and cause a set mash that blocks the flow of liquid down through the filter bed; either a set mash or a runoff that doesn't clear may be due to ineffective crushing and mashing.

Sparge Liquor

A volume of liquor roughly 25 percent greater than the liquor used for mashing-in is heated to 170 to 176 degrees F (77 to 80 degrees C) in preparation for sparging.

The temperature of the sparge liquor is critical because sugars flow more freely in hot solution than in cold. Its temperature must be maintained throughout the sparging to dissolve and rinse free the extract cupped in the hulls or adhered to the malt particles.

Excessive temperatures in the mash itself, however (above 170 degrees F [77 degrees C]), rupture balled native-starch particles and decompose the protein sludge, causing them to be carried away in the runoff. Because only very simple protein and carbohydrate fractions can be managed by culture yeast, none of these more complex fragments should be allowed in the wort. Runoff temperatures above 170 degrees F (77 degrees C) also cause extraction of husk polyphenols and marked astringency in the beer.

If necessary, the salt content or acidity of the sparge liquor should be adjusted, preferably with calcium salts or lactic or phosphoric acid, to limit extraction of harsh-tasting malt fractions and improve clarity. The pH of the runoff should never rise above pH 6; better results are achieved when the runoff pH does not rise above 5.8.

Carbonate waters are not useful for sparging, because they induce haze fractions and silicates into solution and may induce renewed enzyme activity. These waters become even more alkaline upon heating. Carbonate ions must be precipitated or disassociated before the liquor is used for sparging.

Preparing to Sparge

The space below the false bottom can be purged of particulate matter by flushing it with clear, 170 degree F (77 degrees C) liquor, either through an inlet below the false bottom, opposite the spigot, or through a tube thrust down through the mash. The inlet and runoff rates must be carefully matched to avoid disturbing the filter bed above. Flushing can be eliminated if the cloudy runoff is refiltered through the mash until it runs clear (vorlauf vehrfahren), or the runoff is starch free.

The degree of clarity that should be obtained in the runoff is a matter of debate. A lot of draff carried into the kettle is a recipe for astringent beer, but a small amount may improve trub coagulation. The majority of brewers recycle until the runoff is no longer heavily clouded; this is generally accomplished in less than ten minutes. Excessive recycling may lead to greater lipid levels in the wort and ought to be avoided.

To set the filter bed and settle the protein sludge, the lauter-tun spigot is opened once the liquid above the grains clears. The liquid is run off very slowly until it stands one-half to one inch deep above the surface of the mash. This liquid level must be maintained throughout sparging. Draining below the mash surface level causes the mash to settle too tightly and the protein sludge to cake. Extract efficiency is reduced and the potential for developing a set mash increases. Too great a liquid depth, on the other hand, acts as weight on the grains and leads to stuck mashes. The mash surface should be periodically leveled and smoothed to fill in all the depressions and vertical channels.

Sparging

The liquid level above the filter bed is maintained by the introduction of sparge liquor. Sparge liquor should be gently and evenly dispersed over the top of the mash so it will evenly percolate through the mash and diffuse all the extract from it. The sparging rate should be free from surges and matched to the runoff rate so that the liquid level in the lauter-tun is not changed.

The sparging/runoff rate may be gradually increased, but not so much so that turbidity is caused in the runoff. Set mashes also result from too rapid a flow rate.

High-husk, six-row barley may be run off in less than an hour (a six-inch-deep bed may be filtered in as little as one-half hour). Maximum extraction, however, is achieved with a very slow runoff rate, a deeper filter bed, and raking the mash to within six inches of the false bottom. Raking restructures the filter bed, ensuring even percolation of the sparge liquor through the grain and complete extraction of the sugars. A mash that is raked, or that is from finely ground malt, or shows a tendency to set, must be run off slowly. Set mashes that don't respond to being stirred must be cut repeatedly during sparging in order to reopen channels of extract flow.

Within 1 1/2 hours, the greater part of the extract will have been leached from the malt. Although the maximum yield is obtained by restricting the runoff rate so that it takes two to four hours to collect the sweet wort, the small percentage of extract gained is not worth the time and effort.

The temperature within the mash should be carefully maintained during sparging and filtering, although the early runoff will usually be well below 168 degrees F (75 degrees C). In the interest of preventing further enzyme activity, the wort collecting in the copper should be heated to above 170 degrees F (77 degrees C) as it accumulates. Where a large amount of evaporation is required, the sweet wort is brought to boiling and partially hopped as soon as it has covered the bottom of the kettle.

As the color of the runoff pales, its extract content is periodically checked with a hydrometer; when the reading drops to below 3 °Plato (SG 1012, corrected to 68/60 degrees F [20/15.56 degrees C]), the runoff is diverted from the wort kettle.

Below this density, the runoff pH is likely to rise above pH 6, increasing the likelihood that malt tannins, lipids, and silicates will be leached into it. Malt tannins give an astringent taste and are harsher flavored than hop tannins. They are more soluble and are not as readily precipitated in the kettle. Lipids interfere with foam stability, increase ester formation, and are precursors to cardboardy, stale flavors in beer.

CHAPTER 11

Boiling the Wort

Vigorously boiling the mash runoff produces several desirable effects: it destroys mash enzymes, sterilizes the wort, and stabilizes salts in solutions. It extracts hop resins, drives off kettle-harsh hop oils, and coagulates and precipitates unstable protein. Boiling also evaporates excess water, lowers the wort pH, and creates a stable medium for controlled fermentation by the culture yeast. Boiling may begin when enough wort has been collected to cover the bottom of the kettle.

Kettle Hops

Hops should be added to the kettle by being scattered over the surface of violently boiling wort. They may be added all at once, but more commonly they are meted out in portions throughout the boil. The actual sequence is determined by the hop character that is meant to be carried over into the finished beer.

Adding hops early on in the boil ensures greater utilization of bittering principles and a more complete precipitation of proteins, hop tannins, and hop particles. A sixty-to-ninety-minute boil succeeds in isomerizing 25 to 30 percent of the alpha resins and in bonding them to the wort as iso-alpha-acids. With pelletized hops, ruptured and better-exposed lupulin glands give greater utilization, even as high as 35 percent. This is the greatest percentage of hop bittering and preservative principles that is normally ever carried over into the finished beer. On the other hand, the bitterness derived from long boiling is coarser than that from a more moderate period; for this reason, it is usual to add only a fraction of the hops at the start of the boil.

Some of the hop polyphenols are transported into the ferment in combination with simple albumins, forming tiny substances-in-solution known as *colloids*. This colloidal matter is not significantly precipitated and is involved in forming the body and head of the finished beer. Because their surface area is disproportionately greater than their volume, colloids do not readily settle out of solution. Consequently, their contribution to the beer's body is not offset by inherent instability, as is the case with noncolloidal protein.

It is common to add 5 to 15 percent of the hops at or before the onset of boiling to break the surface tension of the wort so that it does not throw up as voluminous a protein head and boil over. When the wort is the product of an infusion mash, it should be boiled vigorously for fifteen to thirty minutes before more of the hops are added to allow the boiling action to decompose and precipitate some of the proteins. If this is not accomplished before the hops are added, then hop polyphenols will combine with the coarse protein flocks and be precipitated out of solution, carrying hop resins with them.

Even an intense initial boil, however, does not eliminate the large proteins as effectively as do the processes of decoction mashing. Although the proteins can be precipitated, they cannot be dissolved into albumin, peptides, and amino acids, because all enzyme activity has been terminated by the boil.

When the wort is the product of a decoction mash, excessive complex proteins aren't usually a problem. The several boilings and rests largely reduce or eliminate them. Decoction-mashed wort can therefore be hopped somewhat more conservatively than infusion-mashed wort, simply because the hops need not overcome a great amount of protein.

All of the aromatic hop character of the beer is lost during a long boil. The hops' volatile essential oils and esters can be preserved by adding hops later in the boil. It is usual, in fact, to add the hops in two, three, or even four portions. Only lightly hopped beers that employ hops for their preservative contribution rather than for their flavor and aroma fully extract the entire quantity of hops during a sixty-minute or longer boil.

Beers that are heavily hopped in the beginning of the boil exhibit a cleaner kraeusen fermentation head and are more stable than beers hopped later, but the hop bitterness will be coarser and less pleasant. It is essential, however, that most of the hops should be vigorously boiled in the uncovered wort for forty-five minutes or more to efficiently isomerize alpha acid and precipitate tannin and proteins. Generally, a small portion of the bittering hops is added to the kettle with the first mash runoff. The largest part is added to boil for forty-five to sixty minutes. A smaller portion may be cast onto the wort fifteen to thirty minutes before the boil ends. Finishing hops, which give the beer a spicy hop flavor and bouquet, may be added within the last minutes of the boil, as the wort is struck from the kettle, or as an extract during fermentation.

Hop Rates

The quantity of hops is determined by several factors: the desired bitterness level, the hop flavor and aromatic character in the finished beer, the alpha-acid content and condition of the hops, and the efficiency of the hop extraction.

Hop acids have limited solubility and ability to isomerize, which lessen with increasing wort gravity. Usual lager hop rates are approximately .2 to .4 ounces of hops per gallon of cooled wort, but may be as low as .15 ounces or as high as .75 ounces per gallon, depending on hop quality, the alpha acidity of the hops, the beer type and its density. Contrary to what might be expected, hop acids become less soluble as wort density increases. Kettle-hop rates may or may not be increased to balance the terminal density of some beers; rather, finishing-hop rates may be increased so that hop flavor, not bitterness, balances the sweetness.

Establishing the Evaporation Rate

As soon as all of the sparging runoff has been brought to a full boil, the wort's extract content and volume can be measured. With the hops fully submerged, correct the volume to 60 or 68 degrees F (15.56 or 20 degrees C). Correct the volume to 60 degrees F by multiplying volume at full boil by .959, to 68 degrees F by .960 (the displacement of wort by the hops is insignificant). These figures can be used to establish the evaporation rate necessary to evaporate the wort to the desired volume and concentration within the prescribed parameters of the boil. The usual evaporation rate in an uncovered boil is 10 percent per hour, although the actual rate depends upon the wort's surface area, surface tension, kettle geometry, the amount of energy applied, ventilation, and the ambient atmospheric pressure.

It may happen that the brewer will need to proceed with a boil that will yield less wort than is needed to satisfy fermenting, priming, topping-up, or kraeusen and yeast-culturing requirements. If a correction must be made, then the volume is generally allowed to vary from what was expected. Too great or too small a volume of sweet wort is of less concern than the correct density. When extract-poor malt, inefficient mashing or sparging, or miscalculation results in a wide disparity between the density that was expected and what occurs, a lighter-density beer must be accepted or the extract content increased with malt-extract or wort, should any be available.

Never boil for less than the prescribed time. The kettle may be partly covered for part of the boil to control evaporation, but the wort must be vigorously boiled, uncovered, for at least the final thirty minutes to drive off harsh, volatile kettle-hop and malt oils, sulphur compounds, ketones, and esters.

Never simmer the wort in lieu of a vigorous boil. Efficient hop-resin isomerization, albumin/resin bonding, and protein/tannin precipitation is achieved only through the agitation of the boil. In fact, a violent boil has the greatest influence on the stabilization of the wort. If movement cannot be induced by the circulation of thermal currents in the wort (heating the kettle asymmetrically improves circulation), then agitation becomes increasingly important. Oxygenation improves flocculation, but at the unacceptable cost of oxidizing and discoloring the wort. Aeration of the mash, wort, or beer at any time except after wort cooling should be avoided.

Once adjustments to the volume of the wort have been made, the pH of the boil should be checked in a sample cooled to 68 degrees F (20 degrees C). Optimum protein flocculation occurs at above pH 5.5, but an initial pH of 5.2 to 5.5 is more appropriate to satisfy the other pH requirements of wort boiling and fermentation. Corrections to the wort acidity should be made with acid or calcium carbonate. Lower pH values produce fewer, smaller flocks; below pH 5.0, the protein does not coagulate. Whenever the pH is less than optimal, agitation and movement within the kettle become increasingly important to flock size.

The pH of the wort drops during boiling as calcium phosphate is precipitated out of solution (sodium and potassium phosphate are unaffected by boiling); usual pH reduction is approximately 0.2 for a sweet wort of 5.5, and .3 for a pH of 5.8.

Hot Break (Kettle Break)

Samples periodically taken from the wort and viewed in a glass container should reveal the progressive flocculation of albuminous protein with hop tannin (polyphenols). Invisible in suspension, they first appear as a mist of tiny flakes that cloud the wort soon after boiling commences. The rolling motion of the boil causes the malt proteins to collide with and adhere to the sticky hop polyphenols. The particles rapidly coagulate into a much smaller number of larger flocks one-eighth inch across, roughly composed of 50 to 60 percent protein, 20 to 30 percent polyphenols, 15 to 20 percent resins, and 2 to 3 percent ash. Upon resting, these large flocks should readily precipitate, leaving the sample brilliantly clear.

Cold Break

As the end of the prescribed boil approaches, samples taken and force-cooled to below 50 degrees F (10 degrees C) are examined. The wort that showed clear when it was hot should cloud slowly as it cools, as previously invisible coagulum loses its solubility in the cooler solution. This cold break should settle, again leaving the wort clear, bright, and sparkling.

The wort must be boiled past a positive cold break in the sample, and flavoring hops should not be added until after the break has been achieved. It is important that the break samples be evaluated; however, boiling should not be extended beyond the recommended time even when the break is poor. A scarcity of flocculum in a well-agitated, strong boil at the proper pH may be caused by malt of poor quality or by either an excessively long or insufficient albumin rest. In the first case, almost all the albumin has been reduced to amino acids or retained in the spent grain, and the beer can be expected to be thin. In the latter case, the protein is too complex to coagulate, and the beer will lack stability and be prone to serious oxidation and taste impairment.

In any case, no correction in the kettle is possible if temperature, pH, and movement of the wort are all satisfactory. The boiling should not be extended unless it is subsequent to a pH or temperature adjustment to the wort.

If a satisfactory break cannot be established because proteolysis has been insufficient, the only recourse is to rack the beer off its sediment several times during fermentation and lagering to separate it from proteins in the trub, and to chill it or tightly filter it before packaging. Even so, the beer may form a chill haze.

Finishing Hops

Finishing hops are usually the very finest hops, chosen for their flavor and aromatics. Generally they are only a fraction of the quantity of kettle hops employed. Fragrant hops are broken up and added to the kettle or the hop back, or an extraction of their hop oils is infused into the cooled wort or fermented beer.

The later in the brewing cycle that finishing hops are added, the greater their bouquet will be. Flavoring hops are commonly added ten or fifteen minutes before the end of the boil for lager beer, so that humulene, carophyllene, and their oxidation products are effectively extracted by exposure to the boiling-hot wort. Late hops contribute little bitterness to the beer and only subdued aroma, but they give the beer a crisp hop flavor. Some aroma hops may be added as the wort is filtered through the hop bed.

Later addition of hops is made only when a distinctive hop aroma is desired. Traditionally, whole hops are added to British ales, even up to the point of packaging, but a hop extract is more appropriate for lager styles. A hop extract can be made by steeping aroma hops for ten minutes or more at pH 5.5 or above in four fluid ounces of wort per each half ounce of hops. An extract is usually added to the wort post-primary, so that none of it is lost in the hop and trub residue and the aroma is not scrubbed out during primary fermentation. Extracts give a cleaner kraeusen head than adding loose or bagged hops post-kettle and present less risk of contamination. The aromatic character of an extract varies substantially from that achieved by dry-hopping; boiling drives off some volatile essential oils (myrecene, thioesters) while extracting others (humulene, carophyllene). Overall, aroma from an extract is milder, spicier, and less grassy/weedy than that derived by dry-hopping.

The hop nose and flavor characteristic of most lagers is obtained by adding loose hops to the wort at or shortly before the conclusion of the boil. Even the very hoppy character of some lagers is attributable to liberal kettle finishing-hop rates rather than to dry-hopping.

Hop nose and flavor are matters of personal preference; finishing-hop rates may be adjusted to suit the brewer's preference, as well as to reflect the aromatic quality of the hops being used.

Straining the Wort

At the end of the recommended boiling period, the wort should be at its desired volume and concentration (both corrected to the reference temperature, 60 or 68 degrees F [15.56 or 20 degrees C]). The hot wort may simply be siphoned off its hop and trub residue, but this causes an unreasonable amount of extract to be lost. Where pellets are used, the wort is generally whirlpooled for several minutes, settled until it is clear (generally ten to fifteen minutes), and then run off from a side outlet. Otherwise, it is more efficient to strain the wort through a loose bed of hops, two inches thick, in a large strainer (hop back) or on a false bottom (for example, perforated with sixteenth-inch holes on eighth-inch centers, or slots .062 inches wide covering 30 percent of the surface). The wort may be recycled, very slowly at first, to settle the hops, and returned to the liquid above the filter bed until it runs clear.

In all cases, the wort should be run off or filtered through the hops before it cools below 170 degrees F (77 degrees C). The first clear runoff may immediately be force-cooled and mixed with the yeast starter to facilitate adaptation of the yeast upon pitching. When all of the clear wort has been run off, the hops can be slightly sparged with up to eight fluid ounces of boiling water per ounce of hops, or until the density of the runoff drops below 5 °Plato (SG 1020). The extract still retained by the hops is insignificant — never attempt to press or wring out the last of it. Great care should be taken to see that only clear runoff is taken for cooling and fermentation.

Cooling the Wort

The clear runoff must be quickly cooled to separate the cold break trub from the wort. Fast cooling is essential; the more slowly the wort cools, the more protein and tannin is trapped in suspension, giving rise to chill haze and harsh aftertastes in the beer. The cold break is generally 10 to 20 percent of the volume of the hot-break sediment, and much less coarse.

Cooling in lager breweries traditionally took place in shallow, open coolships to present maximum surface for air cooling. Better flocculation is achieved, however, by force-cooling the wort and employing a deeper settling tank, closely covered against contamination. Below 145 degrees F (63 degrees C), great care must be taken to prevent contamination of the wort by airborne wild yeast and bacteria or unsterilized equipment. The wort should be force-cooled to below 50 degrees F (10 degrees C) to secure the maximum break. Complete precipitation of tannin/proteins — and thus brilliantly clear beer — is achieved by cooling the wort until it becomes slushy, but cooling to 39 to 43 degrees F (4 to 6 degrees C) before racking the beer off of its settlement is generally sufficient.

Since boiling the wort drives its oxygen out of solution, it must be aerated to force oxygen back in. Yeast require considerable (4 to 14 ppm) molecular oxygen during respiration; without it, they cannot reproduce. Cells that survive an oxygen-starved respiratory phase taint the ferment with abnormal, estery flavors. Their lag phase is characteristically shortened, reproduction is limited, and their fermentation is sluggish. Oxygen starvation produces "petite mutants," which ferment weakly and often incompletely, giving a peculiar and cloying diacetyl taste and other off-flavors.

In an oxygenated wort, the yeast splits the sugar molecule in such a fashion that it produces more CO_2 than alcohol. The carbonic gas rising to the surface quickly forms a blanket above the ferment, which insulates it from airborne infection. It may also carry with it a film of debris that can be readily skimmed from the head during the kraeusen stage of fermentation.

Aeration by rousing the wort when it is hot saturates the wort more completely than does aeration of the cooled wort. The risk of airborne contamination is less while the wort is above 145 degrees F (63 degrees C), and aeration of the hot wort causes some of the oxygen to combine with protein fractions, improving the cold break. It would seem that the wort should be aerated when hot, but oxidative polymerization of polyphenols to tannins and oxidation of wort constituents create very objectionable flavors. The color darkens when the hot wort is aerated and flavor suffers irreversible oxidation damage. Aerating the cooled wort (at 60 degrees F [16 degrees C] or below) is always preferred to aerating hot wort, and it yields satisfactory dissolved oxygen (up to 8 ppm). It is essential that the air or oxygen be sterile to preclude contamination of the extract.

If a settling tank is being employed, the cold break should be well settled before the wort is racked into the fermenter. The pH of the wort should be 5.0 to 5.5. With infusion-mashed and ale worts, a pH of 5.0 to 5.2 is usual, but for lager beers a cooled-wort pH of 5.3 to 5.5 is still considered normal.

CHAPTER 12

Fermentation

Any successful fermentation proceeds along a predictable course dictated by the composition of the wort and the characteristics of the yeast strain. The amount of extract, its dextrin/maltose ratio, the amount and complexity of the nitrogenous matter, the availability of yeast nutrients, the pH, and the oxygen saturation and biological purity of the wort are values that have been fixed by mashing particular malts and boiling, cooling, and aerating the wort.

The only significant influences upon the fermentation that can be manipulated by the brewer are those of the yeast — its character, purity, vitality, quantity, and its rousing — and the temperature and duration of the ferment. Changes in any one of these can affect the residual sugar, mouthfeel, clarity, aroma, and flavor of the beer.

Preparing for Pitching

The fermentation cycle should never be started with a weak yeast; such yeast will only be made weaker upon being diluted into the wort. The yeast to be pitched

pH in Typical Lager Brewing

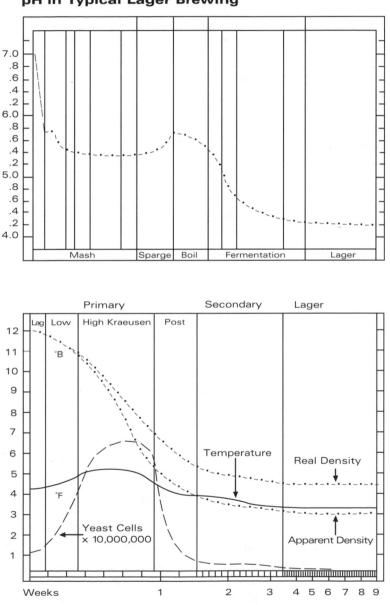

should have been cultured in a wort similar to that being brewed. Yeast that must undergo significant adaptation suffers a high rate of mortality, causing fermentation to start slowly and be relatively weak. The likelihood of contamination increases and decomposition of dead yeast cells mars the beer flavor.

Sugar solutions should not be used to culture yeast. When yeast is cultured in solutions lacking maltose, it loses its ability to absorb maltose, and suffers from unreasonably long periods of adaptation upon being diffused into the wort.

Approximately .5 to .6 fluid ounces (10 to 14 grams) of pasty, thick yeast is needed for each gallon of wort to be pitched to give 12 to 15 x 10^6 cells per milliliter of wort. Up to one fluid ounce (21 grams) of yeast is necessary for each gallon of wort when a very strong start is needed, or when the yeast is a weak fermenter. That much is also needed for worts of very low or high extract content. In the first case, more yeast ensure an adequate start in the nutrient-poor environment, and in the latter case are needed to ferment the greater amount of extract.

Pitching too much yeast, however, overtaxes the supplies of dissolved oxygen, simple sugars, and yeast nutrients and can result in yeast autolysis (self-digestion). The rapid fermentation and premature autolysis can result in fusely, estery and rubbery, yeasty and sulfurous flavors.

Less yeast than the amount recommended above should be pitched when the yeast strain has proven to be a very strong fermenter. A good culture should require only .4 fluid ounces (8.5 grams) of yeast slurry per gallon of wort. Conservative pitching rates (.8 to 1 x 10^6 cells/milliliters per each °Plato of the wort) of healthy yeast are the rule unless experience dictates otherwise.

Conservative pitching rates should not be confused with inadequate pitching rates. Pitching too few yeast results in long lag and reproductive phases, estery aromas, and increased risk of contamination. English ales are commonly pitched at far lower rates (.6 to .8 x 10^6 cells/milliliter per each °Plato of the wort) where esters are meant to be prominent in a beer's aroma. In lager brewing, ester formation is repressed in part by limiting reproduction through higher pitching rates. Ale yeasts may grow to five to eight times the amount pitched, while lager yeasts generally increase three to five times.

The pitching yeast should be clear, white-to-tan, its sediment should be thick and rich, and its aroma pure and pleasant. If the culture is collected from the parent ferment at the height of kraeusen and repitched reasonably quickly, the sediment will be composed mainly of healthy yeast. Regular rousing of the culture produces more yeast and a richer sediment. Dusty yeast that remains suspended and does not form a rich sediment by the time it has thrown up a rocky foam cover is unsuitable for pitching.

The yeast culture can be the most significant source of microbial infection to the ferment. A culture that smells or tastes off will produce disastrous results if pitched. Yeast must be handled carefully, so that the brewing strain is cultured, not wild yeast or bacteria.

If a dry yeast absolutely must be pitched, then slurry two to four grams of granulated yeast per gallon of cooled wort into twice its volume of sterile 100 degrees F (38 degrees C) water to minimize shock excretion while the desiccated yeast resuscitates. Cover it and rest it for thirty minutes. It should be raising a frothy head before it is pitched.

(A note of caution: granulated dry yeast may be contaminated by significant quantities of bacteria. It is probably the least viable and most often contaminated source of brewing yeast. Subculturing from a slant, frozen, or liquid culture, or kraeusening from a healthy ferment is more likely to produce a satisfactory fermentation cycle.)

Before pitching, the yeast can be forcefully roused into the first clear runoff from the kettle (force-cooled to the pitching temperature and racked off of its sediment). The purpose is to aerate and evenly distribute the yeast, and allow it to adapt to the extract while the rest of the wort is being force-cooled and sedimented.

Cooled wort in excess of that to be fermented can be run off into the containers in which it will be stored until it is used for topping-up, priming, kraeusening, or for yeast culturing. The amount of wort removed should at least be equal to the requirements listed in table 14. Refrigerate the tightly capped containers until needed; they will keep for at least six months at 33 degrees F (1 degree C).

Kraeusening

Kraeusen is the German word used to describe the infusion of a strongly fermenting young beer into a larger volume of wort or beer that is past the stage of strong fermentation. Kraeusen beer introduces vigorous yeast in its own sugar-rich substratum. It is characterized by the active raising of a tightly knit or rocky foam head. Yeast colonies should visibly cloud the liquid below.

Kraeusen beer should be taken only from ferments that exhibit textbook characteristics. Although successive kraeusening may encourage the culturing of wild or dusty yeast, it still remains the best method by which fermentation may be induced in the cooled wort.

The culture must be strong, so that it is neither overwhelmed by the larger volume of wort nor unable to renew active fermentation in a well-aged, extract-depleted beer. Kraeusen is traditionally obtained from a strong primary fermentation, but it may be made from wort and a yeast culture *(yeast starter)*. Sterile wort is pitched with a culture, and its volume is increased to at least 5 percent of the wort volume by doubling. (The starter volume is built by adding wort in up to a ten-to-one ratio each time vigorous fermentation becomes apparent.) It should be in full kraeusen when it is pitched.

When 10 percent new beer (just coming into high kraeusen) is used to induce fermentation in the cooled wort, the yeast lag-phase is virtually eliminated. The yeast, having adapted to the solution, require no respiratory phase to develop a cell membrane and enzymes appropriate to the given wort. Initial fermentation is stronger. Employing kraeusen beer to top up the secondary (lager) fermenter induces a strong temporary fermentation and reduces diacetyl and the risk of oxidation and contamination at racking.

When wood chips are used to clear the lager beer, *aufkraeusening* is absolutely necessary. There must be movement of the aged beer so that every part comes into contact with the latticework of chips. The introduction of kraeusen beer at a temperature 5 degrees F (3 degrees C) warmer than the aging beer and the subsequent fermentation create the necessary movement of the whole volume of beer. The chips alone would not otherwise clarify an aged beer.

Kraeusening also reduces lagering time by introducing vigorous fermentation, capable of more rapid metabolism of the small amount of fermentable sugar in the aging beer than the few yeast cells already in the solution.

Good sanitary procedures are an absolute necessity, and whether it is being mixed with wort or with aged beer, the new beer should be well roused in.

Pitching the Yeast

For lager beers, yeast is generally pitched into wort that is at or near the lower end of the intended fermentation temperature range. Although yeast will generally reproduce more quickly if pitched into relatively warmer wort, it will also produce more diacetyl, fusel alcohols, and esters.

Where practical, it is advisable to separate the chilled wort from the cold break in a settling tank. The yeast may be pitched in the settling tank up to twelve hours before the wort is transferred to a fermenter, or during the transfer. The wort temperature is generally allowed to rise to 39 to 43 degrees F (4 to 6 degrees C) before it is racked off the cold break into the fermenter along with the yeast starter, slurry, or kraeusen beer. Where a settling tank is not employed, the wort is generally pitched at 42 to 47 degrees F (6 to 8 degrees C).

The pitching yeast is commonly added at a temperature up to 5 degrees F (3 degrees C) warmer than the wort, and well roused into it in an aerating fashion. Because brewers' yeast requires considerable dissolved oxygen (eight to twelve milligrams/liter) to synthesize fats to cell-wall consituents, a stream of air is often used to effect this mixture of yeast and wort. An aeration stone or other device that increases air-to-wort surface contact improves oxygenation. Gentle rousing should be continued throughout the transfer to achieve an intimate admixture and to dissolve oxygen into the wort.

Care should be taken that the wort's trub sediment is not disturbed, especially as its draining nears completion. Good hot and cold breaks are meaningless if a significant amount of trub is carried into the ferment. Racking should cease as soon as the runoff shows the least bit cloudy; trub carried into the ferment taints the beer with objectionable flavors and aromas.

Proteinaceous precipitate from the hot and cold breaks forms the greatest part of the trub. Although amino acids are absolutely necessary for yeast metabolic functions, yeast react to an excess of simple protein by generating aromatic fusel alcohols. Even more of these volatile carbonyl compounds are excreted when the wort has been underoxygenated. Fusel alcohols are subject to esterization, which produces fruity and solventlike odors that are inappropriate in a lager beer, and to oxidation, forming "stale"-tasting aldehydes.

Trub also contains polyphenols, ketones, and sulfur compounds that may be absorbed into the ferment. Polyphenols give astringent-tasting, mouth-puckering flavors. Volatile sulfur compounds (H_2S, DMS, thiois, and mercaptans) produce rotten-egg, skunky, onionlike, rubbery, and burnt-match flavors and odors.

The Fermentation Lock

Although the release of carbonic gas from the fermentation gives it some measure of protection against oxidation and contamination, covering the fermenter immediately after pitching and fitting it with a fermentation lock is advisable. The airlock allows the pressure created by the carbonic gas to push past the liquid in the lock without allowing air in. This prevents the reverse passage of airborne wild yeast and bacteria into the culture-yeast fermentation. Oxygen trapped within the fermenter by the lock is readily driven off by the rising blanket of heavier carbon dioxide produced by the ferment.

The liquid in the lock should be maintained at a constant level, but not so deep that it puts the fermenting beer under any appreciable pressure. During the primary fermentation, it is essential that virtually no carbon dioxide remain in solution, since it carries malt and hop debris into the head and sulphur compounds and esters out of the ferment.

The purpose of the fermentation lock is to prevent infection. It must be kept perfectly clean. The trap can be filled with an antiseptic solution in which microbes cannot exist, a practice that is advisable during later fermentation. Of course, this solution must not contact the ferment either by splashing caused by excess pressure or by careless handling.

Primary Fermentation

Five to twelve days may elapse from the time the yeast is pitched until vigorous fermentation abates; six or seven days is usual. Ales are fermented at higher temperatures over a relatively shorter period of time to develop characteristic esters and other fermentation flavors. Lagers are suited by lower temperatures, which retard fermentation times and ester development.

The duration of the primary fermentation is also subject to the strength and reducing characteristics of the pitched yeast strain. Nonselective strains that completely ferment the extract work very quickly but produce a thin, inferior-tasting beer. Temperamental strains such as Saaz yeasts incompletely convert the extract during a relatively long, weak ferment but produce a richer-tasting and fuller beer.

Normal primary fermentation is verified by its characteristic low, high, and post-kraeusen stages. Where deviations are encountered, the source of the irregularity should be investigated, identified, and corrected as soon as possible.

Temperature

The temperatures quoted here apply to dextrin-rich lager worts of 10 °Plato (SG 1040) or greater, producing full-bodied beer. If a high-maltose wort relatively free of haze-forming protein fractions is being fermented, or if a top-fermenting yeast strain is used, temperatures should be higher by 6 to 20 degrees F (3 to 10 degrees C). Fermentation times will be correspondingly foreshortened.

Do not exceed the recommended temperatures when fermenting a dextrinous wort with lager yeast. The yeast requires the longer fermentation time at the lower temperatures to break down and convert the less readily fermentable dextrinous sugars. Moreover, higher temperatures invariably cause an increase in esters, fusel alcohols, and solventlike flavors that are inappropriate in lagers.

Temperature Control

Fermentations generate heat. The temperature of any ferment must be monitored and the excessive heat drawn off by lowering the ambient temperature. In no case should the internal temperature of a lager ferment exceed 60 degrees F (15 degrees C), and it should be limited to a cumulative increase of 7 to 14 degrees F (4 to 7 degrees C) relative to the starting temperature.

Ideally, the maximum temperature should not rise above 47 to 52 degrees F (8 to 11 degrees C) when employing traditional lager strains. The maximum temperature may be maintained through high kraeusen until yeast nutrients are depleted, yeast activity slows, and heat generation ends, or even raised for "diacetyl" rest, but it is usually lowered soon after the maximum temperature is reached.

Controlling the temperature at the beginning of fermentation is more important than controlling the temperature near the end of fermentation, because esters and fusel alcohols are largely produced when the yeast is respiring, during the lag and reproductive phases of fermentation.

Temperature changes at any stage of the fermentation should not exceed 5 degrees F (3 degrees C) daily. Abrupt reduction in temperature will shock the yeast and may arrest fermentation completely. The sudden death of many yeast cells deleteriously affects flavor; moreover, yeast mutations tend to adapt to a sudden temperature change more readily than culture yeast. Temperature maintenance and modification must be handled carefully.

Convection currents within the ferment (formed by asymmetrical cooling of the fermentation vessel) improve temperature distribution and yeast performance, producing a more even fermentation.

Density and pH Monitoring

The acidity of the ferment increases as the yeast adapt and respire glucose to succinate and other organic acids. With top-fermenting yeast, the pH drop during respiration is dramatic; it falls .4 to .6 within twelve hours of pitching and to pH 4.0 within twenty-four hours, before it levels off as fermentation begins in earnest. With lager yeast, the pH drop is much less precipitous; for a wort of pH 5.3, a .5 drop requires forty-eight hours, and the pH only falls to 4.5 or so by the end of primary fermentation. One measure of consistent yeast performance is its effect on the pH of the extract solution. To this end, monitoring the pH is critical during the lag phase of a top-fermenting culture, and at the low, high, and post-kraeusen stages of a lager ferment.

The liquid pressure of the fermenting beer also makes its most dramatic drop during primary fermentation and should be regularly checked and logged to define yeast activity and pinpoint racking time.

Primary Fermentation: Lag Phase

After pitching, yeast take some time adapting to the conditions of their new environment. During this "lag" phase, there is little visual evidence of their activity. How successfully the yeast culture adapts to the wort depends upon the number and condition of the yeast cells and the nature of the wort itself. Temperature, density, glucose/maltose content, amino acid availability, and the level of dissolved oxygen all influence yeast behavior.

At pitching, yeast rely on free oxygen, wort fatty acids, and glycogen, an intracellular carbohydrate reserve, to provide energy for the synthesis of wort-specific enzymes and a permeable cell membrane. Glycogen is structurally similar to the amylopectin of malt starch, but with a greater number of shorter branches. Without adequate glycogen reserves, the pitched yeast cannot survive until they can develop the ability to absorb and metabolize wort sugars and nutrients.

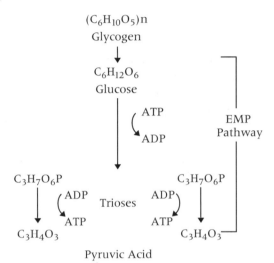

$(C_6H_{10}O_5)n$
Glycogen

$C_6H_{12}O_6$
Glucose

ATP

ADP

EMP
Pathway

$C_3H_7O_6P$ $C_3H_7O_6P$

ADP   Trioses   ADP

ATP   ATP

$C_3H_4O_3$ $C_3H_4O_3$

Pyruvic Acid

During the lag phase, yeast employ a complex enzyme system to hydrolyze the polymeric glycogen to glucose. The glucose molecule is phosphorylated and its carbon links broken (glycosis) to yield two triose phosphates. These simpler three-carbon compounds are oxidized to pyruvic acid (pyruvate, an important yeast oxo-acid) with the release of energy by formation of energy-rich ATP, adenosine triphosphate, from energy-depleted ADP.

An inadequate starch reserve may be characteristic of a particular yeast strain, but more often this is due to depletion of glycogen from storing a culture for too long or at too warm a temperature. A culture that survives glycogen deprivation produces abnormal levels of vicinal diketones (especially diacetyl), marring the beer flavor. Fermentation takes longer and is less vigorous, because there are fewer cells, and consequently, slower yeast growth.

Yeast cells also store simple acids, alcohols, nitrogen, and phosphates catabolized from compounds assimilated during culturing. At pitching, yeast employ other enzyme groups to combine these simple chains, synthesizing many of their complex structural and metabolic requirements. Pyruvic acid is reduced to oxaloacetate, from which amino acids and proteins may be synthesized, or to acetyl Co A, an acyl Co A, an acetic-acid-related sulfur compound that can be oxidized to a host of fatty acids, triglycerides, and lipids required for cell-membrane synthesis. Molecular oxygen is required for these reactions. The synthesis of a ten-fold increase of sterols in the yeast to make cell walls permeable requires oxygen. Unless there is sufficient dissolved oxygen in the wort, the formation of a cell wall able to react to and regulate uptake of the particular sugars and nutrients in that wort will cease. Unable to selectively absorb nutrients from solution, many yeast cells will autolyze, and surviving cells will not develop normally. Both scenarios produce off-flavors in beer.

Lacking dissolved oxygen, acetyl Co A esterifies alcohols, including fusel alcohols. These solventlike and harsh-tasting "higher" alcohols are intermediate products of amino-acid metabolism and are normally oxidized back to organic oxo-acids. When respiring yeast lack oxygen, fusel alcohols may be excreted or dehydrated by acetyl Co A to esters. The principle ester formed is ethyl acetate, which irreversibly flavors the beer with fruity/solventy aromatics.

Inadequate oxygenation also causes pyruvic acid, fatty acids, and amino acids to be decarboxylated to aldehydes. These too are normally metabolic intermediates, but without enough oxygen, brewers' yeast must absorb trub to fuel sterol synthesis, and "staling" compounds are excreted. They may be reabsorbed by the yeast during fermentation, but they are just as likely to be further decarboxylated to fusel alcohols or remain after fermentation ceases. Acetaldehyde, the aldehyde of pyruvic acid, usually predominates, giving an odor like green apples.

As the yeast depletes its glycogen reserves, it starts to absorb glucose and fructose from solution and begins to manufacture the enzymes and permeases necessary to reduce other wort sugars. Only the monosaccharides and sucrose in wort can be absorbed by yeast that have not adapted to the wort into which they have been pitched.

Permeases are enzymelike transports that carry specific compounds through the plasma membrane and into the yeast cell. The yeast must synthesize permeases to absorb maltose and maltotriose, and the enzyme a-glucosidase to hydrolyze them to glucose. Lager yeast (*S. uvarum*) synthesize and excrete melibiase to split and absorb the disaccharide melibiose. Other inducible enzymes are formed and secreted to the yeast's outer cell-membrane surfaces after maltose and maltotriose are depleted. These sever glucose molecules from dextrins to fuel subdued metabolism.

The lag and respiratory phases are generally longer when yeast have not been cultured in a solution similar to the wort into which they will be pitched. Prolonged adaptation, common with granulated dry yeast, can lead to the increased formation of fusel alcohol and esters. Culturing in solutions that contain a high percentage of corn sugar or glucose inhibits the formation of maltose permeases. Worts high in corn sugar suffer prolonged lag phases; some yeast strains even lose the ability to ferment maltose in high glucose worts (catabolite repression, or the glucose effect).

The first evidence of yeast activity is usually the formation of wisps of lacy white foam on the surface of the beer eight to twenty-four hours after pitching. Gradually this foam forms a wreath at the rim of the fermenter, and the beer below becomes milky-white from the haze of suspended yeast colonies. Carbon dioxide production is prodigious, although attenuation of the wort is slight. Most of the CO_2 is being released as a byproduct of pyruvic acid decarboxylation to acetyl Co A and oxo-acids; the carbon source for this reaction is glycogen, and only very little of the wort sugar is being metabolized.

If the yeast lag-phase extends beyond twenty-four hours, and the wort and yeast starter were originally well roused and oxygenated, then more yeast should be pitched. Rousing the quiet beer may cause the yeast to start fermenting, but as a rule, more yeast should be pitched. If the extended lag phase appears to be character-istic of the yeast strain, it should not be recultured; if it is due to prolonged storage of the culture before pitching, or to wort composition, the problem should be remedied.

As the yeast build cell walls and reserves up during the lag phase, they begin reproducing. As long as dissolved oxygen remains available in the wort, the yeast will utilize it to fuel anabolic reproduction. This respiratory period marks the period of greatest culture growth. Yeast growth, then, is most dramatic in a well-oxygenated wort.

Low Kraeusen

Although free molecular oxygen is not necessary for yeast growth, it does facilitate it. Yeast can utilize carbon as an energy source fourteen times more efficiently by respir-ing molecular oxygen than it can by fermenting it anaero-bically. Yeast cells reproduce more rapidly in an oxy-genated solution, but normally continue reproduction at least until maltose is depleted.

The yeast begin budding as the lag phase ends, and rapidly scavenge the free oxygen from the wort in the early part of the low-kraeusen stage. As long as readily assimilable nutrients remain, the yeast continues reproduc-ing, albeit at a gradually slowing rate.

As they deplete the molecular oxygen, the yeast begin anaerobic wort metabolism. Within six to thirty-six hours of pitching, the foam wreath should begin to migrate toward the surface center, marking the commencement of the low kraeusen stage of primary fermentation. It characterizes the start of intense catabolism of maltose, the uptake of a wide range of wort amino acids, the gradual transition from respirations to anaerobic fermentation, and a period of exponential yeast growth.

Low Kraeusen

As the head rises to form low, rich mounds and curls of foam, it carries with it protein, hop residues, and degenerated yeast cells, which are visible as a brown scum that collects on the head and at the surface edge. In closed fermentations, the scum may be eliminated by being "blown off" along with some of the liquid supporting it, or allowed to drop. In open systems, it is eliminated from the fermenter by skimming. If oxidized scum is allowed to fall back into the ferment, it will impart harsh, bitter tastes to the beer and provide a nutrient source for bacterial contaminants. Care must be taken that the fermentation is not contaminated if it is exposed for skimming. A low humidity improves atmospheric purity, reducing the likelihood of contamination.

Anaerobic Glucose Fermentation

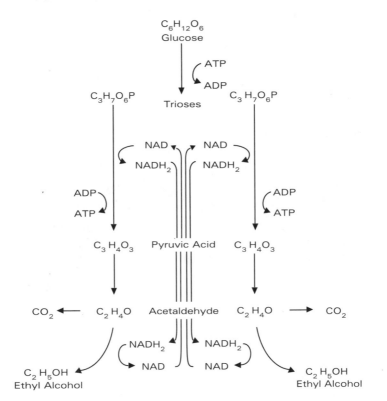

The ferment may be topped-up with sterile wort or liquor to compensate for evaporation and blowoff or skimming losses, although it is more practical to compensate for these losses by increasing initial wort volume.

At this point, the yeast have completely adapted to the conditions of the ferment and are rapidly multiplying. Extract reduction should be about .5 °Plato (SG 1002) during this brief low-kraeusen phase. The pH also declines as organic acids are released as by-products of the yeast metabolism of amino acids.

The major fermentation products are ethyl alcohol (ethanol) and carbon dioxide, but even during a normal fermentation cycle, other compounds are excreted by the yeast. The metabolism of the yeast is fueled primarily by the hydrolysis of carbohydrates, but amino acids and fatty acids from the wort also serve as energy sources. Normal carbohydrate metabolism follows the EMP pathway to pyruvic acid so that ATP may be regenerated to fuel, continuing biosynthesis of the yeasts' metabolic requirements. The ADP-ATP cycle, however, cannot continue if pyruvic acid buildup is left to block it. Pyruvic acid in excess of that required for acetyl Co A and oxaloacetate synthesis is metabolized to CO_2 and acetaldehyde by the yeast enzyme pyruvate decarboxylase. The CO_2 is excreted. Acetaldehyde is hydrated to ethyl alcohol by the enzyme alcohol dehydrogenase so that hydrogen buildup blocking the ADP-ATP synthesis can also be eliminated.

Nitrogen metabolism is closely related to glucose hydrolysis. The yeast enzymatically split amino acids in the wort and separately absorb the nitrogenous amino groups (NH_2) and oxo-acid skeletons. These can be reassembled as amino acids, or as proteins, appropriate to the yeasts' requirements. Oxo-acids necessary for amino acid synthesis may also come from carbohydrate metabolism, and similarly there are several other ways in which oxo-acids are used with consequences affecting beer flavor. They may be decarboxylated to aldehydes, and the aldehydes hydrated by the enzyme alcohol dehydrogenase to form fusel alcohols. Lack of dextrinous sugars, trub in the yeast cake, and elevated temperatures all contribute to the formation of piquant, solventlike, and highly aromatic harsh fusel alcohols.

Oxo-acids may be metabolized to acetohydroxy acids, which are not metabolized by the yeast and are therefore expelled by them. During low kraeusen, this provides for the elimination of oxo-acids (primarily from pyruvic acid), which carbohydrate metabolism is producing in excess.

Excreted into solution, acetohydroxy acids can be oxidized to vicinal diketones, principally diacetyl (dimethyl diketone, $C_4H_6O_2$). Diacetyl has a perceptible buttery flavor, which is objectionable in amounts above .15 ppm; during low kraeusen it may be as high as .35 ppm. That there is some oxygen in the ferment during low kraeusen and that the temperature is not unreasonably depressed in later fermentation are both important to diacetyl control, because after yeast growth has slowed, healthy cells reabsorb vicinal diketones and metabolize them to harmless diols. When the acetohydroxy acid is not oxidized to vicinal diketones during vigorous early fermentation, later diacetyl formation may irreversibly mar beer flavor. The presence of dissolved oxygen later in fermentation also increases the likelihood of oxidation of acetohydroxy acids to diacetyl; vigorous anaerobic fermentation after the low kraeusen stage is essential to diacetyl control.

High Kraeusen

With top-fermenting yeast, a thick head of clumped yeast covers the beer soon after intense fermentation becomes apparent. At their normal operating temperatures, top-fermenting yeast have largely metabolized the sugars in solution at a time when lager yeast are still undergoing growth. Not until eighteen to seventy-two hours after the mounds of foam begin to form (two to four days after pitching) do the lager yeast weave a tightly knit cover over the surface of the beer. This cover rises further and finally breaks into cream-colored, less dense, "rocky heads."

In a lager fermentation, extract reduction approximates 1 °Plato (SG 1004) daily over the two to five days of high kraeusen, while the yeast may still be reproducing logarithmically. The temperature must be exactly controlled.

High Kraeusen

Although 60 degrees F (16 degrees C) is given as the maximum allowable temperature, with most lager yeast strains every effort should be made to hold it to 47 to 52 degrees F (8 to 11 degrees C). When this temperature is reached within the ferment, the ambient temperature can begin to be lowered if diacetyl levels in the beer are not a problem. The temperature should not be lowered more than 5 degrees F (3 degrees C) daily and should be reduced to 38 to 40 degrees F (3 to 4 degrees C) over several days. The temperature at the conclusion of a traditional kraeusen fermentation is usually about 45 degrees F (7 degrees C).

The continued release of organic acids during high kraeusen reduces the pH, depending on the yeast strain and wort characteristics, to 4.0 to 4.5. If the pH drops too rapidly, the yeast will settle out of suspension prematurely; if the pH drops too slowly, it may prevent the beer from clearing properly.

Post Kraeusen

The extract is largely metabolized by the yeast during high kraeusen. As the yeast activity slows, carbonic gas production slows, and consequently the agglutinated yeast colonies sink out of suspension and the foam head is no longer formed.

Late Kraeusen

At this point, all of the head can be floated, siphoned, or skimmed off, even as more is forming, so that it does not fall back through the beer. An exception to this procedure is made when a low-extract, quickly maturing beer is being brewed. Such a beer requires the peptides and amino acids from clean foam for yeast nutrients and for body. The increase in the alcohol content of the beer induces the reabsorption of the albuminous matter into solution. Only a clean head should be allowed to fall back through the ferment. Residual scum gives the beer a harshly bitter background flavor. The stability of the beer is invariably less than if the head is removed or the beer is quickly separated from its trub after the head falls.

Generally, four to six days after high kraeusen begins (six to ten days after pitching), the formation of the foam cover ceases. As the availability of fermentable extract drops during the post-kraeusen stage, the yeast adapt to changing conditions by accelerating their secretion of extracellular enzymes capable of splitting off glucose from dextrins in solution. Reasonable levels of diacetyl and the related dike-tone 2,3-pentane dione are also absorbed and metabolized by the yeast. It is important that the fermentation tempera-ture not be prematurely lowered and that the beer not be racked off its yeast sediment until the diacetyl has been reabsorbed. With a clean fermentation, it is usual for the beer to be held in the primary fermenter for two or three days after the kraeusen head has fallen, with the tempera-ture being lowered from 45 degrees F (7 degrees C) to 38 to 40 degrees F (3 to 4 degrees C). The extract drop over the final twenty-four-hour period of primary fermentation should be about .5 °Plato (SG 1002), and the density should be about one-third what the wort density (OG) was.

An entirely different approach is relatively common in modern fermentation cycles. When the density drops to about 1.5 °Plato (SG 1006) above the target terminal gravity, the brewer raises the temperature of the post-kraeusen beer to 52 degrees F (11 degrees C) or higher, and holds that temperature for two to seven days for a *diacetyl rest* to reinvigorate the yeast culture so that it will metabolize diacetyl, removing it from solution.

Because fermentable extract is rapidly consumed at the higher temperatures of the diacetyl rest, subsequent conditioning can be foreshortened. Secondary fermenta-tion will be both subdued and brief, and lagering may require only fourteen to twenty-one days to achieve the same clarity and flavor stability (but not the same flavor development) that would be expected with the usual five-to-seven-week secondary fermentation and lagering.

Real and Apparent Attenuation

Normal primary fermentation ends when head for-mation ceases; this may take as few as five days when the wort is below 10 °Plato (SG 1040), or eight to ten days for a very rich and dextrinous wort. Roughly 50 to 65 percent of the extract will have been converted to alcohol and carbon dioxide, although the hydrometer may show a 65 to 80 percent reduction in density ("one-third gravity"). The difference between the real attenuation of the beer and the apparent attenuation as gauged by the hydrometer is usually about 15 percent. This phenomenon occurs because the hydrometer measures liquid pressure, and does not reflect the fact that this pressure has been reduced by the formation of alcohol as well as by the reduction of the fermentable extract. Because alcohol is far lighter than water (the liquid pressure of pure water is SG 1000; of alcohol, 798), the hydrometer sinks further into a solution in which alcohol is present, and the hydrometer reading is lower than the extract loss alone can account for.

The real attenuation can be determined. First, a volume of beer is measured at the temperature the brewer's hydrometer is calibrated to, usually 60 or 68 degrees F (15.56 or 20 degrees C), and is decarbonated, usually by membrane filtration. This volume of beer is raised to a temperature of 173 degrees F (78 degrees C) or slightly higher and roused for thirty to sixty minutes to drive off the alcohol. The sample is cooled to 60 degrees F and topped-up to its original volume with distilled water. The volume of water required to replace the lost volume of beer, divided by original volume, is equal to the percent alcohol by volume of the beer. The hydrometer reading of the dealcoholized sample, after topping-up, accurately reflects the real extract content of the beer. The real attenuation is measured by subtracting this reading from the original °Plato (OG) of the wort.

Racking

The beer is carefully racked off its settlement when its density is one-third or less of the wort density (OG) and its drop over the preceding twenty-four hours is .5 °Plato (SG 1002) or less. A reducing-sugar analysis usually shows less than 5 percent. The beer should be free of any foam cover. The transfer to a closed secondary fermenter should be made under antiseptic conditions, and all equipment should be sanitized before use.

The purpose of racking is to separate the beer from decaying yeast cells and flavor-impairing precipitates. Care should be taken that no yeast sediment or trub is carried along into the secondary fermentation. Siphoning or decanting must be terminated just as soon as the runoff becomes the least bit cloudy.

Employing up to 5 percent strongly fermenting kraeusen beer at racking produces a stronger start of secondary fermentation and a better overall fermentation. This absolutely must be done when yeast performance during primary fermentation has been poor, as it replenishes the degraded culture.

Racking must be done without rousing or splashing to prevent oxygen from entering the solution. Oxygen in beer past early kraeusen poses serious consequences to the beer flavor: oxidation of acetohydroxy acids in the secondary fermenter produces diacetyl that the yeast may not reabsorb; alcohols may be oxidized to aldehydes; amino acids may be oxidized to fusel alcohols; acids may oxidize alcohols to esters; and phenolic material may polymerize and become haze fractions. It is also advisable that the secondary fermenter be topped-up with kraeusen beer or wort so that only enough airspace remains to allow for very mild foaming. Cone-bottomed "unitank" fermenters preclude the necessity for racking to a secondary fermenter/lagering tank. Trub is discharged from the bottom outlet throughout the course of the primary fermentation, and yeast is collected as it sediments.

Gauging Yeast Performance

A sample of the beer at racking should show very clear and bright. It should demonstrate a good break. When held up to the light, it should show clear. When agitated, distinctly visible suspended yeast colonies may float about, but upon resting, should settle out rapidly and firmly. Such a yeast is satisfactory for collecting to be repitched and for employment in a long secondary and lager fermentation.

Only "break," or *Bruchhefen,* sedimentary yeast form colonies as the yeast nutrients in the beer diminish. Powdery or dusty *Staubhefen* yeast do not sediment in so clean a break and are likely to remain as a foam cover on the beer surface even after measurable attenuation falls off.

Dusty yeast ferment more of the extract than do break yeast, and do so more quickly. Beer brewed with dusty yeast is unsuitable for long secondary fermentation and lagering, because the yeast have largely eliminated the less readily fermentable extract necessary to support aging. Lagering must be conducted at lower temperatures (as low as 30 degrees F [-1 degree C]) to increase sedimentation and retard fermentation. The beer should be racked into the secondary/lagering fermenter before the density has dropped much below one-third that of the wort (OG).

The appearance of dusty yeast in a ferment is usually due to the propagation of an inferior strain and/or harvesting late in the fermentation cycle. It should not be used for repitching.

Yeast Collection

Fermentations displaying normal characteristics and desirable flavors are the best sources of yeast suitable for culturing. If the yeast have deteriorated (the beer is tainted with burnt-rubber or sulfury flavors, or fermentation is sluggish), are unable to reabsorb diacetyl (buttery taste and aroma), or are contaminated by wild yeast (cloudy beer after kraeusen, medicinal flavors) or bacteria (abnormal, sour, vegetal, or rancid-butter taste and aroma), the culture is not suited for repitching or culturing.

Seed yeast for subsequent brewings, culturing, and bottle priming should be collected only from the middle layer of the primary-fermentation sediment. The sediment should be relatively clean; an undisturbed sediment is composed of three distinct layers. The very thin, dark upper layer and the bottom layer of dead, inferior cells and trub sandwich between them the active, healthy, white yeast, or *barm*. Barm has the best fermenting qualities — strong cells that agglutinate well and settle out properly. Where an open fermenter is used, after the beer is transferred from the primary fermenter, all of the top layer is scraped aside before the middle layer is gathered up into a sterile container. When a closed fermenter that has no yeast-collection system at its base is used, the entire sediment is washed out and the barm separated from the trub by several rinsings, which float off the dead cells and organic residues. With cone-bottomed fermenters, collection begins when the sediment begins to run clean, and ceases when it becomes discolored again by settling trub.

Yeast collected for repitching can be covered with very cold, biologically clean water and agitated into suspension. When most of the yeast has settled, the water is decanted off, taking with it dead cells and trub. The rinsing is repeated. A subsequent acid wash with phosphoric acid or ammonium persulfate solution destroys bacteria, but the yeast culture may need to be recultured to restore its normal fermentation characteristics.

Depending upon the strain, yeast covered with sterile wort in a container fitted with a fermentation lock can be stored at 32 to 40 degrees F (0 to 4 degrees C) for from seven to twenty-one days without significant deterioration.

If the seed yeast will not be pitched within that time, it must be fed again, or drained, pressed, and frozen.

Again depending upon the strain and the sterility of the conditions, lager yeast may be subcultured through as many as twenty successive brewings if they are repitched within twenty-four hours of collection. If the period between repitching is longer, or the strain is prone to mutation, it may be usable for only four or five intermittent brewings. As a general rule, the greater the frequency of use, the more times a strain may be directly subcultured.

Secondary Fermentation

Whether or not a beer will be extensively lagered, a secondary fermentation in a closed fermenter allows for the slow reduction *(conditioning)* of the remaining fermentable extract. In the secondary fermentation stage of lagering, the beer is free from the flavor impairment of sedimented trub and degenerating yeast cells. Seven to twenty-one days may be required for the yeast to deplete the fermentable sugar left after the kraeusen period has ended. Traditional lagering entails holding the beer for a further two to seven weeks for clarification and stabilization.

During the secondary fermentation phase, the beer is slowly attenuated. It is slowly cooled to 33 to 37 degrees F (1 to 3 degrees C) — or to as low as 30 degrees F (-1 degree C) to settle dusty yeast — to allow the yeast to settle thoroughly and to inhibit the activity of any microorganisms possibly contaminating the ferment.

Because the potential risk of airborne contamination is great during the slow, cold ferment, the beer absolutely must be protected from contact with the atmosphere by being fermented in a closed vessel fitted with a fermentation lock. Contamination is otherwise a major risk at this point; yeast activity is slow, because the beer no longer contains abundant extract and nutrients, yet bacteria may be capable of significant dextrin, protein, or yeast-waste fermentation. Even though the pH is below their optimum, given a warm enough temperature even a few wild yeast or lactic-acid bacteria might rapidly propagate and ruin the beer.

Reproduction by the culture yeast will have entirely ceased during this stage of fermentation; further attenuation relies solely on the metabolic activity of the relatively few remaining yeast cells. It is imperative that conditions be conducive to the continued metabolism of the fermentable extract by these yeast cells and that they not be subjected to temperature shock. If the yeast culture needs regeneration, then an active starter culture or 5 percent kraeusen beer is added.

The duration of the secondary fermentation and the temperature at which it should be conducted are determined by the maltotriose and dextrin content of the post-kraeusen beer. If its reduction in density has naturally slowed and the hydrometer reading is still about one-third the value of the original wort reading, then the beer is rich in dextrins. It should be fermented out in the secondary at 33 to 41 degrees F (l to 5 degrees C), depending on the temperature preferences of the yeast strain, for at least fourteen days. When the post-kraeusen density is much less than one-third the value of the wort density, it indicates that the beer is lacking in dextrins and should undergo a secondary fermentation at 34 to 37 degreesF (1 to 3 degrees C) for not more than ten days before the temperature is reduced for lagering. Lagering times will also be shortened.

Long fermentations often darken the color of the beer. Consequently, when lagers are brewed for paleness, secondary fermentation may be carried out at higher temperatures (36 to 39 degrees F [2 to 4 degrees C], but not above 40 degrees F [5 degrees C]) over the shorter time period.

Since beer for draft need not be brewed for a long shelf life, it may also be fermented at higher temperatures (34 to 41 degrees F [1 to 5 degrees C]) and for a shorter period of time. When the hydrometer reading drops less than .2 °Plato/1 degree of gravity over a twenty-four-hour period and is within .4 °Plato/2 degrees of gravity of its anticipated terminal gravity, it can be assumed that there is just enough yeast and fermentable extract left in solution to support cask carbonation. The beer is racked into a keg or cask.

Lagering

A long, cold, post-fermentive rest is usually employed when the wort is from a decoction mash. It yields a more stable beer with a smoother flavor.

Lagering mellows harsh flavors by the combined effects of the falling rate of yeast metabolism, increased acidity, and low temperatures. Astringent tannins coagulate with haze-forming proteins, precipitating these and other, sulfurous compounds out of solution.

Yeast cells are not usually decomposed during lagering, but the culture becomes progressively dormant as fermentable extract (and to varying extents, glycogen reserves) are depleted. With the decline in available carbohydrates, the yeast reabsorb some of the esters and sulfur compounds from the beer.

Successful lagering requires that the beer not be subjected to temperature fluctuations or oxygenation.

Oxygen in nearly fermented beer causes the irreversible formation of diacetyl and the oxidation of fusel alcohols and lipids. Where lagering temperatures are too warm, aldehyde formation is accelerated.

"Staling" aldehydes give beer stale, papery, cardboardy or sherrylike flavors. When higher temperatures decompose yeast cells, sulfury, stale, and soapy flavors arise.

When the kraeusen tradition is being followed, a lattice of beech chips is laid on the bottom of the secondary fermenter and covered with the nearly fermented, or *ruh*, beer. From 5 to 15 percent new beer at up to 39 degrees F (4 degrees C) is roused into it. Where tank construction permits pressurization, and the tank is fitted with some manner of pressure relief, it is common to lager the beer under .2 to 2 atmospheres (3 to 28 psi) of pressure, after the vessel is purged of the atmosphere in the headspace. This can be accomplished by various pressure-regulating arrangements.

$$C_2H_5OH$$
Ethyl Alcohol
$$\downarrow$$
$$C_2H_4O \longrightarrow H_2O$$
Acetaldehyde

The lagering period is determined by referring back to the mash program, the hydrometer reading of the cooled wort, and the primary fermentation time and temperature. Dextrinous beer from a decoction mash should undergo a secondary fermentation and lagering period of seven to twelve days at 33 to 34 degrees F (1 to 2 degrees C) for each 2 °Plato (SG 1008) of cooled-wort hydrometer reading (OG). Lighter beer, lacking dextrins, is usually held for only three to seven days for each 2 °Plato of the wort density. Very strong, kraeusened beer, on the other hand, may be lagered for six to eight months before it is bottled.

Reducing the temperature to near freezing several days after secondary fermentation falls off reduces lagering time; in fact, the decrease in the solubility of body-forming colloids at 30 to 33 degrees F (-1 to +1 degree C) necessitates a briefer lager period.

Fining

Whether or not the beer is being lagered, fining improves its head retention, lacing, and clarity, and reduces aging times. It precipitates degenerated yeast cells, haze proteins, and tannins out of the beer. Gelatin and isinglass act as fining substances by enveloping suspended particles in their matrix, and gelatin further combines with tannic acid to form an insoluble precipitate. Either brewers' gelatin, unflavored 95-percent-pure gelatin, or isinglass may be used, so long as it is dry, smooth, pale colored, and odor free. Finings spoil if they absorb moisture during storage.

Isinglass finings are made from the shedded air bladders of certain fish. They are even more subject to spoiling than gelatin finings, and have a more limited shelf life. Isinglass works quickly and is generally added to the beer only two or three days before the beer will be racked. Isinglass precipitates lipids and can dramatically improve head retention.

When the beer has fermented out, it is ready for fining. A reducing-sugar analysis should show less than 2 percent. The beer must be colder than 50 degrees F (10 degrees C) for gelatin to react with the ferment; the closer to freezing temperature the beer is, the more efficient the action of gelatin finings will be.

Isinglass finings act more rapidly than gelatin finings do under the same conditions, and far better at warm temperatures. Isinglass can be used at up to 60 degrees F (16 degrees C), although it performs better in colder beer.

Dissolving finings into beer, wort, or water must be intelligently handled so that the finings are completely liquefied. They need to be evenly dispersed into the aged beer in a sanitary fashion. Finings cannot combine with yeast, polyphenols, and albumins unless they come into intimate contact with them. To accomplish this, the finings must be diffused throughout the entire volume of beer.

Where the beer is to be filtered, insoluble polyvinylpyrrolidones, such as Polyclar, and polyamides, such as nylon, can be used to remove polyphenols, especially chill-haze anthocyanogens, by bonding to them. Other media used are diatomaceous earth (kieselguhr) and silica gel. Diatomaceous earth selectively removes particles of a certain and greater size and is the filtering agent most commonly used by small breweries. Silica gel absorbs large polypeptides and proteins, removing them from solution so they cannot combine with polyphenols.

If a strong hop aroma is desired in a lager, liquid hop extract may be added with the gelatin finings, or before other treatment. Even with British ales, hops for strong aroma are never usually added after fining. Hops, and especially extracts, when added with finings, can improve the clarification of beer from a well-mashed and boiled wort by increasing the polyphenols available for coprecipitation with albumin.

If the bottled beer lacks a good foam head or is thin, then the clarifying treatment should be reduced in future batches. Use of particular malts and brewing techniques precludes the need for clarifying.

Clarifying with Beech Chips

Beech or hazelnut chips one-eighth inch thick by one-half inch wide are laid on the bottom of the lagering vessel to form a loosely woven lattice. As the wood absorbs moisture, extract coats the many surfaces of the chips, bonding weak yeast cells to them and thus clearing the beer.

The chips are first soaked and then boiled for twelve to twenty-four hours in a sodium bicarbonate solution (1 1/2 pounds/gallon) before being rinsed. The process is repeated, sometimes substituting bisulfate of lime. Finally, the shavings are rinsed in a cold-hot-cold water cycle. The pH of the last rinse should be neutral, indicating that all of the bicarbonate has been washed from the chips. They may be washed and reused until they crack from age.

Real Terminal Extract

When the aged beer is ready to be bottled, its real-extract content can be determined by boiling off the alcohol from a measured volume of the beer, topping it up to its original volume with distilled water, and gauging its density with a hydrometer. The liquid pressure exerted by the fermented beer (sugar analysis less than 2 percent) is due to unfermentable dextrins, maltotetraose, and soluble nitrogen. Taking a hydrometer reading of a dealcoholized sample is the only means by which the "real extract" may be quantified with absolute accuracy, by removing the "apparent density" effect of alcohol from it.

The amount of unfermentable extract remaining in the finished beer is the direct result of the duration and effectiveness of the proteolytic, alpha-amylase and beta-amylase mash rests, the amount and nature of malt used, the effectiveness of protein/polyphenol bonding in the boil, and the ability of the yeast to ferment maltotriose and isomaltose. Typical bottled lagers have a real density of 3.0 to 5.0 °Plato (SG 1012 to 1020); richer types average 5.5 °Plato (SG 1022) to 6.5 °Plato (SG 1026). Bocks may range even higher. The real density of a fully fermented beer is generally 40 percent greater than its apparent density.

Full-bodied beers should show 45 to 60 percent real attenuation, light beers up to 70 percent. Apparent attenuation is usually 60 to 75 percent in the former case and up to 85 percent in the latter.

Bottling

Naturally carbonated beer must be racked off its sediment into a sterile, closed container and mixed with a quantity of actively fermenting kraeusen beer or priming solution sufficient to produce the desired bottle pressure (see table 23). When corn sugar (dextrose) is used to carbonate the bottled beer, it should be made up into a solution; dry primings are not recommended. High-quality dextrose should be the only sugar employed for bottling.

Whether kraeusen beer or sugar fuels bottle carbonation, measurements need to be exact, and the solution mixed with the aged beer very thoroughly, without splashing, or inconsistent carbonation results. The character of the finished beer is greatly influenced by the degree of carbonation.

Mixing the kraeusen beer or priming solution into the aged beer should not be done in an aerating fashion but should raise a foam head, indicating CO_2 release. This aids in the prevention of oxidation and contamination of the beer at bottling by forming a protective blanket of carbonic gas above the beer and driving some atmosphere from the head space above.

The bottles into which the beer is siphoned must be biologically as well as physically clean. Commercially, bottles are washed with 3 percent caustic soda, rinsed, then sterilized at above 170 degrees F (77 degrees C), drained, and rinsed. Clean bottles may be "pasteurized" by soaking them for at least thirty minutes in clean water at above 140 degrees F (60 degrees C) or placing them wet in an oven at 200 degrees F (93 degrees C) for twenty minutes before they are inverted to dry and be inspected.

Any type of bottle may be used, so long as it can be sealed and can withstand the pressure of bottle fermentation. Carbonation in excess of three atmospheres requires the use of a heavy-gauge bottle. Under carefully controlled conditions, thin-walled, "nonreturnable" bottles are sufficient when brewing lager beer of normal carbonation.

Each bottle should be filled to within at least three-quarters of an inch of the top and be left to rest, loosely capped, for several minutes before the caps are secured. This allows air trapped in the neck space to be driven off by the release of carbonic gas. Oxygen that is not displaced may be scavenged by the yeast, but it is possible that where there is a significant amount of air it may be absorbed into the beer and diminish its stability and mar its flavor. Oxygenation at bottling from splashing the beer or from trapping air in the neck space can be a problem as serious as contamination.

The bottled beer should be held at 50 degrees F (10 degrees C) or above for several days to allow fermentation to be established within the bottle before lowering the temperature. Temperature reduction should be gradual, not exceeding 5 degrees F (3 degrees C) daily. Bottle conditioning should take place away from direct sunlight, and the bottles should not be subjected to major temperature fluctuations.

The beer should be aged in the bottle for an absolute minimum of ten to fourteen days, and preferably thirty days, before serving. Lagered, bottle-conditioned beers usually keep for at least several months. There is an optimum storage period for every beer, when chemical changes within the bottle produce the best taste and aroma, and this should dictate the length of the bottle-aging period.

Imbibing

Handcrafted beers are not usually consumed with the same carelessness as a can of beer at a ball game. They are brewed to be drunk at the right temperature, with discernment and appreciation for the subtler aspects of their character. When bottle-conditioned beer is ready for drinking, it should be carefully poured so that the yeast sediment is not disturbed; a good yeast strain cakes solidly on the bottom of the bottle.

A beer is judged by its flavor, aroma, body, head, color, and clarity. All of these values are subjective, and various standards depend on the type of beer being brewed, the balance of one characteristic against another, and the predisposition and preference of the consumer.

Areas for taste

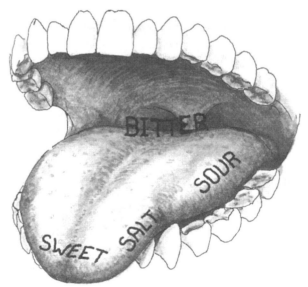

Color, clarity, head formation and retention, and aroma can be assessed before the beer is even tasted. The aroma is usually sampled by swirling the glass and holding it under the nose. The cleanliness and sharpness of the hop bouquet, the balance of roastiness or maltiness, and the intensity and character of fermentation products are the major criteria by which aroma is judged. Aroma may be characterized as being ethereal, aromatic, floral, spicy, malty, roasty, nutty, yeasty, fruity, vegetative, sulfury, buttery, phenolic, solventy, or musty.

Flavor is evaluated by the first sensation, the taste, then by the aftertaste once the beer is swallowed. The body of beer is judged by its fullness and texture, and is closely related to "mouthfeel." The palate fullness of beer is mostly due to the low molecular weight albumins and dextrins carried over to the finished beer, and its viscosity.

Taste perceptions are very generally classified as sweet, sour, bitter, or salty. *Sweetness* is produced by unfermentable sugars and the breakdown of simple dextrins by saliva. *Sourness* (acidity) is directly affected by the pH of the beer, and below pH 4.0 it becomes both noticeable and in most cases, objectionable. *Bitterness* is due to the iso-alpha acids from the hops, and from roasted malt. *Saltiness* is formed by the mineral content of the wort and generally complements bitterness and accentuates dryness.

Because our taste perceptions are highly sophisticated, we can differentiate between far more flavor characteristics than the four basic tastes can account for. Olfactory perceptions greatly affect flavor assessment. Beer flavor is likely to be expressed using olfactory terms such as malty, roasty, caramel, grainy, hoppy, vegetative, medicinal, metallic, sulphury, skunky, burnt, nutty, yeasty, buttery, and fruity.

In the final analysis, the character of the beer should cater to the preferences of the ultimate consumer.

CHAPTER 14

Planning the Brew

Before each brewing cycle is begun, prepare everything that will be needed so the operation may proceed smoothly and without interruption. Make sure that an adequate volume of healthy yeast are available.

Be aware that density and pH readings vary with temperature, so the hotter the mash or wort sample is, the lower the density and pH appear to be. The pH and density should both be gauged at the reference temperature they are calibrated at, whether that is 60 or 68 degrees F (15.56 or 20 degrees C).

Where periods of time are quoted, the longer times generally suit full-bodied, fully lagered beer, or the mashing, sparging, and boiling of difficult malts. The shorter times favor light, quickly maturing beer and beer made from well-modified malt.

If you have not read the whole text, do so before beginning to brew. The procedural outline immediately following is inadequate by itself; the brewer should be familiar with the wider scope of information found elsewhere in the text.

A Note on Mixing

Whenever two substances are to be mixed, mixing should be accomplished gradually to ensure even distribution. When one of the substances is liquid and the other is dry, the dry substance is gradually and evenly moistened before it is flooded with the liquid. Unless this precaution is taken, dry "balls" may become isolated by being encased in paste.

Always mix by the gradual dilution of the smaller amount of any two substances by the larger. Always mix liquids into dry substances, and mix them gradually.

To oxygenate any solution, rouse it splashingly and force air into it, as by pushing downward with an inverted spoon. To rouse a solution without aerating it, very gently rock the vessel or stir slowly, pivoting the spoon at the surface level of the solution to prevent vortexing and splashing.

Planning

Paperwork is probably not your favorite pastime, but predicting a beer's density, color, and flavor and achieving reasonable batch-to-batch consistency are only possible by planning. Use the worksheets in the following tables to plan any recipe and brew, using the text and tables to calculate requirements. Worksheets are provided rather than formulas, because many brewers are not comfortable with algebra.

Due to the cumbersome nature of parenthetically including all the varying units of measurement commonly used by brewers (barrels, hectoliters, liters, kilograms), weight is only given in pounds or avoirdupois ounces, and volume in U.S. gallons. For brewers who use other units of measurement other than pounds, ounces and gallons as given, use the weights and measures in appendix D to convert results to other units of measure. Where EBC color is given in a malt lot analysis, convert it to °Lovibond/SRM by the formula EBC(.375) + .46 = SRM. Where extract potential is given as liter°/kilogram 7 Miag, convert it to percent extract/gallon by the formula L°/kg/385.65 = % extract/gal.

Table 14

Planning
Batch Parameters
1. Beer style: _____
2. Liquor mineral character: _____
3. Wort density (OG), °Plato: _____
4. Beer density (FG), °Plato:_____
5. % ABV (OG-FGx .52): _____
7. Wort color, SRM: _____
6. Hop bitterness, IBU:_____
8. Carbonation, volumes/CO_2: _____
Wort Volume
9. Beer, bottling volume: + _____
10. Kraeusen beer, volume (optional, usually 10%):   - _____
11. Blowoff/racking losses, volume (3–5%):   + _____
12. Wort removed for kraeusen, starters (optional):   + _____
13. Cooled wort, volume required: = _____
14. Wort boil, duration: _____ hours
15. Evaporation rate per hour (.10 av.): .____x 14:____ = _____
Evaporation loss: + _____
16.Wort retained in the hops; oz./hops x .045 gal. (pellets .02): + _____
17. SWEET WORT, VOLUME REQUIRED: = _____

Planning Data

18. Mash rests, temperature and duration: 1 _____ _____

                                              2 _____ _____

                                              3 _____ _____

                                              4 _____ _____

                                              5 _____ _____

19. Mash-liquor temperature: For infusion mashes and mashes doughed-in at 95° F (35°C) or warmer, heat liquor to 10 to 15°F (6 to 8°C) warmer than the rest temperature. For decoction mashes doughed-in cold, dough-in with liquor at 57 to 70°F (14 to 2°C) and then heat liquor to boiling. Use boiling liquor to raise the temperature of the cold mash to the next rest. Volumes of mash to be pulled for each decoction can be predicted by completing this worksheet:

A. Total lb. of malt in mash: _____ x 3.33 = _____

B. Total volume of liquor in mash: _____ x 8.32 = _____

C. Add lines A and B: _____ = _____

D. Temperature of next mash rest: _____°F

E. Temperature of mash before decoction: _____°F

F. Subtract line E from line D. Temperature rise: = _____°F

G. Multiply line C by line F: _____

H. Subtract line E from 212°F: _____°F

I. Divide line G by line H: _____°F

J. Divide line I by line C: _____

K. For a thick mash/thick decoction, multiply line J by 1.25; for a thin mash/thick decoction, multiply line J by 1.4: _____

Line K is the percentage of the mash that should be withdrawn for the decoction.

20. Decoction 1, volume: _____ Rests at: _____°F _____°F _____°F.

      Boil for: _____minutes. Next rest temperature: _____°F.

      Decoction 2, volume: _____ Rests at: _____°F _____°F _____°F.

      Boil for: _____minutes. Next rest temperature: _____°F.

      Decoction 3, volume: _____ Rests at: _____°F _____°F _____°F.

      Boil for: _____minutes. Next rest temperature: _____°F.

21. Sparge liquor temperature (c.170–175°F): _____°F.

22. Cooled wort/pitching temperature: _____

23. Wort aeration method, amount:: _____

24. Yeast strain: _____ Yeast/kraeusen, amount: _____

25. Primary fermentation, maximum temperature: _____

26. Rack to secondary at: _____ °Plato (see table 22)

27. Secondary fermentation, temperature: _____ duration: _____

29. Lagering/aging, temperature: _____ duration: _____

30. Finings, type: _____amount: _____

31. Primings, type: _____amount: _____ (see table 23)

Table 15

Grain Bill

1. Wort volume required (table 14, line 17): _____

2. Wort color desired, homebrew color units: HCU/lb. _____

Convert SRM color to linear HCU color scale. At 1–10°, SRM equals HCU. At more than 10 °SRM, convert to HCU:

SRM:	10.5	11	11.5	12	12.5	13	13.5	14	14.5	15
HCU:	10.8	11.6	12.4	13.3	14.1	14.9	17.7	18.6	20.5	22.4

SRM:	15.5	16	16.5	17	17.5	18	18.5	19	19.5	20
HCU:	24.3	26.2	28.1	30	32.9	35.8	38.8	41.9	45	47.8

3. Multiply line 1 by line 2: TOTAL HCU REQUIRED = _____

4. Wort density (table 14, line 3)_____ divide by 11.47.

(For specific gravity, divide by 46.16) LB. EXTRACT/GAL.: _____

5. Multiply line 1 by line 4: TOTAL LB. OF EXTRACT REQUIRED = _____

Begin formulating any recipe with the specialty malt or adjunct that has the most critical impact on flavor. Follow with specialty malts and adjuncts in diminishing order of effect on flavor, and then color. List each one, and subtract its color and extract contribution from lines 3 and 5. Where no lot analysis is available, skip lines 10, 11, 18, and 19, and use values from table 16, columns 3 and 5 for lines 7, 12, and 20.

SPECIALTY MALT or ADJUNCT _____ Lot number: ____

6. Pounds: _____

7. Color, °L: x_____

8. Multiply line 6 by line 7: HCU COLOR CONTRIBUTION =_____

9. List color contributions, line 8, of all specialty malts and adjuncts as they are accumulated:

_____ + _____ + _____ + _____ =_____
TOTAL HCU COLOR CONTRIBUTION

10. Specialty malt/adjunct, extract potential, DBCG: . _____

11. Moisture content: /1. _____

12. Divide line 10 by line 11: as-is coarse grind extract = . _____

13. Brew-house efficiency (usually .85–.95): x . _____

14. Multiply line 12 by line 13: Extract contribution/lb. = . _____

15. Multiply line 14 by line 6: EXTRACT YIELD = ___ . _____

16. List extract yields, line 15, of all specialty malts and adjuncts as they are accumulated:

_____ + _____ + _____ + _____ = _____

                                                                 TOTAL EXTRACT YIELD

Repeat lines 6 through 16 for each specialty malt or adjunct, then go on to calculating the amount of base malt you will need:

BASE MALT: _____ Lot number: _____

17. Subtract line 16 from line 5: REMAINING EXTRACT REQUIRED = _____

18. Base malt, extract DBCG: _____

19. Base malt, moisture content: /1. _____

20. Divide line 18 by line 19:   as-is coarse grind extract = _____

21. Divide line 17 by line 20:   LB. OF BASE MALT = _____

22. Base malt color, °L: x _____

23. Multiply line 21 by line 22:
                    BASE-MALT COLOR CONTRIBUTION = _____

24. Add line 23 to line 9: TOTAL HCU COLOR CONTRIBUTION = _____

Line 24 should match table 14, line 7.

Table 16

Brew-house Yield from Various Sources

Brew-house yield is the actual extract that can be expected from a given source in a given brewery. It reflects the extract potential of the malt or adjunct and its moisture content, as well as the degree of crushing, the skill of the brewer, and the efficiency of the brew-house equipment.

This table can be used to predict brew-house yield when no grain analysis is available.

Columns 3 and 4 give typical color and extract-potential values for the grains and adjuncts shown in column 1. Column 4, dry basis coarse grind extract (DBCG) reflects the extract potential of grains given a usual brew-house crush, but does not account for the grain's moisture content or the brew-house efficiency; it is the yield at 100 percent brew-house efficiency if the malt were oven-dry.

Grains usually have a moisture content of 2 to 5 percent, and usual brew-house efficiency is 85 to 95 percent. As-is coarse grind (AICG) is the value derived by adjusting the DBCG of grains to reflect the moisture content but not the brew-house efficiency. Column 5 gives the AICG for grains, assuming a moisture content of 4 percent. Columns 7 and 8 are provided for novice brewers to use in simplified recipe formulation. They give the brew-house yield one could expect from average grains processed with reasonably good efficiency (92 percent brew-house efficiency for grains to be mashed, except for infusion-mashed lager and wheat malts, which are given at 90 percent); for kettle adjuncts, extract efficiency is assumed to be 100 percent.

Brew-house Yield from Various Sources

Source	Modification	Color, °L/ASBC (Avg.)	Extract Potential DBCG	AICG	Mash Type	Brewhouse Yield 1Lb./1Gal., 92% °P	SG
Lager malt, 2-row tradit'l	Low	1.4	80.5%	77.4%	Multi-rest	8.2	1033
					Infusion	8.0	1032
Lager malt, 2-row European	Moderate	1.6	80%	76.9%	Multi-rest	8.1	1033
					Infusion	8.0	1032
Lager malt, 2-row American	Full	1.7	79.5%	76.4%	Multi-rest	8.1	1032.5
					Infusion	7.9	1032
Lager malt, 6-row American	Full	1.7	77.5%	74.5%	Multi-rest	7.9	1031.5
					Infusion	7.7	1031
Pale malt, 2-row British	Full	2.4	80%	76.9	Infusion	8.1	1033

Brew-house Yield from Various Sources, continued

Source	Modification	Color, °L/ASBC (Avg.)	Extract Potential DBCG	AICG	Mash Type	Brewhouse Yield 1Lb./1Gal., 92% °P	SG
Diastatic, 6-row	Moderate	1.3	80.5%	77.4%	Infusion	8.2	1033
Wheat malt, Red winter	Full	2.0	82.5%	79.3%	Multi-rest Infusion	8.4 8.2	1034 1033
CaraPils	Sacch'r	3.0	78%	75.0%		7.9	1032
Vienna	Moderate	5.0	80%	76.9%		8.1	1033
Munich	Moderate	9.0	80%	76.9%		8.1	1033
C-30	Sacch'r	30	77%	74.0%		7.8	1031.5
Crystal	Sacch'r	55	77%	74.0%		7.8	1031.5
C-80	Sacch'r	80	76.5%	73.6%		7.8	1031
C-120	Sacch'r	120	76%	73.1%		7.7	1031
Amber	Over	25	77%	74.0%		7.8	1031.5
Brown	Full	55	75%	72.2%		7.6	1030
Chocolate	Low	400	70%	67.3%		7.1	1028.5
Black malt	Low	600	70%	67.3%		7.1	1028.5
Roast barley		450	70.5%	68.8%		7.3	1029
Flaked barley		1.5	60%	57.7%		6.1	1024.5
Flaked wheat		2.0	87%	83.7%		8.8	1035.5
Flaked corn		1.0	88%	84.6%		8.9	1036
Oatmeal		1.0	62%	59.6%		6.3	1025
Rice		0.5	88%	84.6%		8.9	1036

Table 16, continued

Kettle Adjuncts					
Source	Color, °L/ASBC (Avg.)	Extract Potential DBCG	AICG	Brewhouse Yield 1Lb./1Gal., 92% °P	SG
Malt syrup, diastatic	3.0	78%		9.0	1036
Malt syrup, light	5.0	78%		9.0	1036
Malt syrup, amber	10.0	78%		9.0	1036
Malt syrup, dark	15.0	78%		9.0	1036
Malt syrup, wheat	3.0	78%		9.0	1036
DME, light	7.5	97%		11.1	1045
DME, amber	12.5	97%		11.1	1045
DME, dark	18.0	97%		11.21	1045
Malto-dextrin	6.0	92%		10.6	1042.5
Glucose		90%		10.4	1041.5
Sucrose		100%		11.5	1046.2
Honey		76%		8.8	1035
CaraPils	3.0	78%	75.0%	8.6	1034.5
C-30	30	77%	74.0%	8.5	1034
Crystal	55	77%	74.0%	8.5	1034
C-80	80	76.5%	73.6%	8.5	1034
C-120	120	76%	73.1%	8.4	1034
Chocolate	400	70%	67.3%	7.7	1031
Black malt	600	70%	67.3%	7.7	1031
Roast barley	450	70.5%	68.8%	7.9	1032

Table 17

Brewing Liquor, Volume, and Treatment

1. Sweet wort, volume required (table 14, line 17): _____

2. Grain bill, total weight (table 15, lines 6 and 21): _____

3. Multiply line 2 by .165 gal.: Wort retained, spent grains +_____

4. Add line 3 to line 1:LIQUOR REQUIRED, TOTAL VOLUME =_____

5. Mash liquor, per lb./grain (.28–.45 gal./lb.): x_____

6. Multiply line 2 by line 5: MASH LIQUOR, VOLUME =_____

   If line 6 is greater than 45% of line 4, recalculate the amount of mash liquor using a lower volume per pound, but not less than .28 gal. per pound of grain.

7. Subtract line 6 from line 4: SPARGE LIQUOR, VOLUME =_____

   If line 7 is greater than 65% of line 4, reduce it to 65%, and add the difference to the wort after it is in the kettle. Regardless of the volume given on line 7, stop sparging when the mash runoff reaches pH 5.8 or drops to 3.0 °Plato (SG 1012) and add the excess liquor directly to the kettle.

To treat any volume of brewing water:

1. List the ions present in your water source as ppm (mg/L) in column 3.

2. Subtract column 3 from the ppm of ions for the style of beer that you are brewing (column 2).

3. Use the figures in column 5 (ppm of ions per gram of salt) to determine which mineral salts to use and how much to add.

4. Multiply column 5 by column 6; list in column 7. Column 7 should be approximately similar to column 4.

5. Multiply column 7 by the gallons of water you will be treating; list in column 8. Column 8 gives the grams of salts to add.

6. Add columns 3 and 7 to display the final treated-liquor profile in column 9 It is not possible, or necessary, to absolutely duplicate the quoted mineral distribution; approximation is all that is needed, so that column 9 more or less equals the chosen water type from column 2.

Table 17, continued

										- 3	= 4
Brewing Liquor, Volume, and Treatment, continued											
IONS	PIL-SEN	DORT-MUND	MUN-ICH	VIE-NNA	BUR-TON	YRK-SHR	DUB-LIN	LON-DON	EDIN-BRGH	Your Water	Differ-ence
Ca	7	225	75	200	275	100	120	90	120		
Mg	2	40	18	60	40	15	5	5	25		
Na	2	60	2	8	25	25	12	15	55		
SO₄	5	120	10	125	450	65	55	40	140		
HCO₃	15	180	150	120	260	150	125	125	225		
Cl	5	60	2	12	35	30	20	20	65		
HDNS	30	750	250	750	875	275	300	235	350		
TDS	35	1000	275	850	1100	400	350	300	650		

*Calcium chloride, dihydrate (CaCl₂•H₂O)

5					6	7 (5x6)	8 (COL 6	9 (3 + 7)
IONS: 1 GRAM ADDED TO 1 GAL.					X GRAMS	= PPM	X GAL.) =	FINAL LIQUOR
CaSO₄	MgSO₄	NaCl*	CaCl₂	CaCO₃	PER GAL.	ADDED	TREATMENT	PROFILE, PPM
61.5								
			72.					
				106.				
	37.							
		104.						
147.4								
	145.3							
				158.4				
	160.3							
			127.4					
HARDNESS ADDED, ONE GRAM/1 GAL.								
CaSO₄ 153.8								
MgSO₄	92.5							
NaCl		0.					0.	0.
CaCl₂			180.					
CaCO₃				106.				
TDS ADDED, ONE GRAM IN 1 GAL.								
CaSO₄ 208.9								
MgSO₄	182.3							
NaCl		264.2						
CaCl₂			199.4					
CaCO₃				264.2				

Table 18

Hop Rates

To calculate hop additions, refer to the utilization chart following the worksheet. Always calculate the bitterness contribution of anti-boilover, aroma, and flavoring hop additions first, so that the remainder of bitterness required can be adjusted by the kettle hop addition(s):

1. Hop bitterness, IBUs, from table 14, line 6: _____
2. Wort volume in U.S. gallons, from table 14, line 17: _____
3. Multiply line 2 by 3.785 to convert gallons to liters: _____
4. Multiply line 1 by line 3:   TOTAL IBUs REQUIRED = _____

Hops added at start of boil to prevent boil over, usually 1/4 oz. / 5 gal., 3/4 oz./bbl.

Variety: _____ **Boil time, minutes:**   _____
5. % alpha acid, as a whole number (5%=5):   _____
6. Amount by weight, as avoirdupois ounces: OZ. OF HOPSx _____
7. Multiply line 5 by line 6:   AAUs = _____
8. Expected utilization, as IBUs per gallon (chart, below):   _____
9. Multiply line 7 by line 8:   _____
10. Divide line 9 by line 2:   IBUs = _____
11. Subtract line 10 from line 4: REMAINING IBUs REQUIRED = _____

Aroma hops, variety: _____ **Boil, minutes:**   _____
Aromatic oils, % by weight: _____
12. % alpha acid as a whole number (5%=5):   _____
13. Amount by weight, as avoirdupois ounces: OZ. OF HOPS x _____
14. Multiply line 12 by line 13:   AAUs = _____
15. Expected utilization, as IBUs per gallon (chart, below):   _____
16. Multiply line 14 by line 15:   _____
17. Divide line 16 by line 2:   IBUs = _____
18. Subtract line 17 from line 11: REMAINING IBUs REQUIRED = _____

Flavor hops, variety: _____ **Boil, minutes:**   _____
Aromatic oils, % by weight: _____
19. % alpha acid as a whole number (5%=5):_____
20. Amount by weight, as avoirdupois ounces:OZ. OF HOPS x_____
21. Multiply line 19 by line 20:   AAUs = _____
22. Expected utilization, as IBUs per gallon (chart, below):   _____
23. Multiply line 21 by line 22:   _____

Table 18, continued

24. Divide line 23 by line 2:   IBUs = _____
25. Subtract line 24 from line 18: REMAINING IBUs REQUIRED =_____

Kettle hops, variety: _____ **Boil, minutes:**   _____
26. % alpha acid as a whole number (5%=5):   _____
27. Amount by weight, as avoirdupois ounces: OZ. OF HOPS x _____
28. Multiply line 26 by line 27:   AAUs = _____
29. Expected utilization, as IBUs per gallon (chart, below):   _____
30. Multiply line 28 by line 29:   _____
31. Divide line 30 by line 2:   IBUs = _____
32. Subtract line 31 from line 25: REMAINING IBUs REQUIRED =_____

Kettle hops, variety: _____ **Boil, minutes:**   _____
33. Expected utilization, as IBUs per gallon (chart, below): x _____
34. Multiply line 33 by line 2:   =_____
35. Divide line 32 by line 34:   AAUs REQUIRED =_____
36. Hop variety, % alpha acid as a whole number (5%=5): / _____
32. Divide line 35 by line 36:   OZ. OF HOPS =_____

Brew-house Utilization and IBUs of 1 HBU/Gal. for Various Densities/Gravities

Wort Density:	8–12.5 °P SG 1032–50		12.5–16 °P 1050–1065		16–18 °P 1065–1075		18–20.5 °P 1075–1085		20.5–23 °P 1085–1095	
Boil Time, Minutes:	UTL'	IBU	UTL'	IBU	UTL'	IBU	UTL'	IBU	UTL'	IBU
Hops 90	31%	22.5	28%	21	27%	20	26%	19.5	24%	18
Pellets 90	33%	24.5	30%	22.5	28%	21	27%	20	54%	18.5
Hops 60	28%	21	26%	19.5	24%	18	23%	17	21%	15.5
Pellets 60	31%	23	28%	21	26%	19.5	25%	18.5	23%	17
Hops 30	15%	11	14%	10.5	13%	10	13%	10	12%	9
Pellets 30	18%	14	17%	13	16%	11.5	16%	11.5	15%	11
Hops 15	8%	6	8%	6	7%	5	7%	5	7%	5
Pellets 15	12%	9	12%	9	10%	7.5	9%	7	8%	6
Hops 5	5%	3.5	5%	3.5	5%	3.5	4%	3	4%	3
Pellets 5	6%	4.5	6%	4.5	5%	3.5	4%	3	4%	3
Hops 0	5%	3.5	4%	3	4%	3	4%	3	3%	2
Pellets 0	5%	3.5	5%	3.5	4%	3	4%	3	3%	2

Table 19

Brew Log

Date: ___/___/___

Brew number: ____ Beer style: _____ Brand: _____

	Lot #	Weight	HCU	Extract Contribution
Base malt:	_____	_____	_____	_____
Colored	_____	_____	_____	_____
malts	_____	_____	_____	_____
and	_____	_____	_____	_____
adjuncts:	_____	_____	_____	_____

Treated liquor: Volume _____ pH _____ Hardness _____ TDS _____

Yeast strain: _____ Generation #:_____

	Time	Temp	pH	Density	Volume	Iodine	Amount
Mash liquor:		____	____		_____		
Dough-in:	____	____	____		_____		_____
Mash-in:	____	____	____		_____		
Decoction:	____	____			_____		
Protein rest:	____	____	____				
Decoction:	____	____					
Sacch' rest:	____	____	____			_____	
	____	____				_____	
Decoction:	____	____			_____		
Lauter mash:	____	____	____				
Recycle:	____	____					
Runoff start:	____	____					
Sparge liquor:		____	____				
Sparge:	____	____					
Runoff end:	____	____	____	_____		_____	
Kettle top-up:					_____		
Wort boil, start:	___	___	___	_____	_____		_____

Table 19, continued

	Time	Temp	pH	Density	Volume	Iodine	Amount
Hopping:	___						___
	___						___
	___						___
	___						___
Copper finings:	___						___
Cast-out:	___	___	___	___	___		
Volume adjustm':		___	___	___	___		
Chill start:	___						
Chill finish:	___	___	___	___	___		
Pitching:	___						___
Oxygenation:	___						___
Lag end:	___	___	___	___			
Yeast growth:	___						___
		___	___	___			
		___	___	___			
		___	___	___			
Kraeusen end:	___	___	___	___			___
		___	___	___			___
Racking:		___	___	___			
		___	___	___			
Dry hops:	___	___		___			___
Finings:	___	___			___		___
Primings:	___	___		___			___
Bottled:	___	___	___	___	___		

Evaluation: Carbonation ____ Color ____ Clarity ____ Head ____
Lace____ Aroma____ Flavor____ Sweet____ Malty____ Roasty____
Bitter____ Hoppy____Sulphur____ Esters____ Phenols____ Fusels____
DMS____ Diacetyl____Smooth____ Fullness____ Other _____

_____

_____

_____

_____

Recipes

Recipes are for five-gallon "closed" fermentation based upon 90 percent brew-house yield, 15 percent evaporation in the kettle, a two-quart yeast starter, 5 percent kraeusen wort added to the secondary, 5 percent racking losses, and corn sugar for bottle conditioning. There should be 5 1/4 gallons of cooled wort present after boiling, of which three quarts should be bottled; one quart for kraeusening at racking to secondary and two quarts for future yeast culturing. Pitch with a two-quart yeast starter. If you are repitching an active strain, remove less wort, so that five gallons are present after pitching. If you are not going to kraeusen the beer, 5 1/4 gallons should be fermented. Where type 90 hop pellets will be used instead of whole hops, reduce kettle-hop rates by 10 percent.

Pilsener
OG 12 °Plato (SG 1048)
FG 3.5 °Plato (SG 1012)
4.5% alcohol by volume
Color 4.5 °standard reference method
40 international bitterness units
Soft water; treat 7.5 gallons with lactic acid to below pH 7.0
6.5 lb. two-row lager malt
1 lb. Munich malt
.5 lb. CaraPils malt
Doughing-in: 7 quarts of liquor
Mashing-in: 3.5 quarts
Saccharification strike temperature: 153°F (67°C)
Rest temperature maintenance: 1.5 quarts
Sparging: 4.5 gallons
1.25 homebrew bitterness units Saaz hops at start of wort boil
7 HBU Saaz for 45 minutes
2.5 HBU Saaz for 30 minutes
.5 oz. Saaz finishing hops 15 minutes before strike
.5 oz. Saaz aroma hops at strike
Neutral or slightly estery lager yeast, $12 \bullet 10^6$ cells/mL

Dortmunder

OG 13.5 °Plato (SG 1054)

FG 3.2 °Plato (SG 1013)

5.4% ABV

Color 5 °SRM

30 IBU

Very hard, high-sodium water (see table 18), treat 7.75 gallons

6.5 lb. two-row lager malt

1 lb. Munich malt

1.25 lb. CaraPils malt

Doughing-in: 7.5 quarts

Mashing-in: 3.75 quarts

Strike temperature: 150°F (65°C)

Temperature maintenance: 1.5 quarts

Sparging: 4.5 gallons

1.5 HBU Hallertau/Perle hops at start of boil

4.5 HBU Hallertau/Perle hops for 60 minutes

1.5 HBU Hallertau/Perle hops for 30 minutes

.25 oz. Hallertau/Perle hops for 15 minutes

Neutral or slightly estery lager yeast, 12–14•10^6 cells/mL

Vienna

OG 13 °Plato (SG 1052)

FG 3.5 °Plato (SG 1013)

4.8% ABV

Color 11 °SRM

26 IBU

Hard water (see table 19), treat 7.75 gallons

4.5 lb. two-row lager malt

3 lb. Munich malt

.25 lb. CaraPils malt

.5 lb. caramel-30 °L malt

Doughing-in: 8 quarts

.25 lb. crystal-50 malt

Mashing-in: 4 quarts

Strike temperature: 150°F (65°C)

Temperature maintenance: 1.5 quarts

Sparging: 4.25 gallons

1.25 HBU Hallertau/Perle at start of boil

6.0 HBU Hallertau/Perle for 45 minutes

3.0 HBU Hallertau/Perle for 15 minutes

Aromatic lager yeast, $10-12 \bullet 10^6$ cells/mL, 50–55°F (10–13°C)

This recipe can be brewed from 100% Vienna malt (8.25 lb.) for a drier flavor.

Add 1/2 oz. of Hallertau/Perle at strike for a hoppier aroma.

Munich Dark

OG 13.5 °Plato (SG 1054)

FG 4.0 °Plato (SG 1016)

5.0% ABV

Color 16.5 °SRM

25 IBU

Carbonate water (see table 18), treat 8 gallons

4 lb. two-row lager malt

3.5 lb. Munich malt

1 lb. crystal-50 malt

.25 lb. caramel-80 malt

.25 lb. chocolate malt

Doughing-in: 8 quarts

Mashing-in: 5 quarts

Strike temperature: 155°F (68°C)

Temperature maintenance: 1.5 quarts

Sparging: 4.25 gallons

1.5 HBU Hallertau/Perle at start of boil

3.0 HBU Hallertau/Perle for 60 minutes

3.0 HBU Hallertau/Perle for 30 minutes

.25 oz. Hallertau at strike

Neutral lager yeast, $14 \bullet 10^6$ cells/mL

This recipe can be brewed from 100% Munich malt (8.75 lb.).

Munich Light

OG 11.5 °Plato (SG 1046)

FG 3.0 °Plato (SG 1012)

4.4% ABV

Color 5 °SRM

23 IBU

Mildly carbonate water (see table 18), treat 7.5 gal. with lactic acid to below pH 7.0

5 lb. two-row lager malt

1 lb. Munich malt

1.25 lb. CaraPils malt

Doughing-in: 6.5 quarts

Mashing-in: 4.5 quarts

Strike temperature: 153°F (62°C)

Temperature maintenance: 1.75 quarts

Sparging: 4.25 gallons

1.5 HBU Hallertau Kettle at start of boil

3.0 HBU Hallertau for 45 minutes

3.0 HBU Hallertau for 30 minutes

.25 oz. Hallertau at strike

Neutral lager yeast, $12 \cdot 10^6$ cells/mL

Hellesbock

OG 16.5 °Plato (SG 1067)

FG 4.5 °Plato (SG 1018)

6.6% ABV

Color 5 °SRM

25 IBU

Soft or hard water, 8 gallons

9 lb. two-row lager malt

1.5 lb. CaraPils malt

.25 lb. caramel-30 malt

Doughing-in: 9 quarts

Mashing-in: 5 quarts

Strike temperature: 152°F (66°C)

Temperature maintenance: 1.5 quarts

Sparging: 4.5 gallons

1.5 HBU Perle at start of boil

1.5 HBU Perle for 60 minutes

3.0 HBU Perle for 45 minutes

.5 oz. Tettnang for 15 minutes

.25 oz. Tettnang at strike

Neutral lager yeast, 16–18•10^6 cells/mL

Bock

OG 16.5 °Plato (SG 1067)
FG 4.5 °Plato (SG 1018)
6.6% ABV
Color 20 °SRM
25 IBU
Soft or hard water, 8 gallons
7.75 lb. two-row lager malt
1.5 lb. crystal-50 malt
.5 lb. caramel-120 malt
.75 lb. brown malt
.5 lb. chocolate malt
Doughing-in: 9 quarts
Mashing-in: 5 quarts
Strike temperature: 150°F (65°C)
Temperature maintenance: 1.5 quarts
Sparging: 4.25 gallons
1.5 HBU Hallertau at start of boil
3.0 HBU Perle for 60 minutes
4.5 HBU Perle for 15 minutes
.5 oz. Hallertau at strike
Neutral lager yeast, $16-18 \bullet 10^6$ cells/mL

Dopplebock

OG 18.5 °Plato (SG 1075)

FG 4.5 °Plato (SG 1018)

7.3% ABV

Color 16 °SRM

22 IBU

Soft or hard water, 8.25 gallons

7.25 lb. two-row lager malt

3.5 lb. Munich malt

1.5 lb. crystal-50 malt

Doughing-in: 10 quarts

Mashing-in: 5.5 quarts

Strike temperature: 150°F (65°C)

Temperature maintenance: 1.5 quarts

Sparging: 4 gallons

1.5 HBU Perle at start of boil

3.0 HBU Perle for 60 minutes

3.0 HBU Perle for 45 minutes

.5 oz. Perle at strike

Neutral lager yeast, $16-18 \cdot 10^6$ cells/mL

CHAPTER 15

Brewing Procedure

The following is a step-by-step guide to the classic lager brewing process, using a three-vessel brew house (mash-tun, lauter-tun, combination decoction/wort kettle). The same program can be followed using either a two-vessel (combined mash-/lauter-tun) or four-vessel (separate decoction kettle) brew house.

Mash temperatures given are for 122 degree F (50 degrees C) and 153 to 155 degree F (67 to 68 degrees C) rests; 131 degree F (55 degrees C) and 158 to 160 degree F (70 to 71 degrees C) rests can be substituted. With well-modified modern malts (over 36 percent SNR, and especially over 40 percent SNR), peptidase activity during a 122 degree F (50 degrees C) rest risks depleting the wort of body- and head-forming polypeptides. A brief, combined proteolysis and saccharification rest at 131 degrees F (55 degrees C) better suits malts with an SNR of 37 to 40 percent than a 122 degree F (50 degrees

C) rest, and the higher temperatures should be substituted in the decoction program.

For infusion mashing, see appendix B. For step mashing, refer to appendix C.

Malt Examination

. Peel the husk away from the dorsal side of twenty or so kernels of malt to expose the acrospire. Chew another dozen or so kernels. Unless the malt is easily chewed and the acrospire has been uniformly grown to from three-fourths to the full length of the kernel, the malt should be step or decoction mashed. This is also true for base malts that are of questionable enzymatic strength, are high in protein, or that are unevenly malted.

Three-Decoction Mash

Expect a three-decoction mash to take from 3 1/2 to 9 hours. Begin by crushing the amount of malt called for in the recipe. The malt should be weighed, but it may be measured assuming that one pound equals 4.25 cups, U.S. liquid measure.

Doughing-In

Dough-in the crushed malt by sprinkling it with small amounts of brewing liquor at roughly 58 to 70 degrees F (14 to 21 degrees C) until twenty-four to twenty-eight fluid ounces of liquor per pound of malt has been kneaded in. For a thin mash, when brewing light, quickly fermenting beer, thirty-two to forty fluid ounces of water per pound are required.

Hold for fifteen minutes (or for up to thirty minutes for steely or enzyme-poor malt). Mix regularly and thoroughly to distribute moisture evenly throughout the mash. The malt should be uniformly and universally solubilized. Check for successful moisture penetration of the coarser grits and hard ends of the kernels by pulverizing several between the fingers. Make sure there are no dry pockets or balled flour within the mash.

Acid Rest

For each pound of malt doughed-in, bring twelve to fourteen fluid ounces of liquor to a boil. For a thin mash, sixteen to twenty fluid ounces should be boiled. Knead it into the grain to raise the mash temperature evenly to 105 degrees F (40 degrees C). After twenty minutes, check the mash pH; if it is at or below 5.8 (preferably 5.2 to 5.5), proceed with the first decoction.

Otherwise, acidifying measures must be taken before mashing should proceed. The mash acidity can be reduced by adding acidified mash from a lactic-acid mash. To make such a mash, one or two days before brewing, mash-in 5 percent of the malt to 155 degrees F (68 degrees C). Rest for one hour. Cover and cool, undisturbed, down to 125 degrees F (52 degrees C). Knead in a small amount of dry crushed malt (to introduce *Lactobacillus delbrueckii*) and cover. No airspace should be left above the mash; cover the mash by pressing food-wrap down over it to seal it from contact with air.

After twenty-four hours at 95 to 120 degrees F (35 to 49 degrees C), the pH will drop below 5. After two days, it will be below 4.5. A lactic-acid mash is most effective when the brewing water is relatively soft. Five percent acidified mash at pH 4.8 can be expected to reduce a mash at pH 6 to below 5.8. At pH 4.5, it will lower the mash pH to about 5.6.

More commonly, the pH of an overly alkaline mash is corrected by employing a portion of sourmalt or cautiously mixing minute amounts of lactic or phosphoric acid into it until the mash pH drops to 5.5. In future brews, adjust the pH of the liquor, rather than the mash, using proportionally similar treatment.

First Decoction

Pull the heaviest one-third part of the mash to the side of the tun and withdraw it to the decoction kettle. The "heaviest" part of the mash means mash with only enough liquid to fill the spaces between the grains, but not so much as to cover them. The decoction should always be thick, with just enough free liquid to prevent scorching. Return any free-standing liquid that settles above the boiler mash back to the main mash. If the mash itself is thin, however, 40 percent or more of the mash volume may need to be pulled for the decoction, and boiling some free-standing liquid with the decoction is inevitable. Use the "Planning Data" worksheet in table 14 to calculate decoction volumes.

Closely cover the cold settlement in the mash-tun and maintain its temperature as nearly as possible at 95 to 105 degrees F (35 to 40 degrees C).

Heat the decoction to 150 to 158 degrees F (66 to 70 degrees C) in ten minutes (or as rapidly as possible), and hold it there for ten minutes to dextrinize it. Heat it to 167 degrees F (75 degrees C) over five minutes, then bring it to a boil in five to ten minutes while lifting the grain up and away from the bottom of the kettle to prevent scorching. Cover and boil it vigorously for five to ten minutes, the longer time being for steely or enzyme-poor malt.

Protein Rest

Return the darkened decoction to the starchy cold settlement by degrees, while lifting and breaking up the mash, over a period of five or so minutes, to evenly raise the temperature of the whole to 122 degrees F (50 degrees C) or within the range of 118 to 128 degrees F (48 to 53 degrees C). Check the temperature throughout the mash, making sure it is even.

Monitor the mash pH; it should drop to pH 5.2 to 5.3. The usual rest period is only five minutes before the heaviest part of the mash is drawn off for the second decoction.

Second Decoction

Withdraw the heaviest 33 to 45 percent of the mash to the decoction kettle (as before, adjust the decoction volume to reflect consistency). Cover both mashes. Heat the decoction to 150 degrees F (66 degrees C) within ten minutes, then through the alpha-amylase range and to 167 degrees F (75 degrees C) over ten to fifteen minutes, and then to boiling, while lifting and stirring. Boil vigorously for five minutes, or for up to twenty minutes for very steely malts, stirring frequently.

Saccharification/Dextrinization Rest

Return the decoction to the rest mash evenly, so as not to scald any portion of the rest mash. Temperature dispersal should be absolutely uniform. The saccharification temperature, usually 153 to 155 degrees F (67 to 68 degrees C), should be reached within five minutes when the beer is to be fully lagered. Returning the decoction gradually, over a period of fifteen to thirty minutes, to a rest temperature of 149 to 151 degrees F (65 to 66 degrees C) favors maltose production when brewing lighter, drier beers.

Hold the saccharification temperature for fifteen minutes; the mash will darken in color.

Test for successful starch conversion. Float tincture of iodine (.02N solution; usual medicine-cabinet variety) drop by drop above a small sample of the mash in a porcelain dish. Check the color at the interface of the iodine and the mash. Continue mashing until there is no color change, or for a sweet, full beer until the reaction is only very faintly mahogany reddish. Disregard discoloration caused by husk particles; it in no way indicates lack of conversion.

Use caution. Iodine is a poison. Do not let it inadvertently taint the mash. Discard all samples and rinse the dish and any equipment that has been contacted by the iodine.

The precise saccharification rest temperature should be maintained. This may be simply accomplished by infusing small amounts of boiling liquor into the mash. Because the mash liquid absorbs a great deal of extract during saccharification, it may become too thick to satisfactorily settle into a well-stratified filter bed. These temperature-maintenance infusions serve to improve filtering of a thick mash and are generally necessary when less than 1 1/2 quarts of liquor have been used to mash-in each pound of malt. Thinning a thick mash assures that its density does not interfere with filter bed settlement in the lauter-tun.

Lauter Decoction

When starch end point has been verified, rack off the very thinnest 40 to 50 percent of the mash. Bring it to a boil. Boil vigorously while stirring for five minutes.

Final Rest

Remix the mashes thoroughly, evenly raising the temperature to near 170 degrees F (77 degrees C). Rouse and mix the mash for five minutes while maintaining the lauter rest temperature to force insoluble mash particles into a temporary suspension. This causes a clearly stratified settlement of first the hulls, then endosperm particles, and finally the protein gums to be formed in the lauter-tun.

Single-Decoction Mash

Part 1. Using malt of 33 to 36 percent SNR, mash-in the malt with thirty-six to forty-eight fluid ounces of liquor at 130 to 135 degrees F (55 to 58 degrees C) per pound of malt (the colder the malt is, and the less the volume of liquor being used, the hotter the liquor temperature will need to be).

After five minutes, pull the heaviest 33 to 45 percent of the mash volume and heat it to 150 degrees F

(66 degrees C) in ten minutes, to 167 degrees F (75 degrees C) in ten to fifteen minutes, and then to boiling. Boil for five minutes.

Return the decoction to the rest mash for a 153 to 155 degree F (67 to 68 degrees C) saccharification rest. After fifteen minutes, begin testing for starch conversion. Maintain the temperature by infusing with boiling water as necessary. Depending on the fullness desired for the beer, conversion at the conclusion of the rest should give a negative to red-mahogany iodine reaction.

As soon as the desired iodine reaction is achieved, add boiling liquor to bring the dilution up to forty-eight fluid ounces per pound of malt and the mash temperature to near 170 degrees F (77 degrees C), then transfer the goods to the lauter-tun as quickly but as gently as possible.

Part 2. Using malt of 37 to 40 percent SNR, mash-in the malt with thirty-six to forty-eight fluid ounces of liquor at 140 to 145 degrees F (60 to 63 degrees C) per pound of malt for a 131 degree F (55 degrees C) protein/saccharification rest temperature.

After five minutes, pull the heaviest 33 to 45 percent of the mash volume and heat it to 158 degrees F (70 degrees C), rest it for ten minutes, and then heat it to boiling. Boil the decoction for five minutes.

Return the decoction to the rest mash for a 158 to 160 degree F (70 to 71 degrees C) dextrin rest. After fifteen minutes, begin testing for starch conversion. Maintain the temperature by infusing with boiling water as necessary.

As soon as the desired iodine reaction is achieved, add boiling liquor to bring the dilution up to forty-eight fluid ounces per pound of malt and the mash temperature to near 170 degrees F (77 degrees C), then transfer the goods to the lauter-tun as quickly but as gently as possible.

Sparging/Filtering

Fill the lauter-tun to one-half inch above the false bottom with sparge liquor. Give the mash one final stirring and transfer it to the lauter-tun. Maintain the temperature at as close to 170 degrees F (77 degrees C) as possible for ten to fifteen minutes while the filter bed forms undisturbed.

In the meantime, bring the appropriate volume of sparging water to 170 to 175 degrees F (77 to 80 degrees C).

After the malt particles (husks, acrospires, and any starch granules) have settled and the liquid above the protein coagulum has cleared, set the filter bed and flush debris from the space below the false bottom by opening the draincock until a steady trickle of runoff forms. Drain the mash until the protein has settled and the clear liquid above it lies only about one-half inch deep. Smooth and level the mash surface. Maintain the liquid depth above the mash by returning the runoff to the lauter-tun until the wort runs clear. When all the cloudy runoff has been recycled, begin sparging. Open the sparging-water tap, matching the trickle of 170 to 175 degree F (77 to 80 degrees C) liquor to the runoff rate. Carefully balance the inlet and outlet flow-rates so that the liquid level above the mash is not disturbed.

Manipulate the flow, balancing the sparging rate to the runoff, so that the filtering takes 1 1/2 hours to complete. Divide the amount of sweet wort to be collected by ninety (minutes) to define the required runoff flow per minute. (Six-row barley with a high husk content may be run off in as little as thirty minutes.) During a slow filtering, carefully rake the lauter mash to within six inches of the false bottom to close vertical channels and improve extract yield. Smooth the mash surface as any cracks appear, and keep the liquid level above the surface of the mash, but not more than two inches deep. Immediately begin heating the wort collecting in the copper to above

170 degrees F (77 degrees C). Sparge until the density of the runoff drops below 3.0 °Plato (SG 1012). Discontinue sparging and allow the mash to drain.

Boiling the Wort

Add a small portion of loosely broken-up boiling hops, to reduce surface tension and the likelihood of boil over, to the sweet wort as soon as all of the extract has been collected.

Check the wort acidity. It should be pH 5.2 to 5.5. If it is below pH 5.0, protein precipitation will be retarded;

Lauter-tun

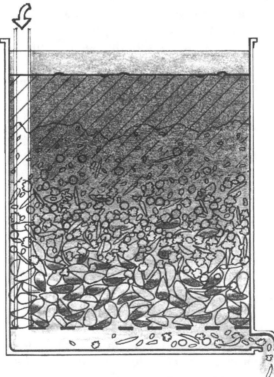

adjust with a carbonate salt if necessary. Measure and record the density, corrected to 68 degrees F (20 degrees C), or 60 degrees F (15.56 degrees C) if that is the temperature that the hydrometer is calibrated at.

Hot Break

Periodically examine samples of the boiling wort to assess protein/polyphenol flocculation. Remove a glassful of wort. The tannin/proteins that mist the wort early in the boil should coagulate into a much smaller number of larger flakes, one-eighth inch long or longer, as the boil progresses. Check the pH. It should drop during the boil to 5.0 to 5.3.

Cold Break

As the end of the boiling period draws near, the flocks in the hot sample should readily precipitate and leave the wort clear. Force-cool the sample; it should slowly cloud again as it cools. This cold break should then settle out from the wort, leaving it clear and bright. If a clean break cannot be established during the designated boil, and the intensity of the boil and wort pH are acceptable, then either the malt or the brew-house program is unacceptable. The finished beer will likely be cloudy and astringent. Do not, however, exceed quoted boiling times, especially when brewing light beers. Longer boiling is not likely to improve clarification unless it is subsequent to a significant correction of the boiling intensity or pH, and will increase the bitterness and discoloration of the wort.

Finishing Hops

Add finishing hops ten to fifteen minutes before the end of the boil, as the heat is shut off, or when the wort is being run from the kettle. The later the addition, the less the bitterness contribution, but the greater the flavor and aroma.

At kettle knock-out, turn off the heat. Check and record the wort acidity. The pH should be 5.0 to 5.3. Measure the wort volume and density, corrected to 68 degrees F (20 degrees C), or 60 degrees F (15.56 degrees C) if that is the temperature that the hydrometer is calibrated at. Correct the volume to the 68 degree F (20 degrees C) reference temperature by multiplying by .96, or by .958 for 60 degrees F (15.56 degrees C). If the density is high, and the volume is less than required, restore it with cold water. Determine extract efficiency using the table below.

Table 20

Brew-house Efficiency	
1. Volume of wort, in gallons, at 68°F (20°C):	1. _____
2. °Plato of wort, at 68°F:	2. _____
3. Multiply line 1 by line 2:	3. _____
4. Divide line 3 by table 15, line 1 (anticipated wort volume):	4. _____
5. Planned °Plato of wort, from table 14, line 3:	5. _____
6. Divide line 4 by line 5:	6. _____
7. Multiply line 6 by line 13, table 15:	7. _____

Line 7 is the actual brew-house efficiency. Use this efficiency in future brews to more accurately predict original gravity.

Filtering and Cooling the Wort

If the wort will be run through a hop back, lay a bed of fresh hops over the false bottom to form a filter bed. If the wort will either be siphoned from the kettle or run off from a side tap, or if the wort was hopped with pellets, whirlpool the wort with a paddle for two to three minutes so that the hops and trub form a cone at the center of the kettle's bottom. Allow the hops and trub to settle for ten to fifteen minutes.

Force-cooling the wort quickly (fifteen to forty-five minutes) gives a more complete break than slow or passive attempering, and reduces DMS development. The colder the temperature the wort is chilled to, the better the cold break will be. A wort chiller should always be used. Where an immersible chilling coil is employed, the wort is cooled before it is run off from the kettle. For lager beers, cooling to at least 39 degrees F (4 degrees C) will reduce the chances of chill haze in the finished beer.

Run off the wort, slowly at first, returning it to the kettle without splashing, until the runoff clears. If the wort is being siphoned from the kettle, keep the pick-up close to the side of the kettle and away from the bottom of the kettle until near the end of the run. Run the wort into the fermenter or settling tank.

If the wort is being run into a closed settling tank, allow it to rest undisturbed for several (two to sixteen) hours before racking it off its trub to the fermenter. Expect the wort to precipitate a cold-break sediment equal to 10 to 20 percent of the hot-break trub. If the wort is being run directly to the fermenter, let it splash in freely to aerate it. Keep the cooled wort covered, and work using as sanitary a method and in as clean, dry, and draft-free an environment as possible.

Decant any wort in excess of the amount needed for primary fermentation into sterile containers. Reheat to boiling, cap and refrigerate until needed.

Pitching the Yeast

Most lagers require the pitching of .40 to .66 fluid ounces (8.5 to 14 grams) of thick, pasty yeast per gallon of wort to be pitched, for a rate of 10 to 15 million cells per milliliter. Up to 1 fluid ounce (21 grams) of yeast may be required to ferment a gallon of wort at greater than 15 °Plato (SG 1061).

Table 21

Calculating Pitching Volume

If the culture vessel is not graduated, the volume of the yeast culture, in fluid ounces, can be measured by the formula $\dfrac{(\pi r''_2)h''}{1.8046}$

1. Diameter of yeast-culture container: $d'' = $ _____

2. Divide line 1 by 2 (r=d/2): $r'' = $ _____

3. Multiply line 2 by itself: $r''_2 = $ _____

4. Multiply line 3 by 3.1416: $\pi r''_2 = $ _____

5. Multiply line 4 by the thickness (depth, in inches) of the yeast sediment: $(\pi r''_2)h'' = $ _____

6. Divide line 5 by 1.8046: $\dfrac{(\pi r''_2)h''}{1.8046} = $ _____

Line 6 gives the fluid ounces of yeast sediment in the starter vessel.

Shake the starter vessel to mix the yeast sediment into a milky solution. Pitch only the amount of yeast necessary to ensure rapid initial fermentation. Any remainder may be frozen, or covered with fresh wort, then capped with an airlock and refrigerated, for use later in the brewing cycle or for subsequent brewings.

Kraeusening

When kraeusening, "new" beer equal to 10 percent of the primary fermenting volume at up to 5 degrees F (3 degrees C) above pitching temperature is used to introduce active yeast for fermentation. Kraeusening produces strong initial fermentation.

Yeast Starter

A yeast starter is the equivalent of kraeusen beer, but made up from a yeast culture roused into ten times its volume of wort. The ten-to-one dilution is repeated each time strong fermentation becomes evident until the starter is at pitching strength (5 to 10 percent of the volume it will be pitched into). Yeast starters, like kraeusening, promote stronger and faster fermentation starts and blanket the ferment with CO_2 much sooner than does pitching yeast sediment.

Yeast starters should be made up one to two days before brewing, from sterile wort and 10 to 20 percent of the pitching volume of yeast. The wort may be from bottled wort saved from a previous brewing, or may be made up in a small brewing to resemble the wort that will be pitched. If the yeast can be aerated, oxygenate it for several hours before pitching to strengthen the culture and reduce the lag phase.

Pitch the yeast as the wort runs into the fermenter. Allow the wort to splash into the fermenter and rouse it splashingly and thoroughly. Fill the fermenter and fit the airlock (blowoff) to it. The temperature at pitching should usually be 42 to 50 degrees F (6 to 10 degrees C). A low initial temperature will produce a beer with less esters and fusel alcohols. To encourage growth, the yeast can be oxygenated by trickling sterile air or oxygen up through the wort for up to an hour after pitching.

Primary Fermentation

Primary fermentation takes five to fourteen days. Temperatures quoted are for full-bodied, dextrin-rich lagers above 10 °Plato (SG 1040) that are to be fully lagered. For maltose-rich wort to be fermented in less time, add 6 to 8 degrees F (3 to 4 degrees C) to the temperature. Do not, however, exceed 60 degrees F (16 degrees C) during primary fermentation and 50 degrees F (10 degrees C) during secondary fermentation if at all possible. Keep the beer out of direct sunlight and avoid drafts and temperature fluctuations.

Check and record the temperature, density, pH, and yeast-cell count of the beer while it is fermenting and lagering only if it can be done conveniently and without any risk of contaminating the beer.

Table 22

Primary Fermentation Temperature/Time Guideline		
Temperature		**Duration**
50–55°F	(10–13°C)	5–8 days
48–50°F	(9–10°C)	6–10 days
41–48°F	(5–9°C)	7–14 days

Every yeast strain has a temperature optimum, where it ferments well and gives the desired fermentation character. Quoted primary and secondary fermentation temperatures should be adjusted to suit the specific requirements of any particular yeast strain.

Hold the pitched wort, covered and fitted with a fermentation lock, at an ambient temperature of 45 to 50 degrees F (7 to 10 degrees C).

A foam wreath forming at the sides of the fermenter indicates that the lag phase is ending. A light shone on the surface reveals active carbonic gas release.

Low Kraeusen

Six to thirty-six hours after pitching, the foam migrates to the center of the beer surface. The temperature should begin rising. Extract should drop approximately .5 °Plato (SG 1002), and the pH should drop noticeably. The foam cover becomes tightly knit. A light shone on the beer reveals even more CO_2 release and a milky turbidity, indicative of the amount of yeast in suspension.

Carboy with Blowoff and Airlock

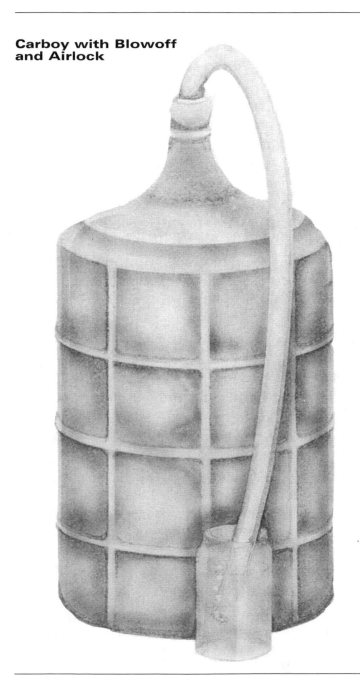

High Kraeusen

Two to four days after pitching, the foam rises up to form looser-knit, cream-colored "rocky heads." When the temperature of the ferment reaches the maximum recommended for the yeast strain, or 55 degrees F (12 degrees C), attemper the fermenter so that the temperature of the fermenting beer does not rise further. The liquid pressure should fall by .75 to 2 °Plato (SG 1003 to 1008) daily. The pH should drop to about 4.5.

Post Kraeusen

Six to fourteen days (six to ten days is usual) after pitching, the foam head begins to diminish as CO_2 production falls off. Extract reduction should slow dramatically, and with a reasonably flocculant yeast strain the cell count will drop below ten million cells per milliliter.

If a diacetyl rest is being employed, force the temperature of the post-kraeusen ferment to rise to 55 to 60 degrees F (13 to 16 degrees C). After two days, lower the ambient temperature again, bringing the beer down to 38 to 40 degrees F (3 to 4 degrees C) at 3 to 5 degrees F (1 to 3 degrees C) per day.

When the extract drop slows to 0.5 °Plato (SG 1002) over twenty-four hours, the head will have completely fallen. Rack the beer into a secondary fermenter/lagering vessel. The beer should be clear and bright. If the yeast does not seem to have largely settled out and still clouds the beer, then the yeast strain is dusty or mutated, the beer may ferment past end point, and it will probably need to be fined.

Make a hydrometer reading of the sample and record it. For beers from worts of 10 to 15 °Plato (SG 1040 to 1060), it should be roughly 30 to 40 percent of what the wort density (OG) was, or 1 to 2 °Plato (SG 1004 to 1008) above the expected final density (FG). Testing with

Dextrocheck (reducing-sugar indicator) should show less than 5 percent reducing sugar. Check and record the pH; it should not have dropped much below pH 4.5.

Secondary Fermentation

Clean and sterilize the lagering vessel, preferably rinsing it with sterile, boiled water. Carefully rack the beer in the primary fermenter off of its settlement into the closed lagering vessel. Take care not to carry along any of the sedimented yeast or trub; cease racking when the runoff becomes the least bit cloudy.

Run the beer into the lagering vessel as quickly as possible, absolutely avoiding splashing. Only enough head space to allow for mild foaming should be left above the nearly fermented beer; if necessary restore the volume by topping-up the fermenter with sterile water. Kraeusen beer should be added to produce the smoothest possible beer. Kraeusening generally reduces diacetyl, corrects poor primary-fermentation yeast performance, entrains CO_2 in the beer, and gives fuller, mellower flavors.

Seed yeast for starters and culturing should be collected from the primary-fermenter yeast cake.

Fit the fermenter with a fermentation lock. If the hydrometer reading at racking is one-third the density of the original gravity or greater, ferment for seven to twenty-one days, reducing the ambient temperature from 38 to 40 degrees F (3 to 4 degrees C) down to 33 to 37 degrees F (1 to 3 degrees C) when carbon dioxide production falls off. If the reading is much less than one-third of the original hydrometer reading, the beer lacks slowly fermenting dextrins and should nearly ferment out in seven to ten days before the temperature is reduced for lagering.

Beer that will not be lagered is usually held in a secondary fermenter for only one to two weeks, and is fermented down to the terminal extract value before being chilled to clarify and sediment it in preparation for packaging.

Lagering

Lager tradition calls for seven to twelve days secondary fermentation and lagering per each 2 °Plato (SG 1008) of the original wort hydrometer reading, with the beer temperature falling to as close to 33 to 36 degrees F (1 to 2 degrees C) as possible. The above notwithstanding, if the hydrometer reading at racking was much less than one-third the value of the wort reading (OG), the beer should not be secondary fermented/lagered for more than one week for each 2 °Plato of the wort reading; four or five days per each °Plato is usual. Lowering the temperature to 30 to 33 degrees F (-1 to 1 degree C) immediately after secondary fermentation reduces lagering times.

Beer that will be bottle-conditioned is lagered at atmospheric pressure. Lagering may be carried out under pressure, but only if the lagering vessel is able to be safely pressurized, is fitted with a pressure-relief valve, and the beer will not be bottle-conditioned. *Do not attempt to lager under pressure in a glass carboy.* Use only a Cornelius keg or the like fitted with a pressure-relief valve. The vessel should be closed when the beer is .2 to .5 °Plato (SG 1001 to 1002) above the anticipated terminal gravity.

Fermentation is complete when the hydrometer reading is at or near the terminal extract value and no drop or visible activity has been experienced in the last five days. A reducing-sugar analysis should show less than 2 percent, indicating that the beer has fermented out.

If the beer is to be fined, prepare the finings. For fining with gelatin, measure out one gram (one-eighth teaspoon) of 95 percent pure gelatin and two fluid ounces (sixty milliliters) of cold water or beer per gallon of beer to be fined. Cover the solution and let the gelatin hydrate for one hour.

Gently heat the solution to 150 to 160 degrees F (65 to 70 degrees C) to dissolve the gelatin; do not let it come to a boil. Do not let it cool below 120 degrees F (50 degrees C) before thoroughly mixing the hot solution into the aged beer as a stream, by stirring, or by rocking the lager vessel for two to three minutes, without aerating the beer. Allow the beer to rest undisturbed for seven to fourteen days at below 50 degrees F (10 degrees C) before racking for bottling.

Prepare isinglass finings by measuring out one-half gram of the finings and four fluid ounces (120 milliliters) of sterile beer or water for each gallon of beer to be fined (for batches of more than one barrel, use five grams of isinglass in .15 gallons, per barrel of beer). Check the pH; reduce the acidity to pH 2.5 to 3.0 with phosphoric acid if necessary. Closely cover the finings while they undergo acid hydrolysis at 55 to 65 degrees F (12 to 18 degrees C) for twenty-four to thirty-six hours. Mix thoroughly into the aged beer.

Isinglass will clear the beer within twenty-four to seventy-two hours. The beer temperature should be held stable or be let rise slightly until it is racked.

Dry hops or hop extract can added either anytime before the finings or with them, but they are not usually added afterward.

Bottling

The ruh beer is usually quietly racked off of its sediment to a third vessel for mixing with the priming solution, whether that be priming sugars, wort, or kraeusen beer. Refer to table 23 for guidelines for the amounts of each to add for a desired level of bottle carbonation.

Table 23

Bottle Priming							
For Bottle Pressure* At: 50°F 32°F 40°F 60°F atmospheres				Approximate: Oz. Dextrose/Gal.	Fl. Oz. Kraeusen/Wort/Gal 10°P 12°P 14°P		
2	1.2	1.5	2.5	1.2	13.5	11	9.5
2.5	1.5	1.9	3.2	1.5	17	14	12
3	1.9	2.35	3.8	1.8	20.5	17	14.5
3.5	2.3	2.8	4.4	2.1	24	20	17

*At sea level. For elevations other than sea level, reduce bottle priming by approximately 3.3% for each 1,000' of elevation. 50°F is the standard temperature at which bottle pressure is gauged.

Bottling should take place in a clean, dry area that is free from drafts. Mix the carefully measured priming solution into the ruh beer without splashing, rousing it for several minutes to ensure uniform dispersal and to induce carbon dioxide to release from and blanket the beer.

Inspect the bottles. Reject any with chipped rims or residue deposits. Wash in warm water, using cleansing solution only if necessary. Thoroughly brush the inside surfaces. Sterilize bottles in a dishwasher on the sanitizer cycle, with live steam by stacking wet bottles in an oven and heating them to 200 degrees F (93 degrees C), in a .2 percent chlorine bath, or in a water bath at above 170 degrees F (77 degrees C). Invert the bottles on clean paper towels to drain.

Carefully dispense the primed beer into the sanitized bottles, filling them at least to within three-fourths of an inch of the rim. Loosely cover the bottles for several minutes to allow carbon-dioxide release to drive off oxygen in the head space before securing the caps and inverting the bottles to disclose leakage.

Hold at 50 to 65 degrees F (10 to 18 degrees C) for fourteen to twenty-one days before beginning to reduce

Soda Keg and Filtering System

Soda Keg

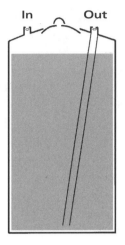

Soda Keg and Filter

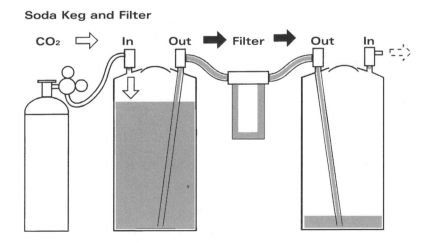

the temperature to 32 to 45 degrees F (0 to 7 degrees C) for conditioning and storage. Do not subject the bottled beer to drafts or temperature fluctuations.

Draft Beer

Clean the keg in the same way you would clean bottles; if the keg is wooden, check its pitch or paraffin surfacing for cracks or deterioration, and melt out the old wax and reline as necessary. Usually beer for draft is drawn into the keg with just less than 1 percent fermentable extract left in it to provide carbonation for cask conditioning. Otherwise, add kraeusen beer or priming solution in sufficient quantity to produce 1.5 atmospheres (20 psi) pressure at 50 degrees F (10 degrees C). Fill the keg to within two inches of the bung hole and rouse thoroughly at priming to induce a mad condition. After several minutes, drive in the bung with a rubber or wooden mallet. Condition for ten to fourteen days at 50 to 65 degrees F (10 to 18 degrees C) before tapping.

A CO_2 source may be used to carbonate the beer. At its simplest, this may be accomplished by applying CO_2 pressure to the keg, with the regulator set for the pressure (psi) called for in the "Volumes of CO_2" table found in appendix D, and shaking the keg several times over a fifteen-minute period, until the flow of CO_2 upon shaking falls off.

Troubleshooting

Mash

Balled starch in mash: Poorly handled doughing-in of the crushed malt; malt too finely crushed.

Mash pH too high: Brewing water overly alkaline; liquor for pale beer not acidified, poor quality malt. Correct by adding acid or mineral salt.

Mash pH too low: Brewing water overly acidic; lactic-acid- or acetic-acid-bacteria-spoiled malt. Correct pH with alkaline mineral salts.

Mash doesn't saccharify: Lack of diastatic enzymes in mash, either destroyed at malting or by mash temperatures above 160 degrees F (71 degrees C); inappropriate pH. Add crushed diasatic malt and continue mashing; check pH. As a last resort, add diastatic enzyme preparation.

Set mash: Poorly converted mash; malt poorly doughed-in; malt too finely crushed; mash poorly stirred up before filtering; too fast a runoff rate. In most cases, correct by thoroughly stirring up the mash and allowing it to resettle; cut the mash to within six inches of the bottom to reopen channels of extract flow in the mash. Press hot water up from under the false bottom. Reduce runoff/sparging rate.

Wort

Low extract: Not enough malt used; poor sparging efficiency; insufficient crushing; balled starch from poorly handled doughing-in; wrong mash pH; insufficient mash enzyme activity. Check for unconverted starch by making an iodine test of a wort sample. Continue brewing the same volume at the lower density.

Poor kettle break: Flocks do not sediment; excessive protein decomposition during malting or mashing; wort agitation insufficient; temperature too low; improper pH; too few hop tannins in the boil; poor quality malt. Increase heat and wort movement. Check pH and hop rate; correct if necessary. If the wort clears but throws very little sediment, then malting or mashing protein digestion may have been overdone.

Poor cold break: Wort cooled too slowly; improper pH; wort lacks tannins; excessive protein digestion. Cool to below 32 degrees F (0 degrees C) to encourage sedimentation.

Wort tastes sour: Wort pH too low; coliform, acetic, or lactic-acid bacteria contamination. Check pH; heat wort to

above 140 degrees F (60 degrees C) and re-cool; pitch quickly. Sourness may diminish with aging or be masked by adding burnt malt, finishing hops, or calcium carbonate.
Sour or vinegar taste/smell: Acetic acid bacteria. As above.

Fermentation

Insufficient lag phase: Wort insufficiently aerated; too much trub carried into ferment; temperature too high. Ferment has strong solvent and fruity aroma. Irreversible.

Excessive lag phase: Too little yeast pitched; yeast weak, degenerated, poisoned, or shocked by temperature change; wort extract too low; inappropriate pH; wort too cold; inadequate oxygenation of wort. Rouse in new yeast. Correct temperature to suit yeast strain.

Sluggish fermentation: Weak or inappropriate yeast strain; yeast degenerated, poisoned, or shocked by temperature change; fermentation temperature too cold; iron, chlorine, or nitrates in the water supply; low wort extract; wort lacking in readily fermentable sugars or soluble nitrogen. Establish correct temperature and pH; repitch.

Spotty low-kraeusen head, unable to support trub: Weak yeast; temperature too low; wort inadequately hopped; deteriorated hops. Raise fermentation temperature; rouse in new yeast.

Fermentation ceases before high kraeusen: Temperature too cold; extract too low or from wort lacking readily fermentable sugars or yeast nutrients. Yeast strain mutated by exposure to too much glucose (catabolic repression) or lack of oxygen (petite mutants). Establish correct temperature; repitch.

Yeast break, head falls prematurely: Temperature lowered prematurely; mutated yeast strain cannot ferment maltotriose; too fast a pH drop in the ferment (bacterial contamination); inadequate extract. Establish correct temperature, pH; repitch.

Poor yeast flocculation; yeast do not settle; porous sediment: Dusty yeast strain; wild yeast contamination; inappropriate pH; temperature too high. Reduce temperatures. Fine the aged beer.

Haze in beer after high kraeusen: Insufficient protein reduction during mashing; inadequate boil; wild yeast contamination; dusty yeast pitched. Reduce temperature before racking and during lagering; fine; as last resort treat with papain or similar proteolytic-enzyme extract.

Yeast floats to surface after high kraeusen: Fermentation contaminated by wild yeast; culture yeast degenerated; brewing water too soft; sudden temperature rise; pH too high. Skim. Degenerated yeast have an unpleasant smell; when yeast performance is poor or abnormal, sample the bouquet.

Bottled or Kegged Beer

Roughness: Abnormal water composition; insufficient boil; excess tannin; excessive/alkaline sparging; insufficient kettle evaporation; hot-side oxygenation.

Fruity aroma/flavor: From esters, higher alcohols, acetates of higher alcohols. The consequence of underoxygenation of the pitching yeast, too high a fermentation temperature, too low a pitching rate, or a deteriorated yeast strain. When unpleasant and combined with vegetal aroma and flavor, from coliform contamination of the wort or yeast culture.

Celery odor: H. protea contamination, probably from tainted yeast culture. Irreversible.

Bitter-vegetable taste: From deteriorated hops (oxidized beta-acids).

Buttery (diacetyl) flavor: Where strong and like rancid butter, from lactic-acid bacteria, significantly *Pediococcus*. Slight or pleasant diacetyl flavor more often from low pitching rate, underoxygenation, petite mutants in culture yeast, or characteristic of the yeast strain; beer racked off its primary sediment too early or oxidized in the secondary.

Cardboardy taste: Oxidation; from too much air in bottle headspace; trub carried into/lipids oxidized in the ferment; warm storage, mishandling; insufficient boil; when with poor head retention, from lipids in the beer.

Sulfury aroma/flavor: Too low a fermentation temperature; poor rinsing of sulfur-based sterilant; from wild yeast, *Zymomonas* or coliform bacteria. May be characteristic of yeast strain, or from autolization of sedimented yeast. Except when from bacterial contamination, may be reduced by aging or by scrubbing with carbon dioxide. Corny aroma and flavor is characteristic of dimethyl sulphide (DMS), from poorly malted barley, especially six-row; high-moisture malt; hot wort not chilled quickly enough; coliform bacteria contamination.

Sour taste: From too low a pH; from acetic- or lactic-acid bacterial contamination.

Medicinal aroma/flavor: From wild yeast or bacteria; chlorine in the ferment; plastic contamination; excess of phenolic material from oversparging or weak wort boil. Accentuated by high fermentation temperatures.

Astringency: Excessive sparging, hot-side aeration, yeast autolization, excessive or oxidized trub.

Skunky odor: Beer light-struck. Avoid direct sunlight during brewing and in package; reduce headspace.

Rotten egg odor: Hydrogen sulphide; yeast-strain characteristic; fermentation by wild yeast; weak fermentation; in bottled or kegged beer, may be from contamination by *Zymomonas* bacteria.

Disagreeable smell/taste; turbidity, acidity: *Pediococcus* or *Bacillus* contamination of the primary ferment. Irreversible.

Green apple flavor: Acetaldehyde, the principle volatile acid in beer. From too high a fermentation temperature; yeast-strain characteristic; bacterial contamination.

Banana aroma/flavor: Acetates. Yeast-strain characteristic; wild-yeast contamination; too high a fermentation temperature.

Thinness: Wort extract too low; excessive mash protein digestion; dextrin-poor extract.

Haze: Poor mash protein digestion; insufficient boil; wild yeast; bacteria; oxidation of beer; poor starch conversion in mash.

Gelatinous precipitate: Excessive sparging; poorly degraded hemicellulose.

Lack of head: Excessive protein rest; overmodified malt; too high an adjunct ratio; lipids in ferment (excessive sparging; autolized yeast); overfoaming in fermentation; overboiling; insufficient or deteriorated hops; contact with oil.

Gushing: Excess of priming sugars; beer not fermented out before packaging; temperature fluctuation; mishandling; old malt; iron; wild-yeast contamination.

Problems encountered with bottled beer can be accentuated by holding a sample at 85 degrees F (30 degrees C) and visually monitoring it for several days, then evaluating the forcing sample. Precipitates or surface formations generally indicate microbial contamination. Culturing or flavor evaluation may pinpoint organism responsible.

Cleaning and Sterilizing

All brewing equipment must be kept scrupulously clean. Wort-cooling, yeast-culturing, and fermenting equipment must also be made sterile. Equipment should be cleaned immediately after each use and all residues and particles washed off before it is sterilized. No abrasives should ever be used to scour brewing equipment, with the exception of copper or stainless steel kettles.

Cleaners should be used sparingly, and then only on equipment that has been badly neglected or is too soiled to be cleaned by being soaked in water and then rigorously scrubbed. Where deposits have formed, only the deposits themselves should be treated for removal, and then preferably by nothing more than a thick paste of fresh yeast.

Sterilizing with boiling water or steam is preferable to using chemical sterilants. Heating equipment to above 140 degrees F (60 degrees C) for twenty minutes eliminates most microbes, while heating to above 170 degrees F

(77 degrees C), boiling, or steaming sterilizes any equipment that does not have impenetrable deposits. For home-brewers, sterilizing wet bottles and small pieces of equipment in an oven at 200 degrees F (93 degrees C) or in a dishwasher with a heat-drying cycle is oftentimes the most practical method.

Sterilizing solutions should only be applied where equipment size, shape, or manufacture — or severe contamination — makes heat sterilization impractical. The cleansers and sterilants specified below should not be misconstrued as being substitutes for prompt and thorough cleaning with hot water or sterilizing with pure, clear 180 degree F (82 degrees C) water. All cleaning and antiseptic solutions should be freshly made up as needed, as most lose their potency during storage.

A thorough rinsing after using a cleanser or sterilant is very important to protect the taste of the beer. Spray or swab all surfaces with rinse water. Grossly inefficient rinsing can be identified by monitoring the pH of the rinse water for change.

The usual cleaning cycle includes a cold-water soaking, either a hot or cold cleaning as appropriate, and a cold rinse. For fermenting equipment, heat sterilization or the application of a sterilant (usually in cold water, followed by a hot rinse) is also necessary. See "Percentage Solutions" in the "Useful Information" section of appendix D for the preparation of percentage solutions. Following is a detailed look at how to clean various materials with different solutions.

Construction

Stainless steel: Clean with 2 to 3 percent hot caustic-soda solution and mild detergent at 170 degrees F (77 degrees C), followed with one or more rinses with water hotter than 140 degrees F (60 degrees C). Use 2 percent phosphoric, sulfuric, or sulfurous acid or 3 percent iodophor as a sterilant. Acid sterilants remove *beerstone*, or deposits of oxalic lime and organic matter and passivate stainless steel.

Copper: Only noncorrosive cleansers should be used. Caustic soda especially must be avoided. As copper is commonly used only for kettle fabrication, it should only need to be scoured with sand or other silica abrasive.

Glass, glazed porcelain: Most cleansers and sterilants are suitable for use on glass or glazed porcelain; only phosphoric acid should not be used, as it can etch glass. A 2 to 3 percent caustic-soda solution is the preferred cleanser. Trisodium phosphate or mild detergents may be substituted. Microorganic contamination may be countered by application of chlorinated trisodium phosphate, or more commonly by a subsequent sterilant application. Household bleach in .2 percent aqueous solution is the most commonly used sterilant, but after a clear rinse, any of the acid sterilants can be used.

Plastics, enamelware: A 2 to 3 percent caustic-soda solution will not harm these surfaces, but mild detergents are more commonly used. Either material requires application of a cleanser more frequently than glass or metal surfaces. Sterilants may be .2 percent chlorine bleach, 5 percent chlorinated trisodium phosphate solution (alkaline), sodium or potassium metabisulfite, 2 to 3 percent phosphoric acid, or 3 percent iodophor (acid).

Aluminum: Only mild detergent with an acid cleanser (2 to 5 percent nitric or phosphoric acid) should be used. Compatible sterilizing agents include nitric and sulfurous acid.

Wood: Rinse and brush wooden articles and then immerse them in boiling water immediately after use. Because of wood's natural porosity, use of cleansers should be avoided. Where absolutely necessary, a hot 2 to 3 percent solution of caustic soda or 5 percent sodium carbonate or bicarbonate can be applied, but it must be rinsed away by several long baths, from hot to cold. Five percent metabisulfite sterilizing followed by several clear-water rinses may be employed, but boiling or steaming is preferred. Any solution applied to wood is likely to leach into it, and is very difficult to coax back out of it.

Do not let wood implements sit damp between brewings. They must be dried thoroughly after cleansing.

Equipment

Malt mills and screen: These need only be cleaned with a stiff brush after every use. The cleaning, however, should be thorough.

Mash and lauter-tuns: These should be kept wet after use and then scrubbed clean, rinsed, and dried. *A false bottom, strainmaster, or grain bag* in the tuns must at least occasionally be boiled in a 2 to 3 percent caustic-soda solution or be scrubbed with an appropriate cleanser.

Brew kettles of copper, stainless steel, or aluminum: Articles of this construction are the only ones used in brewing upon which an abrasive should be used. In fact, they benefit by its employment. The abrasives not only scour away calcified deposits, but pitting and etching of the kettle surface improves heat transfer and protein coagulation during wort boiling. A thick paste of fresh yeast should be brushed onto any stubborn deposits and kept moist before scrubbing. The yeast is finally rinsed away with clean, cold water.

Immersible heating elements: These must periodically be soaked in 10 percent trisodium phosphate solution and then scrubbed to remove scale.

Fermentation locks: The locks should always be soaked in a detergent or caustic-soda solution and then flushed clean after every use. Use of an antiseptic solution in the fermentation lock is not necessary, but it is advisable. A fermentation lock should be changed as soon as it becomes dirty.

Fermenters: Insofar as possible, fermenters should only be cleaned by a thorough brushing in cold water after use and then be heat sterilized before their next use. Any beerstone deposits that do not come free should be covered with yeast paste. A mild detergent or cleanser (3 percent caustic soda, 5 percent trisodium phosphate, or 2 percent nitric or phosphoric acid) may be added. The paste should be kept moist for a day and then the deposit scrubbed away. Where a cleanser is necessary, use caustic soda. Where a sterilant is necessary, use household bleach, 2 to 3 percent phosphoric acid, or 1 percent iodophor.

Plastic tubing: Used for wort cooling or siphoning, plastic tubes should be boiled in caustic soda and thoroughly flushed. Hydrogen peroxide can also be used to clean and sterilize tubing very effectively. Storing tubing in a sterilant solution largely eliminates the risk of contamination, but bleach turns tubing opaque, and iodophor discolors it, although this is not a serious problem to most brewers.

Bottles: Clean-looking bottles can be washed in 170 degree F (77 degrees C) water, boiled, or steamed. Dirty bottles should be soaked and then scoured with 2 to 3 percent caustic soda, 5 percent trisodium phosphate, or a mild detergent solution, followed by several rinses with water hotter than 140 degrees F (60 degrees C).

Alkaline Cleansers

Sodium hydroxide: Caustic soda, NaOH. It is effective only when it is used hot. A most effective solvent, it hydrolyzes most malt and wort residues. It may, however, leave calcium salt residues, except when it is applied with a detergent or the sequestering agent EDTA ($C_{10}H_{12}N_2Na_4O_8$). It is highly corrosive and should not be used on copper or aluminum surfaces. It dissolves skin and burns mucous membranes; use only with rubber gloves and adequate eye protection. Potassium hydroxide gives the same results.

Sodium carbonate: Washing soda, $Na_2CO_3 \cdot 10H_2O$. It is applied hot. It is far less effective than other cleansers mentioned.

Sodium bicarbonate: Commonly called baking soda, $NaHCO3$, similar to sodium carbonate in effect.

Trisodium phosphate: A common household cleanser, TSP, $Na_3PO_4 \cdot 12H_2O$, is a very effective solvent, especially for calcified deposits such as boiler scale. Chlorinated trisodium phosphate adds some bactericidal capability to its cleansing.

Acid Cleansers

Nitric acid: Called aqua fortis, HNO_3, this substance is caustic but does not corrode aluminum. It is corrosive to other metals. It can also be used as a sterilant, or to passivate steel.

Phosphoric acid: Phosphoric acid, H_3PO_4, is a very effective bactericide at below pH 3.0 (2 to 3 percent solution). It passivates steel, dissolving scale deposits and protecting it from oxidation. It is a substitute for nitric acid when cleaning aluminum. Do not use on porcelain.

Alkaline Sterilants

Sodium hypochlorite: Common household chlorine bleach, Chlorox, or chlorinated soda, $NAClO \cdot 5H_2O$. It is a very effective sterilant. It is usually used in strengths less than 1 percent in aqueous solution, but it is effective in distilled water at less than .05 percent (.3 fluid ounce in five gallons) with reasonable contact time. Usual dilution is .2 percent/one fluid ounce in four gallons; at this concentration, the sterilant does not need to be rinsed, so long as objects are well drained.

Caution: This cleanser produces poisonous chlorine gas in contact with acid compounds. This reaction also strongly corrodes stainless steel.

Acid Sterilants

Iodophor: Iodine combined with phosphoric acid. One-half fluid ounce of iodophor per gallon of solution (four milliliters/liter) is an effective sterilant with thirty minutes' contact time at below 120 degrees F (49 degrees C). At this concentration it does not require rinsing.

Phosphoric acid: A commonly used acid sterilant. It is very effective at 2 to 3 percent concentration (pH 2.0 to 3.0), and residues at this strength may not mar beer flavor. Phosphoric acid passivates stainless steel against corrosion.

Hydrogen peroxide: H_2O_2 is an oxidizing sterilant that is also a very effective solvent for cleaning flexible tubing in 2 to 3 percent solution.

Sodium metabisulfite: $Na_2S_2O_5$ is antifermentive, not bactericidal. In the presence of acids, it produces noxious sulfur dioxide (burnt-match) odor. It is not widely favored by brewers as a sterilant.

Potassium metabisulfite: $K_2S_2O_5$ is similar to the sodium salt.

Calcium sulfite: $CaSO_3 \bullet 2H_2O$ was once commonly used by commercial breweries. In contact with the atmosphere, it oxidizes to $CaSO_4$.

Sulfuric acid: Sulfuric acid, H_2SO_4, is corrosive to most metals. As sulfurous acid, SO_2, it is commonly used in commercial breweries in 6 percent aqueous solution.

Alcohol, ethyl or isopropyl: This is useful only for sterilizing small articles. It is effective only with reasonable contact time.

Quaternary ammonium sterilants: Should be avoided, as the residues from these compounds negatively affect foam retention.

CHAPTER 17

Equipment

The following is a list of equipment used for home-brewing. It is by no means complete, comprehensive.

pH papers: These indicate acidity/alkalinity by gauging the color change of the paper wetted with a solution against a scale. Homebrewers commonly use wide range, pH 2 to 10, and narrow range, pH 4.2 to 6.2. Narrow range 5.2 to 6.8 and 5.2 to 7.4 are also available. The best papers are only accurate to pH .2 at best, and most are less accurate. Inexpensive digital pH meters are generally only accurate to ±pH .2, and so are only an improvement over papers because they are easier to read. More accurate (± pH .1 or better), calibratable pH meters are used by commercial brewers but exceed the budgets of most homebrewers. Temperature compensation accounts for the drift in readings made at other than the reference temperature, but readings made at other than 68 degrees F (20 degrees C) still need to be factored back to that temperature to be compared with standard brewing pH values. The decision to purchase any meter should be based upon the unit's accuracy.

Water test kits: Kits are available to test for hardness, alkalinity, calcium, sulphate, chloride, chlorine, nitrite, nitrate, ammonia, iron, and pH. Many are inexpensively available at aquarium-supply shops, and others through laboratory-supply houses. Test kits, especially for water hardness, are more valuable to any brewer — and more versatile — than municipal water-supply analyses, the moreso when the two are used in conjunction.

pH Papers

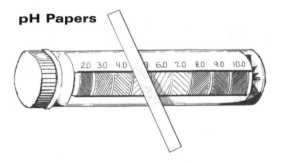

pH and Hardness Test Kit

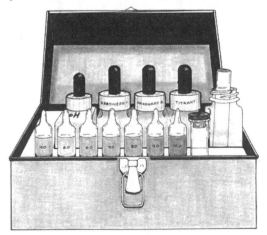

Kettle for water treatment: For boiling or mineral-salt treatment of brewing water. The brewing kettle is generally used.

Gram scale: A gram scale is necessary for accurately dispensing mineral salts. These are usually quite inexpensive, but because the accuracy of a cheap scale is likely suspect, it should be calibrated using a substance of known weight to correct inaccuracies.

Constructing a Balance Scale

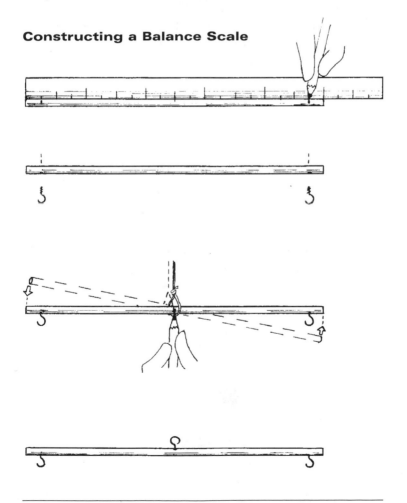

Construction of a simple balance scale can eliminate the need to purchase this or any scale. To use the balance scale, suspend a substance known to be of the weight desired from one side, and add the substance being measured to the other side until the loads level. Coins in good condition make excellent balance weights; a U.S. dime weighs 2.27 grams, a penny weighs 3.1 grams, a nickel 5 grams, and a quarter 5.6 grams.

Covered liquor-storage vessel: For treated water. Any idle fermenter or food-safe bucket can serve the purpose.

Graduated one-quart measuring cup: A Pyrex cup is more serviceable than either glass or plastic. Use it to

Mill

measure and dispense water, malt, and mash. It is indispensable as a dipper and for mixing during mashing and wort boiling.

Malt scale: Some brewers use malt scales in the one-to-ten-pound range; however, malt may be measured by volume with reasonable accuracy to eliminate the need for this piece of equipment.

Malt mill: Unless crushed malt is purchased, some sort of a mill is necessary. Countertop grain/maize mills such as that pictured yield a satisfactory grist, but roller mills give the best grist of any of the home mills. Coffee mills and others equipped with cutting blades are wholly unsatisfactory. Roller mills specifically constructed for crushing malt give the best results, but at a dear price.

Screens: Screens are used to gauge the degree of crushing. A kitchen colander, sieve, or flour sifter, or various gauges of screening can be used to separate several proportions of malt particle sizes. A rough comparison can then be made against separation by standard screens to guide mill adjustments.

Sourmash-tun: Used when a lactic-acid mash is being made to reduce pH prior to brewing. A well-insulated thermos, jug, or picnic cooler maintains temperature well during the long rest; it should be sized to the volume of the sourmash.

Mash-tun: This may be a food-safe plastic bucket, kettle, or insulated plastic picnic or beverage cooler. Capacity should be roughly equal to fermenter capacity.

If it is to double as a lauter-tun, it needs to be equipped with a spigot and a false bottom or filter bag. Some brewers equip the lauter-tun with the means to flush the space below the false bottom. On the whole, it is far easier to manage mashing and filtering in separate containers; this leaves the mash-tun to be fitted with a spigot from which to dispense the sparge water.

The most important criteria for any mash-tun are that it hold heat well and be readily and thoroughly cleanable. Food-safe, insulated, hard-plastic picnic chests hold mash temperature exceedingly well. High temperatures may distort the surfaces, however (high-density polyethylene at 170 degrees F [77 degrees C]); check the manufacturer's specifications.

Large stainless steel pails or kettles are easy to clean, rugged, and lightweight, but they cannot maintain rest temperatures unless they are insulated. A jacket cut from Styrofoam or a wrapping for the tun from any of the myriad insulating materials will improve its performance. It should be used to stabilize the temperature of a stovetop mashing.

A heating element, whether it is integral or a hand-held immersible unit, is somewhat effective, but even temperature dispersal can be achieved only by demonic stirring. Some overheating and caramelization of the mash is inevitable and cleanup may be tedious.

An alternative to the immersible heating element is the RIMS (Recirculating Infusion Mash System), utilizing a picnic cooler, pump, heating element in copper tubing, and electronic parts to fabricate a temperature-controlled mash-tun capable of upward-infusion mashing. Its fabrication is described in *Zymurgy*, Special Issue 1992, Vol. 15, No. 4; it is also available as an off-the-shelf unit by a homebrew manufacturer.

Rigid plastic pails and buckets hold heat somewhat better than do those of stainless steel, but not as well as is required. They are very inexpensive and can be fitted with an insulating jacket and a hardware-store spigot with relative ease. Use only food-safe, heat-resistant plastic.

Enameled steel kettles should be avoided as they chip easily and expose the mash to certain iron contamination.

Lauter-tun: This is the most sophisticated piece of equipment required by the homebrewer. It should be

Picnic Cooler as a Mash-tun

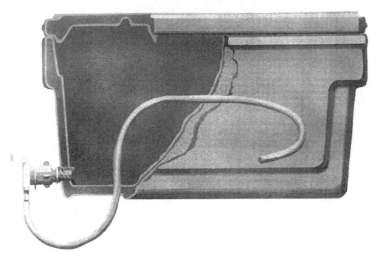

either insulated or constructed of material having insulating properties. It should be of the proper diameter for optimal mash thickness, and at its base it must have a spigot and some manner of false bottom or filter bag set above it. The means to flush the space between them may improve the clarity of the runoff collected from it.

A fine-mesh bag, or one fashioned of canvas sides and a mesh bottom, is commonly used for holding the mash, but presents several disadvantages. These literally "bag" at their bottoms, even when resting on a slotted or perforated base such as is used for steaming vegetables, encouraging uneven percolation of the sparge water through the mash. With canvas-sided bags, the loss is compounded by sparge water flowing down outside of the bag. False bottoms fitted tightly to the inside of the lauter-tun, and one-eighth to two inches above its base, are employed by commercial brewers. Similar designs available to home-brewers give excellent results.

Lauter-tun

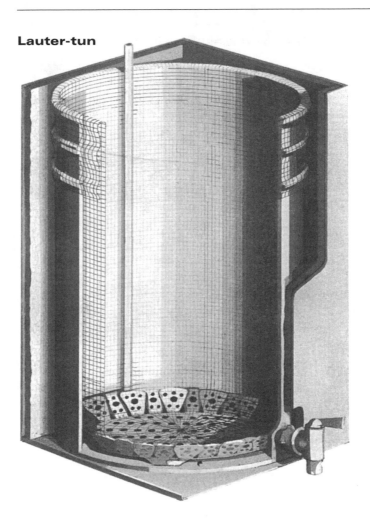

A mash strainer can be used instead of a false bottom to separate the wort from the spent grains. It can be constructed from one-half-inch PVC or copper pipe, using hardware-store fittings. Fitted to an insulated picnic chest, the mash strainer allows mashing and sparging to be accomplished in the single vessel.

False Bottom Cross Sections

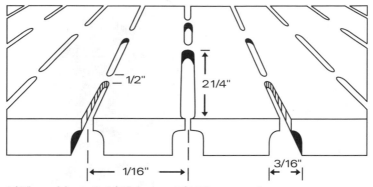

1/2" end bar, 2 1/4" long, 3/16" on centers
Slot Widths: .020" decoctions, 1/32" infusion

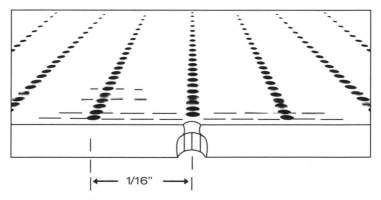

1/32" dia. side-staggered perforations on 1/16" centers

The lauter-tun should be of roughly the same capacity as the mash-tun and must be selected with consideration for the effect of its diameter upon mash depth. Mashing ten pounds of malt at grain depth of six inches requires a diameter of fourteen inches; for a twelve-inch-deep filter bed, a diameter of ten inches is needed, and for eighteen inches, a diameter of eight inches. For twenty

Lauter-tun

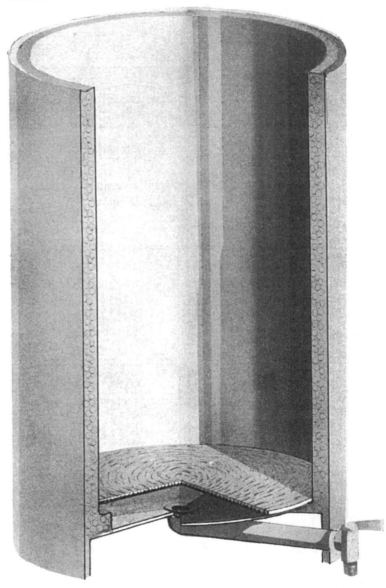

Sparging System

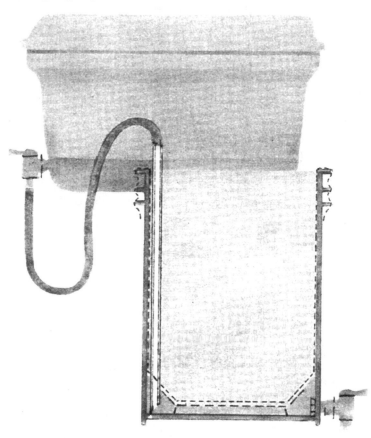

pounds of malt, these figures become twenty inches, four-teen inches, and twelve inches.

Some manner of spigot is also a prerequisite of any lauter-tun.

A dedicated means of flushing the space under the false bottom and above the lauter-tun floor is not generally necessary; either an inlet set opposite the spigot or a tube thrust down through the mash to the false bottom suffices.

Sparger: Any manner of introducing a regulated flow of liquor at 170 to 176 degrees F (77 to 80 degrees C) evenly over the top of the mash, without unduly disturbing it, serves the purpose of a sparger. A perforated stainless steel, copper, or plastic tube or sprinkling head attached by a length of flexible tubing to the mash-tun, a pail, a kettle, or a jug with a spigot serves well as a sparger. Any method of introducing the sparge liquor that does not "drill" the liquor into the mash is entirely suitable.

An insulated mash-tun, filled with the hot sparge liquor while the mash is setting in the lauter-tun, makes the most economical and easily managed arrangement. This fact should greatly influence the selection of the mash-tun.

Large stainless steel spoon: Preferably of one-piece construction. It is used throughout the brewing. Use the spoon to calibrate your kettle by standing the long-handled spoon in the kettle, adding water one quart at a time, and scratching calibration lines into the spoon's handle after each addition.

Mesh strainer: Useful for pulling the goods for a decotion, because the free liquid drains off through the mesh.

Making a Paddle

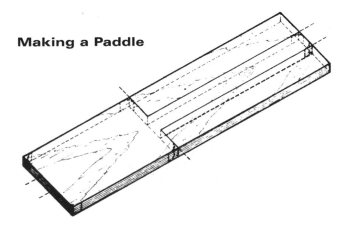

Floating Thermometer

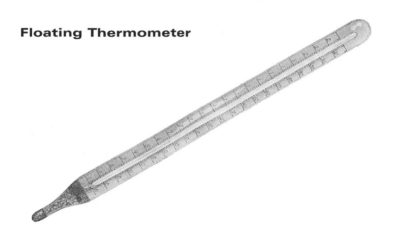

   Paddle: Can be used to stir the mash and boiling wort; it is easier to use and more effective than a paddle. It may be cut from a hardwood board.

   A good combination is using the one-quart measuring cup to mix the mash and the long-handled paddle for keeping extract from caramelizing on the kettle's bottom.

   Immersible thermometer: In the 32 to 212 degree F (0 to 100 degrees C) range, this is indispensable. The floating type that is sealed in a concentric Pyrex bulb offers the best alternative, as it may be readily cleaned, fits through the neck of a carboy, and floats in the mash-tun. Digital electronic thermometers are preferred, if they are accurate to .25 percent of the scale.

   Caution: Mercury is highly toxic; never use a cracked or damaged thermometer, and always handle it carefully. Should mercury taint a brew, the brew must be discarded! Alcohol thermometers are vastly preferred.

   Decoction kettle: The kettle should be roughly 50 percent of the capacity of the mash-tun. Stainless steel or copper is best for boiling decoctions and, in British mashing, for boiling water for infusions.

Porcelain plate: This is essential for starch-conversion testing with iodine. It should be kept solely for this purpose and washed and rinsed separately.

Hydrometer/saccharometer: Measures sugar in solution by displacement, sinking less deeply into solutions of increasing density. A hydrometer measures specific gravity. A saccharometer is marked with a scale in degrees Balling, Plato, or Brix; otherwise, saccharometers and hydrometers are functionally identical. One equipped with an integral

Hydrometer

thermometer is handy, although better accuracy is obtained by heating or cooling the solution to the reference temperature of the instrument.

A hydrometer may be retained within a trial tube and immersed directly into the wort or beer to make a reading, or set into a beaker filled with a sample of the wort or beer.

Scrub brush, sponges: For cleaning brewing equipment. Use only a soft-bristled brush on plastic; a stiffer brush should be used on porcelain, metal, and glass.

Wort kettle: This is usually of 40 to 50 percent greater capacity than the closed fermenter. The kettle may be equipped with a spigot — and a false bottom, stainless steel or copper "scrubby," or cheesecloth pressed down over the kettle's outlet — to filter hop and break residues from the wort. If the kettle has no spigot, filtering may be accomplished by siphoning the wort through flexible tubing and a racking cane fitted with a stainless steel or copper

Copper Jam Boiler

scrubby. For grain brewers, pouring the wort into the lauter-tun and using it as a hop back gives excellent results. Where hop pellets are used, the wort can be whirlpooled and then siphoned off its trub.

A kettle is best fabricated from copper for heat-transfer efficiency, but stainless steel is far easier to obtain, clean, and maintain. The exception here is the not-uncommon copper jam boiler, which makes an excellent asymmetrically heated kettle for five-gallon brewing. At this volume any metal kettle may be set directly on a range top to heat (although electric heating elements may not be able to heat five or six gallons of wort to boiling). Nontoxic plastic boilers (polypropylene or Teflon) equipped with integral heating elements also perform satisfactorily, although they are more difficult to maintain.

Calibrate your kettle by making one-quart additions of water to it and etching calibration lines with each new addition into the handle of a long-handled spoon.

The brew kettle is commonly used to boil the brewing water where carbonate salts need to be precipitated.

Wine thief: For taking samples from the kettle or the ferment. It should be of Pyrex or glass manufacture.

Hop scale: Used to dispense hops by weight. An inexpensive plastic "calorie-counter" scale suffices. Calibrate it with an object or substance of known weight.

Wort chiller: The usual practice of cooling the wort by setting the kettle into a tub of ice or cold running water is woefully ineffective. Slow cooling doesn't precipitate the cold break well, and prolongs the time the wort must spend at temperatures conducive to bacterial growth.

Running the wort through twenty-five feet of three-eighths-inch inside diameter copper tubing coiled into chipped ice will reduce wort temperature from boiling down to at least 90 degrees F (32 degrees C). A concentric-tubing cooler can be made by jacketing such

Hop Scale

tubing with five-eighths-inch inside diameter tubing or garden hose, using a "running tee" for the connection where the inner tubing emerges, and filling the space between with pressurized tap water running in counter-flow to the bitter wort. Wort run through a concentric tubing cooler can be cooled to within 10 degrees F (5 degrees C) of the tap-water temperature.

The arrangement is more simply constructed than might be expected. However, it is difficult to rinse the cooler

Counterflow Wort Chiller

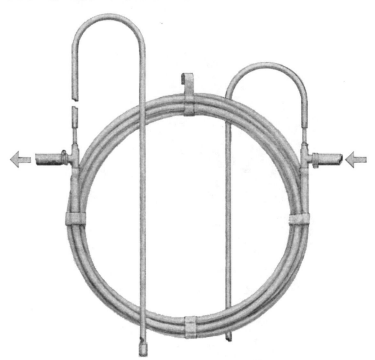

free of extract deposits and impossible to know whether or not one has. The copper tubing must be thoroughly flushed with water immediately after use, followed by rinsing and storage with iodophor or an acid sterilant solution.

An immersion wort chiller can be made up of fifteen to thirty feet of copper tubing coiled so that it can be set directly into the wort kettle. Because tap water is run through the tubing, not wort, it is easier to sanitize. It allows the cold break to be precipitated in the kettle, eliminating the need for running the wort into a separate cooling and settling tank. Wort cooling is, however, less efficient than running the wort itself through copper.

Immersion Chiller

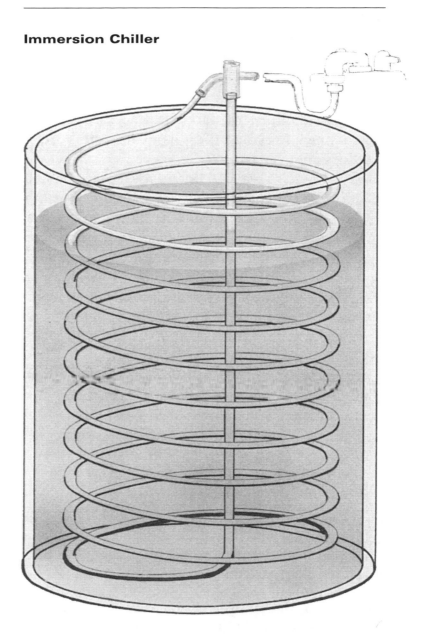

Wort-storage jars: For a five-gallon brewing, vacuum seat canning jars of half-pint, pint, or quart capacities should be used. Several quart jars are needed to hold wort for kraeusening or topping-up. Otherwise, ordinary beer bottles may be used.

Yeast-culturing equipment: This equipment is needed to culture yeast to pitching strength by repeatedly doubling volumes with sterile wort. Unless the yeast strain is very strong, for a five-gallon batch, half-pint, pint, quart, and half-gallon glass containers or Erlenmeyer flasks are needed. Preferably, containers should have constricted necks and should be fitted with a stopper and fermentation lock. Culturing from a single cell requires petri dishes and test tubes, a stainless steel loop, and culture medium (agar-agar or pure vegetable gelatin). A 600X to 1200X microscope fitted with a precision graduated stage, as well as slides and cover glasses, complete a professional lab. A good-quality used lab microscope with glass lenses is superior to any department-store model and can be bought for about the same price. The expense, however, can equal the cost of all other equipment combined. If you want to avoid staining cultures to differentiate lactic-acid bacteria, you will need a phase-contrast or dark-field microscope, and such specialty scopes are expensive.

Culturing from a single cell is usually approximated by thinning the parent culture with wort and streaking a nutrient, bacteria-inhibiting culture medium with the parent culture. Any isolated colonies that develop can be assumed to be from a single cell. Streaking the culture onto a yeast-suppressant medium to disclose bacterial contamination largely eliminates the necessity for a microscope. Prepared staining, yeast-or-bacteria-suppressant nutrient agar in sterile petri dishes is available.

Glass bottles or jugs for culturing yeast to pitching strength should be fitted with fermentation locks; for

twelve- and sixteen-ounce bottles, you will need No. 1 and
No. 2 drilled-and-tapered rubber stoppers; for quart bottles,
use a No. 3 stopper.

Pump-spray or squeeze bottles: These are for dispensing
freshly made-up cleaning and antiseptic solutions.

Primary fermenter: The primary fermenter should be
constructed of easily cleaned material.

For closed-fermentation systems, a six-gallon carboy
with a fermentation lock is preferred. For "blowoff"
systems, a five-gallon carboy fitted with three feet of one-
inch-interior-diameter flexible tubing is used. This Burton-
Union inspired arrangement was developed to separate
top-fermenting yeast and trub from the ferment.

Inverted-carboy single-stage fermentations reduce
the risks of contamination and oxidation and allow for
easy trub separation and yeast collection. These carboy kits
allow the homebrewer to mimic commercial unitank fermentations, with similar benefits.

An "open" fermenter should not have a constricted
neck, but must be of up to 25 percent greater volume than
the beer and be covered by a close fitting lid equipped with
a fermentation lock. Food-safe plastic pails are inexpensive,
but are a nuisance to clean and sterilize after a bit of use.
They must be replaced or relegated to use as mash-tuns or
the like as their surfaces become badly abraded.

A fermentation lock must be fitted through the
cover of the primary fermenter so that all exchange
between the fermenter and the atmosphere takes place
through the airlock. It should be of adequate size to
allow the release of copious amounts of carbon dioxide
produced during the primary fermentation without
splashing the liquid within the lock. The concentric type
serves best. The traditional chemist's airlock is more
appropriate for use during the less volatile secondary fermentation and for yeast culturing.

Five-Gallon Glass Carboy

An inexpensive adhesive-backed liquid-crystal thermometer strip should be attached to the fermenter so that the temperature of the fermentation can be easily monitored.

Refrigeration: Unless the heat produced during primary fermentation is attempered by an appropriate ambient temperature, a refrigerator is necessary for controlling lager fermentation temperatures. Serviceable but cosmetically second-class refrigerators may be found at

Carboy Cap and Chemist's Lock

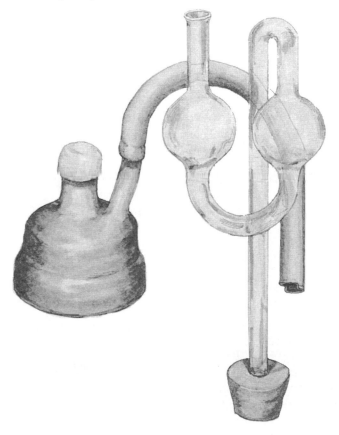

Carboy Brush

reasonable prices. Tighter temperature control can be had by adding an after-market controller with a wider and higher range of set temperatures and tighter differential than a refrigerator's internal thermostat is capable of.

Siphon tubing: To rack wort or beer off its sediment, a four-foot length of flexible tubing is affixed to Pyrex or rigid-plastic tubing fitted with an end cap. Plastic tubing should be replaced as it becomes discolored, cracked, or stiff with use.

Secondary/lager fermenter: This should have a constricted neck to reduce airspace above the ferment. Glass presents the most readily cleaned surface. For five-gallon brewings, the traditional glass carboy is the uncontested choice (and presents a compelling reason for brewing in five-gallon batches). Use a carboy cap or No. 6 1/2 or No. 7 tapered neoprene or rubber stopper to seal the carboy and hold the fermentation lock.

For lagering under pressure, use a Cornelius keg that is equipped with a pressure-relief valve.

When selecting any closed fermenter, bear in mind that its capacity determines the relative sizes of all other brewing vessels.

Cornelius Keg System

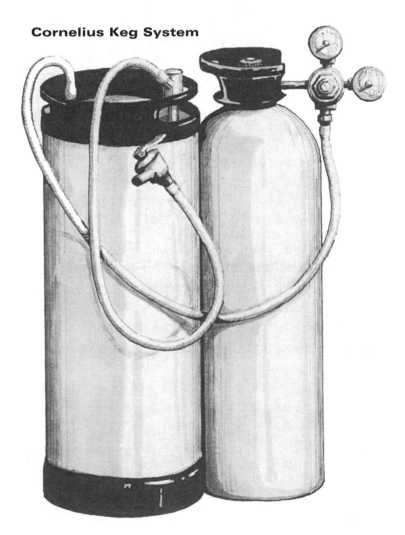

Carboy brush: Used to scour the inside of carboys or other closed-neck containers. It should be roughly two feet long.

Reducing-sugar analysis kit: This positively identifies when aged beer has fermented out. Dextrocheck and other urine-sugar reagents are inexpensive and available at any pharmacy. Glucose-specific analysis kits can be useful indicators of the glucose content of worts and green beer.

Priming bucket: For rousing priming solution into aged beer in preparation to bottle. A fermenter can be employed, but a bucket equipped with a spigot is vastly preferred.

Keg: For draft beer, a five-gallon pre-mix syrup tank (Cornelius keg) used by the soft drink industry is the first choice of homebrewers.

Bottle filler: When the priming tub has no spigot, the beer will need to be siphoned into bottles. A bottle filler with a shut-off valve opens only when it is pressed against the bottom of a bottle. This reduces foaming and oxygen uptake by the beer, and makes bottling less messy.

Bottles: Bottles should be clean, with unchipped rims. Heavy "bar bottles" are preferred over the lighter gauge retail bottles, but in a carefully controlled fermentation, the

Bottle Filler

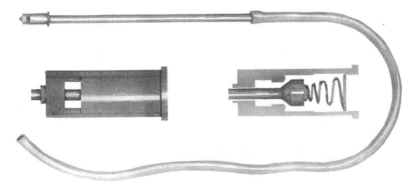

Bottle Brush and Bottle Rinser

latter are sufficient. Bottles with porcelain/plastic swing-tops and PET plastic soft-drink bottles with screw-tops are also commonly used; a cap designed to fit PET bottles allows the homebrewer to artificially carbonate beer in the bottle.

Bottle brush: A brush that reaches the bottom of the bottle is used to scour them during cleaning. A bottle-washer faucet attachment or a multiple-bottle washer made from copper tubing may also be handy.

Bottle rack: A bottle rack holds inverted empties after the work of emptying them is done. A Christmas-tree type rack conserves counter space.

Caps (or other suitable stoppers): Crown-type caps are commonly used for sealing bottled beer.

Capper: To secure crown-type caps. It should be chosen for its ability to evenly seal bottles without chipping their rims or cracking the bottle necks. The best arrangement is the bench-type; other cappers may not be so expensive, but neither do they work so well.

APPENDIX A

Basic Homebrewing from Malt-Extract Syrup

Brewing from grain requires a fair amount of time, expertise, and specialized equipment. It is not really practical or possible for everybody to brew from grains. For beginners, it is not even advisable. Learning about brewing is facilitated by simplifying the process and mastering one step before progressing to another.

Brewing can be reduced to its simplest elements with malt extract syrup, which is simply condensed wort. The homebrewer reconstitutes it with water so that it can be boiled, cooled, pitched with yeast, and fermented. This allows the novice homebrewer to master the mechanics of fermentation and hopping, uncomplicated by crushing, mashing, and sparging grain.

For most hobby brewers, malt extracts present the best choice for producing their beer without giving up the better part of a day each time they brew. An extract brew can be started at noon and the cleanup finished by three. By using unhopped extract, hop pellets, and small amounts of specialty malts in the wort kettle, the homebrewer can create any one of a wide variety of excellent beers in under four hours.

In brewing good beer from extracts it is important to substitute Dry Malt Extract (DME) for any cane or corn sugar called for in the recipe. Sugar increases the alcohol content of a beer without a balancing increase in flavor and fullness. Moreover, sugar gives beer a peculiar flavor, often characterized as "cideriness," that is unpleasant. For every pound of sugar called for in the recipe, substitute 1 1/4 pounds of dry malt extract or 1 1/2 pounds of liquid malt extract.

The best beers are generally produced by boiling the full amount of wort for 1 1/2 hours, but most households do not have a twenty-four- to forty-quart/liter stainless kettle and a wort chiller among the pots, pans, and kitchen widgets. Many homebrewers and virtually all novices boil a more concentrated wort in a twelve- to twenty-quart/liter stockpot for forty-five to sixty minutes and dilute that high-gravity wort down with sterile, chilled water.

For a five-gallon (nineteen liters) batch, the malt extract is boiled with two gallons (eight liters) of liquor, and that high-gravity wort is cooled down with three gallons (eleven liters) of sterilized, chilled liquor as the wort is transferred to the fermenter.

Brewing really needs to begin with planning and preparation. You must choose a recipe and purchase suitable ingredients. Unless you will be pitching granulated dry yeast, you will need to activate liquid or harvested yeast at least twenty-four hours before you pitch it. And you need to sterilize three gallons of water and give them enough time to chill down to 35 degrees F (2 degrees C) or so (the colder the better).

The beginning brewer also needs to accumulate three plastic one gallon spring-water jugs or six two-liter PET soda bottles to hold the chilled liquor. Rinse out soda bottles immediately after they are emptied, put a little detergent and hot water in each, screw the rinsed lids on, and shake them well. Uncap each bottle and pour out the detergent solution, then rinse them several times with very hot water.

Measure out three-quarters of a teaspoon of bleach into each two-liter bottle, or one teaspoon into each gallon jug. Fill the bottles with tap water to the top, cap them, and let them sit and sterilize until needed.

In addition to containers for the liquor, you will need to collect bottles to package the beer into. Heavy glass bottles, such as are used by most import beers, are preferable to light weight bottles. For five gallons, you will need fifty 12-ounce bottles, or forty 16-ounce, or twenty-eight 22-ounce bottles. Rinse each bottle several times just as it is emptied.

If you are pitching liquid yeast, prepare it the day before brewing, or as appropriate for the amount of yeast on hand. At least a quart of starter, or its equivalent volume of yeast, should be actively fermenting on brew day.

On the day before brewing, heat 3 1/2 gallons of water in a clean pot(s) to a boil. Empty the sterilant solution out of your sterilized bottles/jugs. With a very clean, just-rinsed funnel and a Pyrex measuring cup for a ladle, pour a cup or so of boiling water into each jug, swirl it around to rinse out chlorine residues, and dump the rinse. Leave your jugs draining on a paper towel.

Put a clean lid on the kettle, stopper up your clean sink, and fill it with cold water. Immerse the kettle into the water bath. After five minutes or so, drain and refill the sink. Once the brewing liquor has chilled to near body temperature, use the measuring cup and funnel to fill the bottles. Cap and refrigerate them.

The beer will be fermented in either a six- or seven-gallon (twenty-four- to thirty-liter) lidded, food-grade plastic pail with no visible scratches, or a five- or six-gallon (nineteen- to twenty-five-liter) glass carboy. These containers are relatively inexpensive and easily sanitized. Overall, beginning brewers are best advised to begin with the cheaper, and more rugged, food-grade plastic bucket and move on to two-stage or inverted-carboy fermentations after they have gained some experience.

The fermenter, and any and all parts and utensils that contact the wort and beer after the kettle boil, need to be sanitized. Put 1 to 1 1/2 ounces of bleach into the bottom of the fermenter and fill it with water. Fill the fermenter one quart at a time and calibrate its volume as you do so by marking the level after each addition on the outside of the bucket with an indelible marker.

It's a good idea to calibrate your kettle, too, by immersing a long-handled spoon into the water and scratching calibration lines into its handle after each one-quart addition.

Fill the fermenter to the brim. Put every part and utensil that won't rust right into the sterilant solution. Cover it and leave it overnight.

On brew day, fill a kettle with two gallons of water and heat it to boiling. Add any mineral salts called for in the recipe. If you are using malt-extract syrup, open the can and set it in a pot of hot water to warm the syrup so that it will run out of the can more readily.

If you are using specialty grains in the recipe, crush them coarsely and place them in a nylon or muslin bag. Suspend the bag in the brew kettle; the contents of the grains will be leached out into solution as the liquor heats up. Only add caramelized or fully roasted grains to the kettle; starchy malts and grains need to be mashed first. Lager, pale, Vienna, Munich, and amber malts should not be used as kettle adjuncts.

Remove the grains when the liquor reaches 165 to 175 degrees F (74 to 79 degrees C), so that harsh-tasting tannins aren't leached from the husks by hotter temperatures. Squeeze all the free liquid from the bagged grains as they are removed.

As the water comes to a boil, use a rubber spatula to scrape the extract out of the can and into the brew pot.

Stir and lift the extract up away from the bottom of the kettle. Scrape the can clean, and mix the wort again until the extract has evenly dispersed.

Add any DME called for in the recipe and part of the kettle hops to your extract, and boil the wort for at least forty-five minutes. The wort boil should be rolling and intense, but not so wild that it boils over.

While the wort boils, heat two quarts or so of water to boiling. Empty the sanitizing solution out of the fermenting bucket, rinse it with a quart or so of the boiling water, and invert the fermenter onto paper towels on a clean drainboard to drain. Keep an eye on the boiling wort and a clock, and make hop additions as the recipe calls for them.

If you are using granulated dry yeast to pitch the brew, wash and rinse out a pint (500-milliliter) glass container or Pyrex measuring cup with hot water, and then pour about four fluid ounces (120 milliliters) of boiling water into it. Cover it tightly with plastic wrap and force-cool it in the freezer. Cool it to 95 to 110 degrees F (35 to 43 degrees C, about body temperature, so that it feels warm, not hot), and uncover it just long enough to pour the granulated dry yeast into it. The yeast will rehydrate in the warm water and should show a frothy head within a half hour or so.

Shut off the heat to the kettle at the conclusion of the boil. Check the volume level of the wort. If needed, make up the volume to 5 1/4 gallons (twenty-one quarts, twenty liters) with cold water. Cover the kettle and remove it from the burner. Stopper up the sink again and fill it with cold water. Place the kettle into it for a few minutes to reduce the heat of the wort from boiling to near 160 degrees F (70 degrees C).

Remove the kettle to a clean counter and block it up on one side so that the bottom slopes. Wait for the trub to settle to the low side of the kettle bottom. Wash your arms and hands and sanitize the area around the kettle.

Set the sanitized and drained fermenter below in the kettle, away from any drafts. Splash the three gallons of chilled liquor into it.

Siphon or ladle the clear wort into the fermenter, letting it splash into the chilled liquor to aerate it. Leave the last trub-laden wort behind in the kettle, collecting five gallons, or a little more, in the fermenter.

Fit the fermenter with its sanitized lid and an airlock. Cool the wort to below 80 degrees F (27 degrees C), preferably by force-cooling the fermenter, as in a sink full of cold water and ice cubes.

Pitch the yeast. Uncover the fermenter, splash the yeast into the wort and re-cover the fermenter. Give the fermenter a few circular twists to disperse the yeast, and set the fermenter out of harm's way at an ambient temperature, or at slightly below, the fermentation temperature called for by the beer style and the yeast strain's preferred operating range. For ales, the general range is 60 to 72 degrees F (16 to 22 degrees C), and 45 to 55 degrees F (7 to 13 degrees C) for lagers. Fermentation temperatures can be inexpensively monitored by applying an adhesive-backed liquid-crystal temperature indicator to the outside of the fermenter.

Fermentation temperatures can be controlled to some extent by evaporative cooling or by insulation. For evaporative cooling, set the fermenter in a pan of cold water, drape a dampened towel over it, and let the towel trail into the pan of water. Evaporative cooling will draw heat out of the fermenter, reducing its temperature by 5 to 10 degrees F (3 to 5 degrees C). Where a higher temperature is needed, wrapping the fermenter with a dry towel or blanket will let the fermentation temperature rise as much as 10 degrees F (5 degrees C) above room temperature.

Once fermentation has subsided, move the fermenter to a cooler location (ideally 50 to 60 degrees F [10 to 16 degrees C] for ales, 35 to 50 degrees F [2 to 10 degrees C] for lagers). The temperature is reduced for conditioning because it produces mellower flavors. One of the first equipment upgrades that most homebrewers make is either a two-stage or inverted-carboy fermentation (using the BrewCap, for instance). The purpose of racking to a secondary fermenter, after intense primary fermentation subsides, is to separate the beer from its trub. Inverted-carboy systems accomplish the same thing by draining trub and yeast as it settles.

Novice brewers are advised to begin using a single-stage fermentation solely because racking to secondary introduces significant risk of contamination; until the beginning brewer learns the importance of sanitation and how to ensure it, a beer with an astringent bite or phenolic character is at least preferable to a contaminated one. Most beer styles benefit by two to ten weeks of conditioning, but a beer that has not been separated from its trub should not remain on it for more than two weeks, even if it can be aged very cold. So for single-stage fermentations, the beer should be bottled a week to two weeks after the fermentation head has dropped and CO_2 generation has ceased. This is not usually a major concern for beginning brewers, who are impatient to try their handcrafted beer anyway.

The first step of bottling is to sterilize all the bottles you have collected. If your dishwasher has a sanitizing cycle, you can load it up with your bottles and let it sanitize them. Or you can soak them overnight in a clean ten- to fifteen-gallon (forty- to sixty-liter) bucket of water treated with the standard sanitizing solution (approximately one fluid ounce/thirty milliliters per each four gallons/sixteen liters). Another method of sanitizing bottles is to put a half ounce/fifteen milliliters of water into each rinsed bottle and stack them in your oven, set at 200 degrees F (94 degrees

C), for an hour to heat-sterilize them. Shut the heat off about an hour or so before you will begin bottling.

A couple of hours before you will begin bottling, carry your fermenter over and place it gently on a countertop with a solid chair below it, in an area that is free from drafts and that will be easy to clean up. Block the fermenter up at a slightly tilted angle with a book to let the yeast sediment settle to the low side. Fill your priming bucket with sterilizing solution, and cover it.

When you are ready to begin your bottling session, measure out your priming sugar and a pint or so of water into a pan or small pot. Set up your sanitized, drained, and lidded priming bucket on the chair below the fermenter. You will need to start a siphon through the racking cane/tubing to get clear beer from the fermenter into the priming bucket.

Homebrewers have devised dozens of methods for starting a sanitary siphon. One of them is to boil a quart or so of water in a pot, and then pour it hot into one of your chilled-water bottles. Cut a two- to three-inch (fifty- to seventy-five-millimeter) piece off one end of your tubing and put both pieces into sterilant solution in a pot or bucket on the counter with the fermenter. Wash your hands very thoroughly (you should do this again before you prime your beer, and again before you bottle), and assemble your racking cane to one end of the tubing. Pull the plastic cap off the working end of the racking cane and slide the short piece of tubing over the end of the cane.

Insert the tubing into the bottle of hot water and suck on the end of the short piece of tubing to fill the tubing. Use your thumb to cap the end of the short tubing, and lower the tubing into your sanitizing solution. Pull the plastic cap off the working end of the racking cane and replace it with the trub cap.

Hot water should be siphoning from the jug to the sanitizing solution. Slide the fermenter and priming bucket lids over slightly to one side, lift the racking cane out of the sanitizer and up into the fermenter, then quickly drop the free end of the tubing into the priming bucket. Water, and then beer should start flowing into the priming bucket. Keep the free end of the tubing submerged in the priming bucket, and keep a watchful eye on the end of the racking cane. Unless it is kept below the beer level, you will lose the siphon; on the other hand, you want to avoid sucking up trub from the bottom. Pull the beer from the uptilted side of the fermenter until the end of the transfer.

As you get near the bottom, watch the end of the racking cane. Leave the sediment, and enough beer to take a hydrometer reading, behind. The hydrometer reading gives you the final gravity (FG).

Cover the priming bucket. Rinse and then disassemble the racking cane from the tubing. Put both back into the sanitizing solution. If your bottling bucket is not fitted with a spigot, you will need to start a siphon again to fill the bottles. Attach the tubing to the bottle filler.

Heat the pint or so of water to boiling, adding the priming sugar to it. Stir until the sugar dissolves, then lift the bottling-bucket lid. With your sterilized spoon, gently stir the beer to mix the priming solution into the beer, without splashing it around. Cover the bucket and give it a series of sharp twists to complete the mixing.

Set up your bottles ready to fill. Drain any water or sanitizing solution out of them. Set up your bag of crown caps and the capper within easy reach.

You are ready to bottle. If you are siphoning, run the sterilant through the tubing and bottle filler to a bottle until beer emerges, then move to another bottle and begin filling. If you are bottling from a spigot, try to let the beer run down the inside wall of each bottle without a lot of splashing, or attach a bottle filler. Fill each bottle until the beer comes up nearly level with the rim of each bottle. Set a cap loosely on top of each bottle after it is filled. Set the first bottles that you fill an arm's length away so that you won't knock the caps off as you accumulate more and more full bottles.

Tilt your priming bucket as you get near the bottom so that you get all the beer you can. When the racking cane sucks air, you will lose the siphon.

Go back and crimp the caps onto the bottles with the capper. Rinse off the bottles, set them in cases, and put them out of the way at room temperature. Thoroughly rinse and clean your fermenter, priming bucket, and equipment, being careful not to scratch the plastic.

Let your beer carbonate in the bottles at room temperature for a week or two before storing them in a cooler place while the bottles condition. Be patient; most homebrew will not come into its prime state until at least three to four weeks after bottling.

APPENDIX B

The Infusion Mash

Infusion mashing follows different principles for extracting malt than decoction or step mashing. Infusion mashes have only one temperature rest; they do not include a protein rest. Only well-modified malts can be infusion mashed. Mashing and sparging generally take place in a dual-purpose tun over a two- to three-hour period.

The classic infusion mash is not stirred. It entrains and retains a great deal of air; consequently, it "floats."

The greatest challenge in an infusion mash is to achieve and maintain a reasonably even saccharification temperature. Unless the mash can be raked during sparging, an infusion mash can't be stirred to disperse temperature evenly, because stirring deaerates the mash, and the lauter mash will set. Entrained air keeps an infusion mash from settling until late in the sparging cycle.

Temperature variation within the mash, then, is almost inevitable, and within limits is considered acceptable. So long as variations do not exceed ±2 degrees F (1 degree C) of the target saccharification temperature, attenuation consistency will be acceptable.

A mash program should not be chosen to suit the style of beer being brewed, with the single exception that a decoction mash is specific to developing the maltiness that is characteristic of some lager beer styles (Munichs, fests, alts). All ales and most lagers can be made from infusion, decoction, or step mashes.

The choice of a mash program is determined by the character of the malt being used. The infusion mash is designed for use with well-modified malt that can be extracted by a single rest in the 149 to 158 degree F (65 to 70 degrees C) range. English pale and mild malts are not the only malts that are suitable for infusion mashing. Most modern malts, including those of continental origin, can be

Traditional Infusion Mash

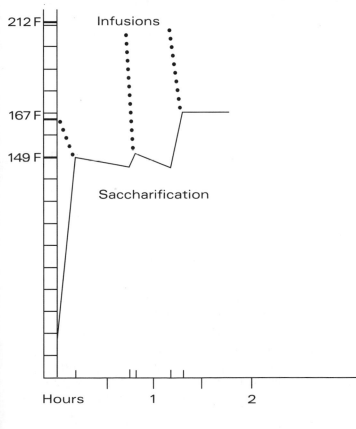

infusion mashed. The criteria for whether or not a malt can be infusion mashed are: a fine/coarse extract difference of less than 1.8 percent, a soluble nitrogen ratio (S/T) of at least 38 percent, and malt that is at least 95 percent mealy. Where no lot analysis is available, acrospire growth examination should give at least 90 percent grown to two-thirds the length of the kernel, and the majority at three-quarters-to-full-kernel length. Beers that will be served very cold may show a protein haze if malt of more than 1.6 percent nitrogen (10 percent protein) with a soluble nitrogen ratio less than 40 percent is mashed without a protein rest.

If the malt is well converted and perfectly crushed, if the saccharification temperature is reasonably uniform, if the mash floats well, if sparging is evenly dispersed, if the lauter mash is raked and the sweet-wort runoff is restricted so that it takes ninety minutes or so to collect, an infusion mash will give nearly the same extract as a step or decoction mash would. In practice, however, infusion mashes give 3 to 10 percent lower extract, depending upon the particular brew house's efficiency.

The saccharification temperature for an infusion mash almost always falls between 149 degrees F (65 degrees C) and 158 degrees F (70 degrees C). And 149 degrees F is the temperature at which malt starch gelatinizes, so the saccharification temperature should be at least 149 degrees F for malt starch to be made easily accessible to diastatic enzymes. Beta-amylase is still very active at 149 degrees F, while alpha-amylase is somewhat subdued, so the maltose-to-dextrins ratio of the wort will be very high, and the wort from a 149 degree F mash will be composed primarily of fermentable sugars. A final gravity (apparent) of 20 to 25 percent of the OG usually results. At 158 degrees F, beta-amylase is almost entirely deactivated, while alpha-amylase is performing at its peak. The greater percentage of maltotriose, maltotetraose, and dextrins in a wort from a 158 degree F mash will give a beer with a high end-gravity (33 to 35 percent of the OG). Mashes within the range bracketed by these temperatures give intermediate results; at 153 to 155 degrees F (67 to 68 degrees C), the FG might be expected to be 28 to 32 percent of the OG.

The duration of the saccharification rest also affects fermentability and flavor. A 120-minute mash is going to eke out every bit of diastatic power that the malt has to offer, while a 45-minute mash at the same temperature is going to leave more large polysaccharides. Consequently, a two-hour mash at 149 degrees F is going to give a beer with a lower final gravity than a 45-minute mash at the same temperature.

Finally, mash thickness will affect fermentability. The thicker the mash, the more effective the enzymes will be, and the longer their power will last. Alpha-amylase is especially sensitive to mash thickness. When brewing for a dextrinous wort, it is important that the mash be kept thick, so that alpha-amylase will not be degraded before all the malt starch is reduced to at least dextrins. The greater the degree of attenuation desired, the thinner the mash should be. It is common to gradually thin an infusion mash with boiling liquor when it is for a well-attenuated beer.

The quality and uniformity of crushing is more important for an infusion mash than for a multitemperature program. The crush needs to be relatively coarse, so the mash will float, but not so coarse that all the kernels aren't at least fully cracked, or the starch won't all hydrolyze. On the other hand, predominantly shredded husks and a high percentage of flour almost ensure a stuck mash.

Historically, the extract of infusion mashes was run off completely after conversion, and the mash was reflooded with hotter liquor and run off a second time in lieu of sparging (double mash). In modern practice, sparging is carried out as for step and decoction mashing, except that the liquid level above the settling grain is not usually lowered as rapidly. Sparging may begin almost immediately after the runoff is begun, and the liquid level may be lowered only gradually.

Since there is little remedy for temperature, thickness, or pH shortcomings in a mash that can only be stirred moderately, the mashing-in for an infusion mash needs to be competently handled. The malt is usually mashed-in with liquor at a strike temperature that is 10 to 20 degrees F (6 to 11 degrees C) hotter than the target mash temperature, depending on the temperature of the malt itself, the ambient temperature, the temperature and insulating properties of the mash-tun, and the mash thickness desired. With a poorly insulated tun, the mash needs to be made up thick, so that subsequent temperature-maintaining liquor infusions won't dilute it so much that the liquid weight forces the grains to sink. In general, where the crushed malt, whether dry or hydrated, drops into liquor/mash in the tun, the mash floats better than if the liquor is added to dry malt in the tun.

The alkalinity of the liquor is critical to the mash pH. When mashing pale malts, the liquor pH needs to be adjusted to below 6.8 for soft waters and as low as 5.8 for hard waters to realize a pH of 5.2 to 5.3 in the mash. As the percentage of dark malts increases in a mash, it becomes less sensitive to the pH of the liquor.

Where very dark or crystallized malts are called for in a recipe, many brewers wait until the end of the mash to add these malts so that exposure to the hot liquid does not unnecessarily extract tannins from the husks. Since these malts do not contain raw starch, they do not need to be saccharified.

Infusion Mash Procedure

Crush the malts. Infuse with 1 1/4 to 1 1/2 quarts of liquor at 160 to 180 degrees F (71 to 82 degrees C) per pound of malt for a saccharification rest at 149 to 158 degrees F (65 to 70 degrees C) and mix gently. Check and record the pH and temperature of the mash. Maintain the rest temperature for forty-five to sixty minutes, or for up to a maximum of two hours for greater attenuation. Make boiling-liquor infusions as necessary to maintain the mash temperature. Crush and hydrate roasted and crystal malts as the end of the mash nears. Confirm the degree of saccharification by iodine testing; for a dextrinous wort, the mash can be concluded once the iodine reaction falls off to a mahogany color.

Begin to run off the sweet wort slowly. Begin sparging with liquor at 170 to 175 degrees F (77 to 80 degrees C) when the grist begins to sink. As the mash level drops, let the liquid level drop proportionally; not more than two inches of liquid should stand above the grains during sparging.

Terminate the runoff when the pH of the sweet wort rises above 5.8 or the density drops to 3 °Plato (SG 1012).

APPEDIX

The Step Mash (Modified Infusion Mash)

The modified infusion method (step mash, temperature-programmed mash) mimics the traditional decoction-mash sequence, but with less satisfactory results (primarily because no part of the mash is ever boiled). It is, however, far more effective in dealing with undermodified malt than an infusion mash, and a great deal simpler and less time-consuming than a decoction mash, taking only 2 1/2 to 5 hours. It has displaced both continental and British tradition in most commercial breweries.

Generally, heat is applied directly to the mash-tun to raise the temperature and to restore temperatures as they fall off during the mash rests. Consequently, a very thick mash can be formed. Caution should be used when applying heat, as rest temperatures can be unwittingly exceeded if not carefully monitored, and if the mash is not constantly and thoroughly mixed.

Crush the malt, dough-in, and bring it to rest at 95 degrees F (35 degrees C), as for decoction mashing. The pH should be near 5.5. After thirty minutes or so, apply heat to the mash-tun to raise the temperature to an even 122 degrees F (50 degrees C) in fifteen minutes; hold it for ten to fifteen minutes. The pH should have dropped to 5.3. Heat to saccharification temperature, quickly for dextrinous

worts, or over a span of fifteen to thirty minutes for highly
attenuable worts. After fifteen minutes begin testing for
starch conversion. When a faint to negative iodine reaction
is observed, infuse the mash with boiling water to raise its
temperature to 167 to 170 degrees F (75 to 77 degrees C).
Hold the temperature and thoroughly mix the mash for five
minutes before transferring it to the lauter-tun for sparging.

Step Mash

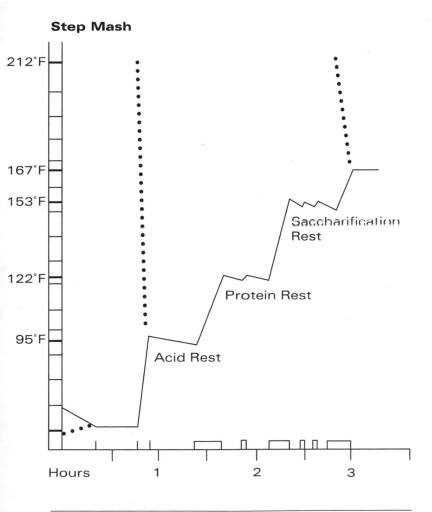

APPENDIX

Weights and Measures

The standard density/specific gravity reference temperature was changed in the United Kingdom from 60 degrees F (15.56 degrees C) to 68 degrees F (20 degrees C) in 1990. The same standard temperature is now used in the British, U.S., and metric systems.

In the same year the Congress of the International System of Units (SI) made corrections to the Celsius temperature scale; what was 20.005 degrees C is now 20 degrees C (68 degrees F), and what was 15.564 degrees C is now 15.56 degrees C (60 degrees F).

The SI size of the liter was changed slightly in 1964. One liter now equals one cubic decimeter exactly, or 99.9972 percent of the pre-1964 liter (the "old" liter was defined as the volume occupied by one kilogram of water at 4 degrees C). Since 1990, the SI standard weight for one liter of pure water in vacuo at 20 degrees C is .998202 kilogram, and in dry air .997151 kilogram. The National Institute of Standards and Technology (NIST) in the U.S. gives the weight of one liter of water at 20 degrees C at one atmosphere, measured in vacuo, as .998232 kilogram, and in dry air as .998229 kilogram. The SI standards are used here.

Abbreviations

U.S. Liquid Measure		Liquid Measure	
dram	dr.	liter	L
fluid ounce	fl. oz.	milliliter	mL
pint	pt.	deciliter	dL
quart	qt.	dekaliter	dkL
gallon	gal.		
barrel	bbl.		

Metric System			Metric System Units	
micro	μ	.0001	gram	g
milli	m	.001	meter	m
centi	c	.01	square meter	m^2
deci	d	.1	cubic meter	m^3
deka	dk	10		
hecto	h	100		
kilo	k	1000		

Capacity

To express any volume in another unit of measure, convert the measure in the left-hand column to any unit in the right-hand column by multiplying by the factor shown.

microliter	= .000 000 1 L
milliliter	= 1 cm^3 = .2705 fl. dr. = .033814 fl. oz. = .001 L = 0.06102 cu. in.= .997151 g of water at 20°C
fluid dram	= 3.697 mL = .125 fl. oz.
centiliter	= 10 mL = .3381 fl. oz. =.01 L
tablespoon	= 14.7868 mL = .5 fl. oz.
Imperial fluid ounce	= 28.4131 mL = .9608 fl. oz. (U.S.)
deciliter	= 100 mL = 3.3814 fl. oz. = .1 L

fluid ounce	= 29.5735 mL = 2 tblsp. = 1.8046 cu. in.
cup	= 236.6 mL = 8 fl. oz. = .2366 L
pint	= 473.176 mL = 16 fl. oz. = 2 cups = .8327 Imp. pt. = .47321 = 28.875 cu. in.
Imperial pint	= 568.29 mL = 20 Imp. fl. oz. = 19.2152 fl. oz. (U.S.) = 1.2009 pt. (U.S.) = .56825 L
quart	= 946.3530 mL - 32 fl. oz. = 4 cups = .8327 Imp. qt. = .94633 L = 57.75 cu. in.
liter	= 1000 mL = 33.8140 fl. oz. = 2.1134 pt. = 1.0567 qt. = .2642 gal. = 997.15lg of water at 20°C = 61.0234 cu. in.
Imperial quart	= 1136.6 mL = 40 Imp. fl. oz. = 38.4304 fl. oz. (U.S.) = 1.2009 qt. (U.S.) = 1.1366 L
gallon	= 3785.4118 mL = 128 fl. oz. = 16 cups = 8 pt. = 4 qt. = 3.7854 L = .8327 Imp. gal. = 231 cu. in. = 8.3216 lb. of water at 20°C
Imperial gallon	= 4546 mL = 160 Imp. fl. oz. = 153.7234 fl. oz. (U.S.) = 4.5459 L = 1.20095 gal.
dekaliter	= 10 L = 2.6417 gal.
1/8 barrel	= 3.875 gal.
1/4 barrel	= 7.75 gal.
1/2 barrel	= 15.5 gal.
hectoliter	= 100 L = 26.4172 gal. = 21.9969 Imp. gal. = .8522 bbl. = .6110 Imp. bbl.
barrel	= 31 gal. = 1.1 735 hL = .717 Imp. bbl. = 7056 cu. in.
Imperial barrel	= 43.2342 gal. (U.S.) = 36 Imp. gal. = 1.63659 hL = 1.3946 bbl. (U.S.)

Submultiples of Capacity (U.S. Liquid Measure)

Gallons	Fl. Oz.	Fl. Pt.	Fl. Qt.
.0078	1		
.0156	2		
.0313	4	¼	
.0469	6		
.0625	8	½	¼
.0938	12	¾	
.125	16	1	½
.1563	20	1¼	
.1875	24	1½	¾
.2188	28	1¾	
.25	32	2	1
.375	48	3	1½
.50	64	4	2
.75	96	6	3
1.00	128	8	4

U.S. and Metric Systems Cubic Measure (Volume)

cubic centimeter = 1 mL at 20°C = .06102374 cu. in.
cubic inch = 16.387064 cm^3
cubic decimeter = 61.0237 cu. in. = 1 L at 20°C
cubic foot = 1,728 cu. in. = 28.317 dm^3 = 28.316846592 cm^3 L = .0283 m^3
cubic meter = 35.31467 cu. ft.

Dry Measure (Volume)

dry pint = 33.6003 cu. in. = .5506 L
dry quart = 67.2006 cu. in. = 2 pt. = 1.1012 L
liter = 61.0255 cu. in. = .9081 qt.
peck = 537.605 cu. in. = 8 qt. = 8.8096 L
bushel = 2,150.42 cu. in. = 32 qt. = 4 pecks = 35.2383 L = .3524 hL

barrel   = 7,056 cu. in. = 105 qt.
hectoliter   = 6,102.5461 cu. in. = 90.81 qt. = 100 L
               = 2.8375 bu.

Weight

microgram = .000 000 1 g
milligram   = .015432 grains = .001 g
centigram   = .1543 grains = .01 g
grain   = 64.7989 mg = .0648 g
gram   = 1,000 mg = 15.432358 grains =
              .035274 oz. (avoir.) = .00220462 lb.
ounce   = 437.5 grains = 28.349523125 g (avoir-
              dupois)
pound   = 7,000 grains = 453.59237 g = 16 oz. =
              .4536 kg
kilogram   = 1,000 g = 35.27396 oz. (avoir.) =
              2.2046226 lb.
short ton   = 2,000 lb. = 20 hundred weight =
              907.18474 kg = .9072 metric ton
metric ton = 1,000 kg = 2204.6226 lb. = 1.1023
              short tons

Linear Measure

millimeter = .03937 in. = .001 m
centimeter = .3937 in. = .01 m
inch   = 25.4 mm = 2.54 cm
decimeter   = 3.937 in. = .1 m
foot   = 30.48 cm = 12 in. = .3048 m
yard   = 91.44 cm = 36 in. = 3 ft. = .9144 m
meter   = 39.370079 in. = 3.28084 ft. = 1.09361 yd.

Square Measure

square centimeter = .1550 sq. in.
square inch   = 6.4516 cm^2 = .006944 sq. ft.
square decimeter = .1076 sq. ft.
square foot   = 929.0304 cm^2 = 144 sq. in. =
                     .0929 m^2

Temperature

°Fahrenheit	°Centigrade	°Réaumur	°Fahrenheit	°Centigrade	°Réaumur
30	-1.11		110	43.33	
32	0	0	113	45	36
35	1.67		122	50	40
39.2	4.0		131	55	44
40	4.44		140	60	48
41	5	4	145	62.78	
45	7.22		149	65	52
50	10	8	155	68.33	
55	12.78		158	70	56
59	15	12	160	71.11	
60	15.56		167	75	60
65	18.33		170	76.67	
68	20	16	176	80	64
70	21.11		180	82.22	
77	25	20	185	85	68
80	26.67		194	90	72
86	30	24	200	93.33	
90	32.22		203	95	76
95	35	28	212	100	80
100	37.78		221	105	84
104	40	32	230	110	88

Conversion

$$°C \text{ to } °F = \frac{(°C) \, 9}{5} + 32$$

$$°R \text{ to } °F = \frac{(°R) \, 9}{4} + 32$$

$$°F \text{ to } °C = \frac{(°F-32) \, 5}{9}$$

$$°R \text{ to } °C = \frac{(°R) \, 5}{4}$$

$$°F \text{ to } °R = \frac{(°F-32) \, 4}{9}$$

$$°C \text{ to } °R = \frac{(°C) \, 4}{5}$$

Density

°Plato (°P; Balling, °B; or Brix) expresses a solution's density as grams of sucrose per 100 grams of solution, measured at 68 degrees F (20 degrees C). 10 °Plato, then, is a 10 percent weight/weight solution. Plato, Balling, Brix and specific gravity are all now commonly calibrated at the international standard of 20 degrees C (68 degrees F). Although 60 degrees F (15.56 degrees C) is being abandoned as a brewing reference temperature, some hydrometers are still calibrated at a reference temperature of 60 degrees F.

Specific gravity (sp gr) measures the density of a solution as compared to the density of pure water (sp gr 1.000). Brewers rarely use specific gravity notation in its usual form. For instance, 1.040 is more often given as "1040" and called "gravity" (SG). British brewers further abbreviate SG 1040 to "40," call it "excess gravity," and write it as "G." Both are useful in simplifying formulas.

Specific gravity is a weight/volume measurement. A 10 percent weight/weight solution gives SG 1040.03 (sp gr 1.04003) at 68 degrees F, rather than 1040 as might be expected, because specific gravity-to-°Plato conversions are not linear.

To convert from specific gravity to °Plato with absolute accuracy requires the use of a regression equation. At 68 degrees F (20 degrees C):

$$°P = 135.997 \times \text{sp gr}^3 - 630.272 \times \text{sp gr}^2 + 1111.14 \times \text{sp gr} - 616.868$$

A simpler formula gives reasonably accurate results:

$$°P = 260 - (260/\text{sp gr}) \text{ and inversely,}$$
$$\text{sp gr} = 260/(260 - °P).$$

Multiplying °Plato by four roughly gives excess gravity (G):

10 °P x 4 = 40 G

Conversely, dividing G by four gives the approximate °Plato:

40/4 = 10 °P

Also:

Extract = G/46.21.   40/46.21 = .866 lb. of extract/gallon required.

Extract is the amount of any substance in solution. In brewing, extract is based on sucrose, dry basis, giving 100 percent yield. What density 100 percent yield gives depends on the ratio of the extract to the volume (or weight) of the solution.

The ASBC laboratory mash assesses extract on a weight/weight basis. In an ASBC mash at 68 degrees F, 100 percent extract gives 11.11 °P, SG 1044.65, and 372.94 L°/kg.

In practice, brewers need to use a weight/volume basis. In the U.S., this is usually pounds per gallon, or pounds per barrel. As one pound in one gallon, 100 percent extract at 68 degrees F is 11.486065 °P, SG 1046.21415, and 385.6458 L°/kg. At 60 degrees F, 100 percent extract/one pound in one gallon gives 11.47 °P, SG 1046.15, and 385.11 L°/kg.

Liter degrees per kilogram (L°/kg) is the IOB (British) standard for extract. It is a metric weight/volume measurement. The most accurate method of converting L°/kg to percent extract is by the formula:

% extract = 10.13 x (.2601 x L° per kg / 10.13 - .03025)

A less accurate but simpler formula is:

.2601 x L°/kg -.3064

Example:

.2601 x 308 L°/kg - .3064 = 79.8% extract

The reciprocal formula is:

L°/kg = 3.845 x % extract + 1.178

For all intents and purposes, °Plato, Balling, and Brix are interchangeable, although the Balling scale was calibrated at 17.5 degrees C. Where a hydrometer calibrated at 60 degrees F (15.56 degrees C) is being used, the reference temperature can be corrected to 68 degrees F (20 degrees C) by the formula:

SG at 60°F x .99548 + 4.53 = SG at 68°F

The reciprocal formula is:

SG at 68°F x 1.00454 - 4.55 = SG at 60°F

For all practical purposes, a hydrometer calibrated at 60 degrees F gives acceptably accurate results, as is seen in the tables below.

The density tables are based upon these values:

1. °Plato = 135.997 x SG_3 -630.272 x SG_2 + 1111.14 x SG - 616.868

2. Extract required for one gallon of solution at a given specific gravity or density: % extract required, at 68°F (20°C) = sp gr x °P x 8.321628; given that one gallon equals 3785.411784 milliliters, and that one milliliter of pure water at 68°F (20°C) in dry air weighs .997151 grams.

A. Gravity and °Plato at 68°F (20°C):

°P	SG	°P	SG	°P	SG
0.000	1000	2.561	1010	5.331	1021
.255	1001	2.815	1011	5.580	1022
.513	1002	3.068	1012	5.829	1023
.771	1003	3.321	1013	6.077	1024
1.028	1004	3.574	1014	6.325	1025
1.284	1005	3.826	1015	6.572	1026
1.541	1006	4.078	1016	6.819	1027
1.796	1007	4.329	1017	7.066	1028
2.052	1008	4.580	1018	7.312	1029
2.306	1009	4.831	1019	7.558	1030
		5.081	1020		

B. Gravity, corresponding °Plato, and pounds of extract required for one gallon of solution at the given gravity, at 68°F (20°C):

For Density of: SG	°P	Lb. Extract for 1 Gal.:	For Density of: SG	°P	Lb. Extract for 1 Gal.:
1031	7.804	.6695	1056	13.805	1.2131
1032	8.049	.6912	1057	14.039	1.2349
1033	8.293	.7129	1058	14.274	1.2567
1034	8.537	.7346	1059	14.508	1.2785
1035	8.781	.7563	1060	14.741	1.3003
1036	9.024	.7780	1061	14.975	1.3221
1037	9.267	.7997	1062	15.207	1.3440
1038	9.510	.8214	1063	15.440	1.3658
1039	9.752	.8432	1064	15.672	1.3876
1040	9.994	.8649	1065	15.903	1.4094
1041	10.234	.8866	1066	16.135	1.4313
1042	10.475	.9084	1067	16.365	1.4531
1043	10.716	.9301	1068	16.596	1.4750
1044	10.956	.9518	1069	16.826	1.4968
1045	11.196	.9736	1070	17.056	1.5187
1046	11.435	.9953	1075	18.198	1.6280
1046.214	11.486	1.0000	1080	19.331	1.7374
1047	11.674	1.0171	1085	20.454	1.8468
1048	11.912	1.0389	1090	21.568	1.9564
1049	12.150	1.0606	1095	22.673	2.0660
1050	12.388	1.0824	1100	23.769	2.1758
1051	12.625	1.1042	1105	24.855	2.2856
1052	12.862	1.1260	1110	25.933	2.3954
1053	13.098	1.1477	1115	27.002	2.5054
1054	13.334	1.1695	1120	28.062	2.6154
1055	13.570	1.1913	1125	29.113	2.7255

C. °Plato, corresponding gravity, and pounds of extract required for one gallon of solution at the given °Plato, at 68°F (20°C)

For Density of: °P	SG	Lb. Extract for 1 Gal.:	For Density of: °P	SG	Lb. Extract for 1 Gal.:
8.0	1031.8	.6869	15.5	1063.26	1.3715
8.5	1033.9	.7324	16.0	1065.42	1.4186
9.0	1035.9	.7758	16.5	1067.58	1.4658
9.5	1037.96	.8206	17.0	1069.76	1.5134
10.0	1040.03	.8655	17.5	1071.94	1.5611
10.5	1042.11	.9108	18.0	1074.14	1.6091
11.0	1044.19	.9560	18.5	1076.33	1.6570
11.486	1046.214	1.0000	19.0	1078.54	1.7054
11.5	1046.28	1.0014	19.5	1080.75	1.7538
12.0	1048.37	1.0469	20.0	1082.97	1.8024
12.5	1050.48	1.0929	21.0	1087.44	1.9004
13.0	1052.59	1.1388	22.0	1091.95	1.9991
13.5	1054.71	1.1850	23.0	1096.49	2.0987
14.0	1056.83	1.2312	24.0	1101.06	2.1991
14.5	1058.97	1.2779	25.0	1105.67	2.3003
15.0	1061.11	1.3245			

D. Gravity and pounds of extract required for one gallon of solution at the given SG, at 60°F (15.56°C)

Density SG	Lb. Extract for 1 Gal.:	Density SG	Lb. Extract for 1 Gal.:	Density SG	Lb. Extract for 1 Gal.:
1031	.6706	1047	.0188	1065	1.4117
1032	.6923	1048	.0406	1066	1.4336
1033	.7141	1049	.0624	1067	1.4555
1034	.7358	1050	.0842	1068	1.4774
1035	.7575	1051	.1060	1069	1.4992
1036	.7793	1052	.1278	1070	1.5211
1037	.8010	1053	.1496	1075	1.6306
1038	.8228	1054	.1714	1080	1.7402
1039	.8445	1055	.1933	1085	1.8498
1040	.8663	1056	1.2151	1090	1.9596
1041	.8881	1057	1.2369	1095	2.0694
1042	.9098	1058	1.2588	1100	2.1793
1043	.9316	1059	1.2806	1105	2.2893
1044	.9534	1060	1.3024	1110	2.3993
1045	.9752	1061	1.3243	1115	2.5095
1046	.9970	1062	1.3462	1120	2.6197
1046.15	1.0000	1063	1.3680	1125	2.7299
		1064	1.3899		

Temperature Corrections for Hydrometers Calibrated at 68°F (20°C).

If Temperature Is: °F	°C	SG: 1010-	1030-	1040-	1050-	1060-	1070-	1080-	1090-
		Adjust Hydrometer Reading By:							
35	2	-2	-2	-3	-3	-3	-3	-4	-4
40	4	-2	-2	-3	-3	-3	-3	-3	-3
50	10	-2	-2	-2	-2	-2	-2	-2	-2
60	15.5	-1	-1	-1	-1	-1	-1	-1	-1
80	27	+2	+2	+2	+2	+2	+2	+2	+2
90	32	+3	+3	+3	+3	+4	+4	+4	+4
95	35	+4	+4	+4	+4	+4	+5	+5	+5
105	40	+5	+5	+5	+6	+6	+6	+6	+6
115	45	+6	+7	+7	+7	+7	+8	+8	+8
125	50	+7	+8	+8	+8	+9	+9	+9	+10

Adjust reading; for example, reading at 80°F is 1055: add 2 = 1057.

Temperature Corrections for Hydrometers Calibrated at 60°F (15.56°C).

If Temperature Is: °F	°C	SG: 1010-	1030-	1040-	1050-	1060-	1070-	1080-	1090-
		Adjust Hydrometer Reading By:							
35	2	-1	-2	-2	-2	-2	-2	-2	-3
40	4	-1	-2	-2	-2	-2	-2	-2	-2
50	10	-1	-1	-1	-1	-1	-1	-1	-1
70	20	+1	+1	+1	+1	+1	+1	+1	+2
80	27	+2	+3	+3	+3	+3	+3	+3	+3
90	32	+4	+4	+4	+4	+5	+5	+5	+5
95	35	+4	+5	+5	+5	+5	+5	+6	+6
105	40	+6	+6	+6	+6	+7	+7	+7	+7
115	45	+7	+7	+8	+8	+8	+8	+9	+9
125	50	+8	+9	+9	+9	+10	+10	+10	+11

Adjust reading; for example, reading at 80°F is 1055: add 3 = 1058.

Temperature Corrections for Saccharometers Calibrated at 68°F (20°C).

If Temperature Is: °F	°C	°P: 2.5- Adjust Saccharometer Reading By:	7.5-	10.0-	12.5-	15.0-	17.0-	19.0-	21.5-
35	2	-.5	-.5	-.8	-.8	-.8	-.8	-1.0	-1.0
40	4	-.5	-.5	-.8	-.8	-.8	-.8	-.8	-.8
50	10	-.5	-.5	-.5	-.5	-.5	-.5	-.5	-.5
60	15.5	-.3	-.3	-.3	-.3	-.3	-.3	-.3	-.3
80	27	+.5	+.5	+.5	+.5	+.5	+.5	+.5	+.5
90	32	+.8	+.8	+.8	+.8	+1.0	+1.0	+1.0	+1.0
95	35	+1.0	+1.0	+1.0	+1.0	+1.0	+1.3	+1.3	+1.3
105	40	+1.3	+1.3	+1.3	+1.5	+1.5	+1.5	+1.5	+1.5
115	45	+1.5	+1.8	+1.8	+1.8	+1.8	+2.1	+2.1	+2.1
125	50	+1.8	+2.1	+2.1	+2.1	+2.3	+2.3	+2.3	+2.6

Adjust reading; for example, °Plato at 85°F is 13.5: add .5 = 14.0.

Alcohol

Expected Alcohol by Volume and by Weight

Apparent Attenuation:		Alcohol by Volume/Weight		Apparent Attenuation:		Alcohol by Volume/Weight	
°P	G	ABV	ABW	°P	G	ABV	ABW
3	12	1.55	1.22	10.5	42	5.42	4.25
4	16	2.06	1.62	11	44	5.68	4.46
5	20	2.58	2.03	11.5	46	5.93	4.66
6	24	3.10	2.43	12	48	6.19	4.86
7	28	3.61	2.84	12.5	50	6.45	5.06
7.5	30	3.87	3.04	13	53	6.71	5.27
8	32	4.13	3.24	14	57	7.22	5.67
8.5	34	4.39	3.44	15	61	7.74	6.08
9	36	4.64	3.65	16	65	8.26	6.48
9.5	38	4.90	3.85	17	70	8.77	6.89
10	40	5.16	4.05	18	74	9.29	7.29

Formulas for deriving approximate alcohol by weight (ABW) or alcohol by volume (ABV) from apparent attenuation (OG-TG):

ABW, °P = [.8192 (OG-TG)]/[2.0665 - (.010665 x OG)]
or:
ABV (v/v), °P = OE-TE x .516
ABW (w/w), °P = OG-FG x .405
ABV (v/v), G = OG-FG x .129
ABW (w/w), G = OE-TE x .102
ABV   = 1.26 x ABW
ABW   = .785 x ABV
True attenuation/fermentability = apparent attenuation x .814

Pressure

Absolute pressure, lb./sq. in. = psi on a gauge + 14.7 psi
Hydrostatic pressure, psi = head, in feet x .434
Head, in feet = psi/.434

Pressure at 50°F at sea level:

1 atmosphere   = water at 212°F, sea level =
                 14.6959 psi = 1.013250 bar =
                 101.325 kilopascals = 760.002
                 mmHg = 1.03323 kg/cm^2 =
                 406.8 inches of H_2O
1 psi (1 lb./sq. in.) = .068046 atmospheres = 6.89476
                 kPa = 70.308 mm/Hg = .0703086
                 kg/cm^2 = 27.68"/H_2O
1 bar   = .9869 atmospheres = 14.5 psi =
                 100 kPa = 750.062 mm/Hg =
                 1.01972 kg/cm^2 = 401.47"/H_2O

Pressure at Various Altitudes

Altitude	psi	Altitude	psi	Altitude	psi
0'	14.70	2,000'	13.67	4,500'	12.45
500'	14.43	2,500'	13.41	5,000'	12.23
1,000'	14.18	3,000'	13.19	10,000'	10.10
1,500'	13.90	3,500'	12.92	15,000'	8.28
		4,000'	12.70		

Volumes of CO_2: Pressure at Various Temperatures

°F	°C	psi 6	8	10	12	14	16	18	20	22	24	26	28
		Volumes of CO_2 at given temperature and pressure:											
30	-1	2.36	2.60	2.82	3.02								
32	0	2.27	2.48	2.70	2.90								
35	1.7	2.14	2.34	2.52	2.73	2.93							
40	4		2.10	2.30	2.47	2.65	2.84	3.01					
45	7.2			2.08	2.26	2.42	2.60	2.77	2.94				
50	10				2.21	2.38	2.54	2.70	2.86	3.02			
55	12.7					2.04	2.19	2.33	2.47	2.63	2.78	2.93	3.01
60	15.6						2.01	2.14	2.28	2.42	2.56	2.70	2.84

At 50°F (10°C):

To carbonate 1 gallon of beer to 1 volume requires 7.5 grams of CO_2.

To carbonate 1 hL of beer to 1 volume requires .2 kg of CO_2.

1 gram CO_2 per 100 mL = 5.06 volumes per volume of beer

1 volume of CO_2 per volume of beer = .198 grams of CO_2 per 100 mL

1 Atmosphere = 14.7 psi = .968 kg/cm^2.

Although the amount of CO_2 in a packaged beer doesn't change as temperature increases, the pressure does.

If bottled beer is let warm up, it may gush upon opening, or even explode if it is overcarbonated:

Pressure Increase at Rising Temperatures					
Volumes of CO_2:	Temperature: 40°F	50°F	60°F	70°F	80°F
2.0	7 psi	11 psi	16 psi	20 psi	25 psi
2.5	12 psi	18 psi	23 psi	28 psi	34 psi
3.0	18 psi	24 psi	30 psi	36 psi	42 psi

Water

At sea level, pure water (H_2O; 11.188% hydrogen, 88.812% oxygen by weight) freezes at 32 degrees F (O degrees C), boils at 212 degrees F (100 degrees C). It is most dense at 39.2 degrees F (3.98 degrees C). One gallon at 60 degrees F (15.56 degrees C) weighs 58,310 grains. At 68 degrees F (20 degrees C), one cubic foot weighs 64.3 lb., one ounce (avoir.) equals .96 fluid ounces, one pound equals .12 gallons, and one cubic inch equals 16.36 grams. At 32 degrees F (O degrees C), water weighs 1.000429 grams/milliliter, but as ice weighs .919 grams/milliliter.

1 mL = 1 cc of water at 68°F (20°C)
1 L   = 1 kg of water at 68°F (20°C)

Density of Water, in Air					
°F	°C	g/cm³ (g/mL)	oz./fl. oz.	lb./gal.	lb./UK gal.
32	0	1.000429	1.043622	8.348982	10.027
39.2	4	1.000693	1.043898	8.351188	10.029
60	15.56	.998772	1.041895	8.335156	10.010
68	20	.997151	1.040204	8.321628	9.994
77	25	.994836	1.037789	8.302309	9.971
212	100	.957344	0.998678	7.989423	9.601

Pressure at Temperatures Other Than 50 Degrees F						
Atmosphere	Temperature At:	50°F lb. per sq. in.	40°F	59°F	68°F	77°F
1.0		14.7	10	20	22	24
2.0		29.4	20	34	40	43
2.5		36.8	25	43	50	53
3.0		44.1	30	52	63	65
4.0		58.8	40	70	79	88

$$CO_2, \text{ volumes } = \frac{4.85 \text{ (lb. per sq. in. } + 14.7)}{\text{temperature, °F } + 12.4}$$

Water Hardness

Parts per million (in metric usage, mg/L) = 1 part $CaCO_3$ per 1,000,000 parts (water = 1 mg/L = .1 parts per 100,000 = .07 °Clark = .0583 gpg (U.S.) = .056 °German

Grain per gallon (U.S.) = 1 part $CaCO_3$ per 58,310 parts water = 17.1497 ppm = 1.2 °Clark

Clark degree (grain per gallon, U.K.) = 1 part $CaCO_3$ per 70,000 parts water = 14.25 ppm = .833 gpg (U.S.) = .8°German = .7 millival

German degree = 1 mg Ca per 1000 L = 1 part CaO per 100,000 parts water = 17.9 ppm as $CaCO_3$ = 1.4285 °Clark

French degree = 1 mg $CaCO_3$ per 1000 L

Millival = .001-ion concentration = 20.357 ppm

Expansion/Contraction of Water:

°F	°C	Relative Volume
32	0	.998362
39.2	4	.998230
60	15.56	.999190
68	20	1.000000
77	25	1.001162
212	100	1.041581

Boiling Point at Various Elevations

Elevation	Boiling Point	Elevation	Boiling Point
-1000	213.8°F (101°C)	5000'	202.9°F (95°C)
sea level	212°F (100°C)	6000'	201.1°F (94°C)
1000'	210.2°F (99°C)	7000'	199.2°F (93°C)
2000'	208.4°F (98°C)	8000'	197.4°F (92°C)
3000'	206.5°F (97°C)	9000'	195.6°F (91°C)
4000'	204.7°F (96°C)	10,000'	183.7°F (90°C)

Boiling point drops approximately 1°F (.56°C) for each 550 feet (170 meters) of increase in altitude.

Boiling Temperature at Various Pressures

Atmospheres of Pressure	Boiling Point °F	°C
1	212	100
1.5	234	112.2
2	249	120.6
3	273	134
4	291	144
10	356	180
17	401	205

Useful Information

One bushel of barley weighs 48 lb.

One bushel of malt weighs 34 lb.

One cup of whole malt weighs approximately 5 oz. (142 g).

After malting, barley yields 85 to 93 percent malt by weight.

Ethyl alcohol boils at 173°F (78.5°C).

No amount of heat applied to a liquid will increase its temperature once it has reached its boiling point. Only pressure can increase a boiling liquid's temperature, by raising its boiling point.

Specific heat at 20°C: Beer = .92, Water = 1.00, Malt = .4.

1 BTU = 1°F temperature change per gallon of water = 2.928 x 10-4 KWH

1 Calorie = 1°C rise per kilogram of water

1 BTU/hr. = 2.931 W

1 Boiler HP = 33.479 BTU/hr.

One gallon per minute equals 225 liters per hour.

For refrigeration load at 68°F: 8.3217 x SG = lb./gal.

Freezing point: -(.42 x ABW + .04 x OG + .2) °C

Approximate Calories in Beer, per 12 Fluid Ounces						
OG	TG 1010	1012	1014	1016	1018	1020
1040	132	132	133	134	135	136
1050	164	165	166	167	168	169
1060	196	197	198	199	200	202

To test or calibrate a thermometer, insert it in chipped ice, and into the steam just above the surface of boiling water; adjust the second reading to account for elevation above sea level.

1 Pasteur unit = 1 minute at 140°F (60°C). Pasteur units increase 10 times for every 12.6°F (7°C) increase in temperature.

Sterilizing at 170°F (77°C) is equal to 268 Pasteur units, at 160°F (72°C) is equal to 45 PU.

Homebrew Sterilant Solutions

Volume of Sterilant Solution:	Add Bleach:
1 gal./4 L	1 1/2 teaspoons or 7 mL
4 gal./15 L	1 fl. oz. or 30 mL
5 gal./19 L	1 1/4 fl. oz. or 40 mL
6 1/2 gal./25 L	1 1/2 fl. oz. or 50 mL

Approximate Displacement Values of Sucrose, Malt, and Hops

1 lb. of sucrose displaces .074 gal. of water

1 g of sucrose displaces .6165 mL of water

1 kg of sucrose displaces .6165 L of water

1 lb. of malt displaces .13 gal. in the mash

1 kg of malt displaces 1.07 L in the mash

1 lb. of spent malt retains .108 gal. of wort

1 kg of spent malt retains .90 L of wort

1 lb. of hops displaces .12 and absorbs 1.8 gal. of wort in the copper

1 kg of hops displaces 1 L and absorbs 15 L of wort in the copper

1 lb. of hops contributes .07 lb. of extract to 1 gal.

1 kg of hops contributes .265 kg of extract to 1 L of wort

1 lb. of spent hops retains .72 gal. of wort

1 kg of spent hops retains 6 L of wort

Percentage Solutions

%	Oz. (Avoir.)	Grams	W/V	W/W Dissolved In (to make up 1 qt.):
1	.33	9.4	in enough water to make up 1 quart of solution	31.66 fl. oz.
2	.67	18.9		31.36
3	1	28.4		31.04
4	1.33	37.8		30.72
5	1.67	47.3		30.4
10	3.33	94.5		28.8

For water, weight/volume (w/v) and weight/weight (w/w) solutions are identical. Otherwise, a w/w% solution at 10% will be 1% stronger than a w/v% solution at 10%.

% solutions:	in 10 mL	100 mL	1 L water
5%	.5g	5 g	50 g
10%	1.0g	10 g	100 g
25%	2.5g	25 g	250 g

Decimal Equivalents

1/64	.015	9/32	.281
1/32	.031	5/16	.312
3/64	.046	11/32	.343
1/16	.062	3/8	.375
5/64	.078	13/32	.406
3/32	.093	7/16	.437
7/64	.109	15/32	.468
1/8	.125	1/2	.500
9/64	.140	9/16	.562
5/32	.156	5/8	.625
11/64	.171	11/16	.687
3/16	.187	3/4	.750
13/64	.203	13/16	.812
7/32	.218	7/8	.875
15/64	.234	15/16	.937
1/4	.250	1	1.000

Percentage/Decimal Equivalents			
%	Decimal	%	Decimal
.01	.0001	5	.05
.5	.005	10	.1
1.0	.01	12.5	.125

Useful Formulas

Diameter of a circle $=$ circumference x .31831
Circumference of a circle $=$ diameter x 3.1416
Area of a circle $=$ diameter^2 x .7854
$=$ circumference^2 x .0796
$=$ radius^2 x 3.1416
Volume of a cylinder $= (\pi r^2)h =$ cu. in., ft., m, etc. $=$
$$\frac{(\pi r"^2)h"}{1.8046} = \text{fl. oz.}$$

Doubling the diameter of a cylinder increases its volume 4 times.

Volume of a dome $= \dfrac{(\pi r^2)\ h}{2}$

Volume of a cone $= \dfrac{(\pi r^2)h}{2} =$ cu. in., ft., m, etc.

Conversions

Gallons (U.S.) to pounds (avoir.) $= (8.33 \times \text{sp gr})$ gal.
Pounds (avoir.) to gallons (U.S.) $= \text{lb.}/8.33$ (sp gr)
Milliliter to grams $= \text{mL}$ (sp gr)
Grams to milliliters $= \text{g/sp gr}$
Milliliters to ounces (avoir.) $= \dfrac{\text{mL (sp gr)}}{28.35}$

Ounces (avoir.) to milliliters $= \dfrac{\text{oz. } (28.35)}{\text{sp gr}}$

BREWERS GLOSSARY

achroodextrins. Simple "border" dextrins, from the reduction of starch (amylopectin) by alpha-amylase; simple a-limit dextrins; negative reaction with iodine.

acrospire. The germinal plant-growth of the barley kernel.

adjuncts. Fermentable extract other than malted barley. Principally corn, rice, wheat, unmalted barley, and glucose (dextrose).

aerate. To saturate with atmospheric air; to force oxygen into solution. Introducing air to the wort at various stages of the brewing process.

aerobic. An organism requiring oxygen for metabolism.

agar. Agar-agar. A nonnitrogenous, gelatinous solidifying agent, more heat-stable than gelatin. A culture medium for microbial analysis.

agglutination. The grouping of cells by adhesion.

airlock. See *fermentation lock.*

airspace. See *ullage.*

albumin. Intermediate soluble protein subject to coagulation upon heating. Hydrolyzed to peptides and amino acids by proteolytic enzymes.

alcohol by volume (v/v). The percentage of volume of alcohol per volume of beer. To calculate the approximate volumetric alcohol content, subtract the final gravity from the original gravity and divide the result by 75. For example: 1.050 − 1.012 = .038/0.0075 = 5% v/v.

alcohol by weight (w/v). The percentage weight of alcohol per volume of beer. For example: 3.2% alcohol by weight = 3.2 grams of alcohol per 100 centiliters of beer. Alcohol by weight can be converted to alcohol by volume by multiplying by 0.795.

aldehyde. An organic compound that is a precursor to ethanol in a normal beer fermentation via the EMP pathway. In the presence of excess air, this reaction can be reversed, with alcohols being oxidized to very complex, unpleasant-tasting aldehydes, typically papery/cardboardy/sherry notes.

ale. 1. Historically, an unhopped malt beverage; 2. Now a generic term for hopped beers produced by top fermentation, as opposed to lagers, which are produced by bottom fermentation.

aleurone layer. The enzyme- and pentosan-bearing layer enveloping, and inseparable from, the malt endosperm.

all-extract beer. A beer made with only malt extract as opposed to one made from barley, or a combination of malt extract and barley.

all-grain beer. A beer made with only malted barley as opposed to one made from malt extract, or from malt extract and malted barley.

all-malt beer. A beer made with only barley malt with no adjuncts or refined sugars.

alpha acid. a-acid. The principle bittering agent of the hop, more soluble when isomerized by boiling. From the alpha resin of the hop.

alpha-acid unit. A measurement of the potential bitterness of hops, expressed by their percentage of alpha acid. Low = 2 to 4%, medium = 5 to 7%, high = 8 to 12%. Abbrev: AAU.

alt. The german word for old. This is an old-fashioned, top-fermenting style of beer that undergoes a cold lagering for maturation.

ambient temperature. The surrounding temperature.

amino acids. The smallest product of protein cleavage; simple nitrogenous matter.

amylodextrin. From the diastatic reduction of starch; ß-limit dextrin; the most complex dextrin from hydrolysis of starch with diastase. Mahogany (red-brown) color reaction with iodine.

amylopectin. Branched starch chain; shell and paste-forming starch. Unable to be entirely saccharified by amylolytic enzymes; a-limit dextrins, or amylodextrins, remain.

amylolysis. The enzymatic reduction of starch to soluble fractions.

amylose. Straight chain of native starch; a-D-glucose (glucose dehydrate) molecules joined by a-(1-4) links. Gives deep blue-black color with iodine.

anaerobic. Conditions under which there is not enough oxygen for respiratory metabolic function. Anaerobic microorganisms are those that can function without the presence of free molecular oxygen.

anion. An electronegative ion.

aqueous. Of water.

attempter. To regulate or moderate process temperature, as by maintaining ambient temperature cooler than the fermentation temperature.

attenuate. Fermentation, reduction of the extract/density by yeast metabolism.

attenuation. The reduction in the wort's specific gravity caused by the transformation of sugars into alcohol and carbon-dioxide gas.

autolysis. Yeast death due to shock or nutrient-depleted solutions.

bacteriostatic. Bacteria inhibiting.

Balling, degrees. A standard for the measurement of the density of solutions, calibrated on the weight of cane sugar in solution, expressed as a percentage of the weight of the solution (grams per 100 grams of solution).

beerstone. Brownish-gray, minerallike deposits left on fermentation equipment. Composed of calcium oxalate and organic residues.

blow-off. A single-stage homebrewing fermentation method in which a plastic tube is fitted into the mouth of a carboy, with the other end submerged in a pail of sterile water. Unwanted residues and carbon dioxide are expelled through the tube, while air is prevented from coming into contact with the fermenting beer, thus avoiding contamination.

brewers gravity. SG. See *gravity.*

buffer. A substance capable of resisting changes in the pH of a solution.

carbonates. Alkaline salts whose anions are derived from carbonic acid.

carbonation. The process of introducing carbon-dioxide gas into a liquid by: injecting the finished beer with carbon dioxide; adding young fermenting beer to finished beer for a renewed fermentation (kraeusening); priming (adding sugar) to fermented wort prior to bottling, creating a secondary fermentation in the bottle; finishing fermentation under pressure.

carboy. A large glass, plastic, or earthenware bottle.

cation. Electropositive ion.

chill haze. Haziness caused by protein and tannin during the secondary fermentation.

chill-proof. Cold conditioning to precipitate chill haze.

closed fermentation. Fermentation under closed,

anaerobic conditions, to minimize risk of contamination and oxidation.

coliform. Waterborne bacteria, often associated with pollution.

colloid. A gelatinous substance-in-solution.

decoction. Boiling, the part of the mash that is boiled.

density. The measurement of the weight of a solution, as compared with the weight of an equal volume of pure water.

dextrin. Soluble polysaccharide fraction, from hydrolysis of starch by heat, acid, or enzyme.

diastase. Starch-reducing enzymes; usually alpha- and beta-amylase, but also limit dextrinase and a-glucosidase (maltase).

diketone. Aromatic, volatile compound perceivable in minute concentration, from yeast or *Pediococcus* metabolism. Most significantly the butter flavor of diacetyl, a vicinal diketone (VDK). The other significant compound of relevance to brewing is 2,3-pentanedione.

dimethyl sulfide (DMS). An important sulfur-carrying compound originating in malt. Adds a crisp, "lager-like" character at low levels and corn or cabbage flavors at high levels.

disaccharides. Sugar group; two monosaccharide molecules joined by the removal of a water molecule.

dry hopping. The addition of hops to the primary fermenter, the secondary fermenter, or to casked beer to add aroma and hop character to the finished beer without adding significant bitterness.

dry malt. Malt extract in powdered form.

EBC (European Brewery Convention). See *SRM*.

enzymes. Protein-based organic catalysts that effect changes in the compositions of the substances they act upon.

erythrodextrin. Tasteless intermediate dextrin. Large

a-limit dextrins. Faint red reaction with iodine.

essential oil. The aromatic volatile liquid from the hop.

esters. "Ethereal salts" such as ethyl acetate; aromatic compounds from fermentation composed of an acid and an alcohol, such as the "banana" ester. Formed by yeast enzymes from an alcohol and an acid. Associated with ale and high-temperature fermentations, although esters also arise to some extent with pure lager yeast cultures, though more so with low wort oxygenation, high initial fermentation temperatures, and high-gravity wort. Top-fermenting yeast strains are prized for their ability to produce particular mixes of esters.

excess gravity. G. A form of expressing specific gravity, for convenience and in formulas, as a whole number: sp gr 1.046 is given as G 46, etc.

extract. Soluble constituents from the malt.

extraction. Drawing out the soluble essence of the malt or hops.

fecal bacteria. Coliform bacteria associated with sewage.

fermentation lock. A one-way valve, that allows carbon-dioxide gas to escape from the fermenter while excluding contaminants.

final specific gravity. The specific gravity of a beer when fermentation is complete.

fining. Clarifying beer, with isinglass, gelatin, bentonite, silica gel, polyvinyl pyrrolidone.

flocculation. The coagulation of phenols and proteins by boiling; the hot break during the boil, and the cold break upon cooling.

germination. Sprouting of the barley kernel, to initiate enzyme development and conversion of the malt.

glucophilic. An organism that thrives on glucose.

gravity. SG. Specific gravity as expressed by brewers; sp gr 1.046 is expressed as 1046. Density of a solution as compared to water; expressed in grams per milliliter (1 mL water weighs 1 g, hence sp gr 1.000 = SG 1000; sp gr 1.046. = SG 1046).

hexose. Sugar molecules of six carbon atoms. Glucose, fructose, lactose, mannose, galactose.

homebrewers bittering units. HBU. A formula adopted by the American Homebrewers Association to measure bitterness of beer. Example: 1.5 ounces of hops at 10 percent alpha acid for five gallons: 1.5 x 10 = 15 HBU per five gallons.

homofermentive. Organisms that metabolize only one specific carbon source.

hop pellets. Finely powdered hop cones compressed into pellets. Hop pellets are less subject to alpha-acid losses than whole hops.

hydrolysis. Decomposition of matter into soluble fractions by either acids or enzymes, in water.

hydrometer. A glass instrument used to measure the specific gravity of liquids as compared to water, consisting of a graduated stem resting on a weighed float.

hydroxide. A compound, usually alkaline, containing the OH (hydroxyl) group.

inoculate. The introduction of a microbe into surroundings capable of supporting its growth.

international bitterness unit. IBU. This is a standard unit that measures the concentration of iso-alpha-acids in milligrams per liter (parts per million). Most procedures will also measure a small amount of uncharacterized soft resins so IBUs are generally 5 to 15 percent higher than iso-alpha acid concentrations.

isinglass. A gelatinous substance made from the swim bladder of certain fish and added to beer as a fining agent.

isomer. Iso-. Organic compounds of identical composition and molecular weight, but having a different molecular structure.

kraeusen. The period of fermentation characterized by a rich foam head. Kraeusening describes the use of actively fermenting beer to induce fermentation in a larger volume of wort or extract-depleted beer.

lactophilic. An organism that metabolizes lactate more readily than glucose.

lager. "To store." A long, cold period of subdued fermentation and sedimentation subsequent to active (primary) fermentation.

lauter. The thin mash after saccharification; its clear liquid. From the German word, to purify/strain.

lauter-tun. A vessel in which the mash settles and the grains are removed from the sweet wort through a straining process. It has a false, slotted bottom and spigot.

lipids. Fatlike substances, especially triacylglycerols and fatty acids. Negatively affect ability of beer to form a foam head. Cause soapy flavors; when oxidized contribute stale flavors.

liquefaction. The process by which alpha-amylase enzymes degrade soluble starch into dextrin.

malt. Barley that has been steeped in water, germinated, then dried in kilns. This process converts insoluble starchs to soluble substances and sugars.

malt extract. A thick syrup or dry powder prepared from malt.

maltodextrin. Isomaltose; also amylodextrin, or an impure mixture of glucose with compounds formed of it.

maltose. A disaccharide of two glucose molecules, and the primary sugar obtained by diastatic hydrolysis of starch. One-third the sweetness of sucrose.

mash, mashing. The process of enzymatically extracting and converting malt solubles to wort, in an aciduric aqueous solution.

microaerophile. An organism that is inhibited in an well-oxygenated environment, and yet requires some oxygen for its metabolic functions.

modification. The degree to which the malt endosperm is converted, manifested by the solubilization of malt protein.

mole. Gram-molecular weight. The sum of the atomic weights of all the atoms of any molecule, in grams.

monosaccharides. Single-molecule sugars.

oligosaccharides. Sugars of more than three molecules, less complex than dextrins.

original gravity. The specific gravity of wort previous to fermentation. A measure of the total amount of dissolved solids in wort.

oxidation. The combination of oxygen with other molecules, oftentimes causing off-flavors, as with aldehydes from alcohols.

pH. A measure of acidity or alkalinity of a solution, usually on a scale of one to fourteen, where seven is neutral.

ppm. Parts per million. Equal to milligrams per liter (mg/L). The measurement of particles of matter in solution.

pectin. Vegetable substance, a chain of galacturonic acid that becomes gelatinous in the presence of sugars and acids.

pentosan. Pentose-based complex carbohydrates, especially gums.

pentose. Sugar molecules of five carbon atoms. Monosaccharides from the decomposition of pentosans, unfermentable by yeast. Xylose, arabinose.

peptonizing. The action of proteolytic enzymes upon protein, successively yielding albumin/proteoses, peptides, and amino acids.

phenols. Aromatic hydroxyl precursors of tannins/polyphenols. Phenolic describes medicinal flavors in beer, from tannins, bacterial growth, cleaning compounds, or plastics.

phosphate. A salt or ester of phosphoric acid.

pitching. Inoculating sterile wort with a vigorous yeast culture.

plasma. Protoplasm. The substance of cell bodies, excluding the nucleus (cytoplasm), in which most cell metabolism occurs.

Plato, degrees. Commercial brewers' standard for the measurement of the density of solutions, expressed as the equivalent weight of cane sugar in solution (calibrated on grams of sucrose per 100 grams of solution). Like degrees Balling, but Plato's computations are more exact.

polymer. A substance having identical elements in the same proportion as another substance, but of higher molecular weight. For example, polyphenols from phenols, polypeptides from peptides.

polyphenol. Complexes of phenolic compounds involved in chill haze formation and oxidative staling.

polysaccharides. Carbohydrate complexes, able to be reduced to monosaccharides by hydrolysis.

precipitation. Separation of suspended matter by sedimentation.

precursor. Matter subject to polymerization.

primary fermentation. The first stage of fermentation, during which most fermentable sugars are converted to ethyl alcohol and carbon dioxide.

priming solution. A solution of sugar in water added to aged beer at bottling to induce fermentation (bottle conditioning).

priming sugar. A small amount of corn, malt, or cane sugar added to bulk beer prior to racking or at bottling, to induce a new fermentation and create carbonation.

protein. Generally amorphous and colloidal complexed amino acid, containing about 16 percent nitrogen with carbon, hydrogen, oxygen, and possibly sulfur, phosphorous, and iron. True protein has a molecular weight of 17,000 to 150,000; in beer, protein will have been largely decomposed to a molecular weight of 5,000 to 12,000 (albumin or proteoses), 400 to 1,500 (peptides), or amino acids. Protein as a haze fraction ranges from molecular weight 10,000 to 100,000 (average 30,000), and as the stabilizing component of foam, 12,000 to 20,000.

proteolysis. The reduction of protein by proteolytic enzymes to fractions.

racking. The transfer of wort or beer from one vessel to another.

reagent. A substance involved in a reaction, that identifies the strength of the substance being measured.

resin. Noncrystalline (amorphous) plant excretions.

rest. Mash rest. Holding the mash at a specific temperature to induce certain enzymatic changes.

ropy fermentation. Viscous, gelatinous blobs, or "rope," from bacterial contamination.

rousing. Creating turbulence by agitation; mixing.

ruh beer. The nearly fermented beer, ready for lagering. Cold secondary fermentation.

saccharification. The naturally occurring process in which malt starch is converted into fermentable sugars, primarily maltose.

saccharometer. An instrument that determines the sugar concentration of a solution by measuring the specific gravity.

sparging. Spraying the spent grains in the mash with hot water to retrieve the remaining malt sugar.

solubilization. Dissolution of matter into solution.

sparge. The even distribution or spray of water over the saccharified mash, to rinse free the extract from the grist.

specific gravity. sp gr. Density of a solution, in grams per milliliter.

SRM (Standard Reference Method) and EBC (European Brewery Convention). Two different analytical methods of describing color developed by comparing color samples. Degrees SRM, approximately equivalent to degrees Lovibond, are used by the ASBC (American Society of Brewing Chemists) while degrees EBC are European units. The following equations show approximate conversions:

$$(°EBC) = 2.65 \times (°Lovibond) - 1.2$$
$$(°Lovibond) = 0.377 \times (°EBC) + 0.45$$

starter. A batch of fermenting yeast, added to the wort to initiate fermentation.

strike temperature. The target temperature of a mash rest, the temperature at which a desired reaction occurs.

substratum. The substance in or on which an organism grows.

tannin. Astringent polyphenolic compounds, capable of colloiding with protcins and either precipitating or forming haze fractions.

terminal extract. The density of the fully fermented beer.

thermophilic. "Heat loving"; bacteria operating at unusually high temperatures.

titration. Measurement of a substance in solution by addition of a standard disclosing solution to initiate an indicative color change.

trisaccharide. A sugar composed of three monosaccharides joined by the removal of water molecules.

trub. Precipitated flocks of haze-forming protein and polyphenols.

turbidity. Sediment in suspension; hazy, murky.

ullage. The empty space between a liquid and the top of its container. Also called airspace or headspace.

v/v. See *alcohol by volume.*

valence. The degree to which an ion or radical is able to combine directly with others.

viscosity. Of glutinous consistency; the resistance of a fluid to flow. The degree of "mouthfeel" of a beer.

volatile. Readily vaporized, especially esters, essential oils, and higher alcohols.

w/v. See *alcohol by weight.*

water hardness. The degree of dissolved minerals in water.

wort. Mash extract (sweet wort); the hopped sugar solution before pitching (bitter wort).

wort gelatin. Culture medium made up from wort as a nutrient source and gelatin to solidify it, for surface-culturing yeast.

BIBLIOGRAPHY

Abel, Bob. *The Book of Beer.* Chicago: 1976.

American Public Health Association. *Standard Methods for the Examination of Water and Wastewater.* Washington: American Public Health Association, 1971.

American Society of Brewing Chemists. *Methods of Analysis of the American Society of Brewing Chemists.* St. Paul, Minn.: American Brewing Chemists, 1976.

Anderson, S. F. *The Art of Making Beer,* New York, 1971.

Bailar, J. C., Kleinberg, J., Moeller, T. *University Chemistry.* Boston, 1965.

Baker, Pat. *The New Brewers Handbook.*

.Baron, Stanley Wade. *Brewed in America.* Boston: Little, 1962.

Berry, C. J. J. *Home Brewed Beers and Stouts.* Andover, England, 1963.

Briggs, D. E., Hough, J. S., Stevens, R., and Young, T. W. *Malting and Brewing Science.* 2 vols. London: Chapman and Hall, 1971.

Burch, Byron. *Brewing Quality Beer.* San Rafael, Calif.: 1974.

Chapman, A. C. *Brewing.* Cambridge, 1912.

Comer, Jay and Tobey, Alan. "Hop Pellets vs. Whole Hops." *A Transcription of the Proceedings of the 5th Annual National Homebrew and Microbrewery Conference.* Boulder, Colo.: American Homebrewers Association, 1983.

Despain, R. O. *The Malt-Ease Flagon.* Berkeley, 1978.

Eckhardt, Fred. *The Essentials of Beer Style,* Portland, Ore.: Fred Eckhardt Communications, 1989.

―――. *Mashing for the North American Home Brewer.* Portland, Ore.: Fred Eckhardt Communications, 1974.

―――. *A Treatise on Lager Beers.* Portland, Ore.: Fred Eckhardt Communications, 1970.

―――. "The Use of Hops in Your Beer." *Amateur Brewer #4.* Portland, Ore.: Fred Eckhardt Communications, 1977.

Ferguson, W. B. "The Chemistry of a Brewer's Vat," *Science for All.* London, 1978.

Findlay, W. P. K., ed. *Modern Brewing Technology.* Cleveland, 1971.

Fix, George. *Principles of Brewing Science.* Boulder, Colo.: Brewers Publications, 1989.

Forget, Carl. *Dictionary of Beer and Brewing.* Boulder, Colo.: Brewers Publications, 1988.

Foster, Terence. "Yeast Culture and Propagation." *Best of Beer and Brewing.* Boulder, Colo.: Brewers Publications, 1987.

―――. "Yeast, An Essential Ingredient." *Zymurgy,* Spring 1984 (Vol. 7, No. 1).

―――. "In the Beginning — There Was Malt." *Zymurgy,* Winter 1984 (Vol. 7, No. 4).

Garret, A. B., Richardson, J. S., Montague, *E. J. Chemistry.* Boston, 1976.

Geraghty, James J. *Water Atlas of the United States.* Port Washington, New York, 1973.

Gold, Elizabeth, ed. *Evaluating Beer.* Boulder, Colo.: Brewers Publications, 1993.

Hahn, Peter C. *Chemicals from Fermentation.* New York, 1968.

Henius, Max. *Danish Beer and Continental Beer Gardens.* New York, 1914.

Hopkins, R. H. and Krause, B. *Biochemistry Applied to Malting and Brewing.* New York, 1937.

Hopkins, R. H. "Brewing; Alcohol; Wine and Spirits." *What Industry Owes to Chemical Science.* Brooklyn, 1946.

Hunt, Brian. "Spoilage and Sanitation in Homebrewing." *Zymurgy,* Summer 1984 (Vol. 7, No. 2).

Jackson, Michael. *The World Guide to Beer.* London: Courage Books, 1977.

Kenny, Stephen T. "Hop Varieties." *Zymurgy,* Spring 1985 (Vol. 8, No. 1).

Kieninger, H. "The Influence of Raw Materials and Yeast on the Various Beer Types." *Best of Beer and Brewing.* Boulder, Colo.: Brewers Publications, 1987.

Lewis, Michael. "Microbiological Controls in Your Brewery." *Best of Beer and Brewing.* Boulder, Colo.: Brewers Publications, 1987.

Line, Dave. *The Big Book of Brewing.* Andover, England: Amateur Winemaker Publications, 1974.

————. *Brewing Beers Like Those You Buy.* Andover, England: Amateur Winemaker Publications, 1981.

Matson, Tim and Lee Ann. *Mountain Brew.* Thetford Center, Vermont, 1975.

Miller, David. *Homebrewing for Americans.* Andover, England: Amateur Winemaker Publications, 1981.

Moore, William. *Home Beermaking.* Oakland: Ferment Press, 1980.

Morgan, Scotty. *Brew Your Own.* San Leandro, California, 1979.

Muldoon, H. C. and Blake, M. 1. *Systematic Organic Chemistry.* New York, 1957.

Nowak, Carl A. *Modern Brewing.* St. Louis, 1934.

Papazian, Charlie. *The Joy of Brewing.* Boulder, Colo.: Avon, 1980.

Paul's Malt, *Brewing Room Book,* 84th edition. Edmunds, Suffolk, 1995.

Peppier, H. J., ed. *Microbial Technology.* New York, 1967.

Porter, John H. *All About Beer.* Garden City, New Jersey: Doubleday, 1975.

Robertson, James D. *The Great American Beer Book.* New York, 1978.

Ross-MacKenzie, John A. *A Standard Manual of Brewing.* London, 1927.

Shales, Ken. *Advanced Home Brewing.* Andover, England, 1972.

Siebel, Ron. "The Origins of Beer Flavor in the Brewery." *A Transcription of the Proceedings of the 5th Annual National Homebrew and Microbrewery Conference.* Boulder, Colo.: American Homebrewers Association, 1983.

Stecher, P. G., ed. *The Merck Index of Chemicals and Drugs.* Rahway, New Jersey: Merck and Co., 1960.

Taylor, E. W. *The Examination of Waters and Water Supplies.* London, 1949.

Thresh, John C. *Water and Water Supplies.* Philadelphia, 1900.

United States Department of Agriculture. *Hop Production.* Washington, D.C., 1961.

Vogel, E. H., Leonhardt, H. G., Merten, J. A., Schwaiger, F. H. *The Practical Brewer.* St. Louis, 1947.

Vrest, Orton. *Home Beer Book.* Rutland, Vermont, 1973.

Wahl, Robert and Henrius, Max. *The American Handy Book of the Brewing, Malting and Auxiliary Trades.* 2 vols. Chicago, 1908.

Weast, Robert C., ed. *Handbook of Chemistry and Physics.* West Palm Beach, Fla.: CRC Press, 1978.

Weiner, Michael A. *The Beer Taster's Guide to Brews and Breweries of the World.* New York: Collier Books, 1977.

ABOUT THE AUTHOR

Greg Noonan is one of the best-known craft brewers in America as well as an internationally recognized expert on brewing. Since 1988, Greg has been the owner and brewmaster at the renown Vermont Pub and Brewery, and in 1994 he founded the Seven Barrel Brewery of West Lebanon, New Hampshire.

Since Greg became brewmaster, the Vermont Pub and Brewery has won a gold medal in 1993 for its Auld Tartan Wee Heavy in the ale strong ale category, and a bronze medal in both 1991 and 1992 for its Vermont Smoked Porter in the smoked flavored beers category at the Great American Beer Festival®.

Greg is author of *Scotch Ale* (Brewers Publications, 1993) and the *Seven Barrel Brewery Brewers' Handbook* (G. W. Kent, 1996), as well as numerous beer style and technical articles for brewing periodicals, including *Zymurgy* and *The New Brewer.* Greg really enjoys good beer.

INDEX

Dextrocheck, testing with, 243
Diacetyl, 101, 175, 183, 185, 188;
    flavor and, 182; formation
    of, 194; kraeusening and,
    243; reducing, 169
Diacetyl diketone, 102
Diacetyl rest, 242; fermentable
    extract and, 185
Diastatic enzymes, 108-9, 134,
    135, 145
Diatomaceous earth, using, 196
Disaccharides, 30
DME. See Dry malt extract
DMS, 20; reducing development
    of, 237
Dopplebock, xx; recipe for, 225
Dortmund, kilning, 117
Dortmunder, xix; mash thickness
    and, 142; recipe for, 219
Doughing-in, 126-29, 135, 144,
    227-28, 304
Dreher, Anton: bottom fermenting
    and, 90
Dry Malt Extract (DME),
    288-89, 292
Dry measures, 309-10

EBC method, 11, 14
Eisbocks, xx
Electron transfer, 49 (diagram)
EMP, 181
Enamelware, cleaning, 256
Enzymes, 107-10; constitutive,
    107; debranching, 109
    (diagram);
diastatic, 108-9, 134, 135, 145;
    extracellular, 107; improving
    effectiveness of, 128;
    inducible, 107; intracellular,

107; nonproteolytic, 138; pH
    and, 47; proteolytic, 108, 145
Equipment, 261-87; cleaning,
    257-58, 297
Equivalence, 60-63
Escherichia coli, 70, 104
Esters, 176, 177, 239
Ethyl, cleaning with, 260
Ethyl acetate, 176
Ethyl alcohol, 181; boiling, 326
Evaporation rates, establishing,
    156-58
Exiguus, 91 (illustration)
Extract efficiency, 138, 236
Extracts: diacetyl rest and, 185;
    expressing, 313;
    post-kraeusen, 184; prob-
    lems with, 249; terminal,
    197-98, 244; unfermentable,
    197; unhopped, 288

False bottom cross sections, 269
    (illustration)
Fatty acids, 33-34, 176; as energy
    sources, 181
Fermentation, 89, 97, 164-90,
    193, 288, 293-94; acidity of,
    174; clean, 185;
    culture-yeast, 171, 192;
    flavor and, 188; gelitanous,
    102; heat from, 173; induc-
    ing, 168; kraeusening and,
    238, 250; lag times for, 110;
    mash thickness and, 140-
    41, 301; problems with,
    250-51; products of, 181;
    ropy, 102, 104; single-stage,
    294; temperature and,
    172-73, 185, 293. See also

BOOKS for Brewers and Beer Lovers

Order Now ... Your Brew Will Thank You!

These books offered by Brewers Publications are some of the most sought after reference tools for homebrewers and professional brewers alike. Filled with tips, techniques, recipes and history, these books will help you expand your brewing horizons. Let the world's foremost brewers help you as you brew. Whatever your brewing level or interest, Brewers Publications has the information necessary for you to brew the best beer in the world — your beer.

- -

Please send me more free information on the following: (check all that apply)

◊ Merchandise and Book Catalog   ◊ Institute for Brewing Studies
◊ American Homebrewers Association®   ◊ Great American Beer Festival®

Ship to:

Name _____

Address _____

City _____ State/Province _____

Zip/Postal Code _____ Country _____

Daytime Phone (_____) _____

Please use the following in conjunction with an order form when ordering books from Brewers Publications.

Payment Method

◊ Check or Money Order Enclosed (Payable to the Association of Brewers)
◊ Visa   ◊ MasterCard

Card Number _____ – _____ – _____ – _____   Expiration Date _____

Name on Card _____ Signature _____

Brewers Publications, PO Box 1510, Boulder, CO 80306-1510, U.S.A.; (303) 546-6514; FAX (303) 447-2825

NBLB

BREWERS PUBLICATIONS ORDER FORM

GENERAL BEER AND BREWING INFORMATION

QTY.	TITLE	STOCK #	PRICE	EXT. PRICE
	The Art of Cidermaking	468	9.95	
	Brewing Mead	461	11.95	
	Dictionary of Beer and Brewing	462	19.95	
	Evaluating Beer	465	19.95	
	Great American Beer Cookbook	466	24.95	
	New Brewing Lager Beer	469	14.95	
	Victory Beer Recipes	467	11.95	
	Winners Circle	464	11.95	

CLASSIC BEER STYLE SERIES

QTY.	TITLE	STOCK #	PRICE	EXT. PRICE
	Pale Ale	401	11.95	
	Continental Pilsener	402	11.95	
	Lambic	403	11.95	
	Oktoberfest, Vienna, Märzen	404	11.95	
	Porter	405	11.95	
	Belgian Ale	406	11.95	
	German Wheat Beer	407	11.95	
	Scotch Ale	408	11.95	
	Bock	409	11.95	
	Stout	410	11.95	

PROFESSIONAL BREWING BOOKS

QTY.	TITLE	STOCK #	PRICE	EXT. PRICE
	Brewery Planner	500	80.00	
	North American Brewers Resource Directory	505	100.00	
	Principles of Brewing Science	463	29.95	

THE BREWERY OPERATIONS SERIES, Transcripts
From National Micro- and Pubbrewers Conferences

QTY.	TITLE	STOCK #	PRICE	EXT. PRICE
	Volume 6, 1989 Conference	536	25.95	
	Volume 7, 1990 Conference	537	25.95	
	Volume 8, 1991 Conference, Brewing Under Adversity	538	25.95	
	Volume 9, 1992 Conference, Quality Brewing — Share the Experience	539	25.95	

BEER AND BREWING SERIES, Transcripts
From National Homebrewers Conferences

QTY.	TITLE	STOCK #	PRICE	EXT. PRICE
	Volume 8, 1988 Conference	448	21.95	
	Volume 10, 1990 Conference	450	21.95	
	Volume 11, 1991 Conference, Brew Free Or Die!	451	21.95	
	Volume 12, 1992 Conference, Just Brew It!	452	21.95	

SUBTOTAL _____

Call or write for a free **Beer Enthusiast catalog** today.
Colo. Residents Add 3% Sales Tax _____
• U.S. funds only.
• All Brewers Publications books come with a money-back guarantee.
P&H * _____
***Postage & Handling:** $4 for the first book ordered, plus $1 for each book thereafter. Canadian and international orders please add $5 for the first book and $2 for each book thereafter. Orders cannot be shipped without appropriate P&H.
TOTAL _____

Brewers Publications, PO Box 1510, Boulder, CO 80306-1510, U.S.A.; (303) 546-6514; FAX (303) 447-2825

NBLB

The Award-Winning
EVALUATING
BEER

Learn more about the beer you drink and brew with *Evaluati*
Beer. Charlie Papazian, George Fix, Gregory Noonan, Jim Ko
and Ron Siebel are among the 13 contributing authors who ma
this book a necessity for every beer lover, brewer and beer judg
Concise text, easy-to-read charts and clear descriptions make be
evaluations easy and fun.

"I read it in *The New Brewer*."

Jerry Bailey, President,
Old Dominion Brewing Co.,
Ashburn, Va.

Industry leaders like Jerry Bailey know that only *The New Brewer* provides the inside information craft brewers from coast to coast depend on. Each issue is packed with vital statistics for business planning, the latest in brewing techniques, alternative technologies, beer recipes, legislative alerts, marketing and distribution ideas — everything you need to succeed in today's competitive market.

Whether you're an established brewery or just in the planning stages, our in-depth coverage will give you information you can put to work immediately. After all, your business is our business.

See for yourself. Subscribe to *The New Brewer* today!

Please complete the following information. We'll rush subscription information your way!

NAME _____

TITLE _____

COMPANY _____

ADDRESS_____ CITY _____

STATE/PROVINCE _____ ZIP/POSTAL CODE _____

COUNTRY_____ TELEPHONE _____

Please return this coupon to: Institute for Brewing Studies, PO Box 1510, Boulder, CO 80306-1510, U.S.A. For faster service, call (303) 447-0816, ibs@aob.org or FAX (303) 447-2825.   NBLB

New Brewer · YOUR INSIDER'S VIEW TO THE CRAFT-BREWING INDUSTRY

We're here for your beer

No, we don't want to take your homebrew away from you (although we'd be glad to sample a few bottles). We at the American Homebrewers Association® want to help you brew the best beer in the world — your own. For more than 18 years we've helped homebrewers of every level brew fantastic beer at home. Whether you're a beginner or an advanced fermentologist, we'll be there for you. (If that means drinking some of your homebrew, all the better.)

MEMBERSHIP BENEFITS INCLUDE:

Five big issues of *Zymurgy*® magazine

Discounts on entries at the annual AHA National Homebrewers Conference

Discounts at the annual AHA National Homebrew Competition

Discounts on select books from Brewers Publications

The Homebrew Club Network

The Members-Only Tasting at the Great American Beer Festival®

Free information for better homebrew

Discounts to AHA Sanctioned Competitions

Members Information Service

Your membership also supports the AHA's educational programs, the new Beer Evaluation Program and the state-by-state AHA Homebrew Legalization Campaign.

The American Homebrewers Association is your partner in better homebrewing.